Mass Unemployment
and the Future of Britain

Mass Unemployment
and the Future of Britain

BILL JORDAN

Basil Blackwell · Oxford

First published 1982
Reprinted 1983
Basil Blackwell Publisher Limited
108 Cowley Road, Oxford OX4 1JF, England

British Library Cataloguing in Publication Data

Jordan, Bill
   Mass unemployment and the future of Britain
   1. Unemployment – Great Britain
   I. Title
   331.13′7941   HD 5765.A6

   ISBN 0-631-13092-6
   ISBN 0-631-13093-4 Pbk

Typesetting by Oxford Verbatim Limited
Printed in Great Britain

Contents

Acknowledgements

I would like to thank the following for a large number of very helpful comments and criticisms made at various stages of the preparation of this book: Bruce Britton, Radford Jordan, John Vincent, Andrew Gamble, Peter Pulzer and Bob Dowse. I am also very grateful to Alex Allan for her outstanding efficiency and stamina in typing several versions of it, and to Mary Brookshaw and Lora Ridger for helping her in this task.

1
The Politics of Mass Unemployment

Unemployment is the most serious internal political problem of the advanced industrialized countries today. It is serious because it is a clear sign that capitalism is not working satisfactorily. A system of production that cannot provide work and income for a substantial proportion of its adult population is evidently faulty.

This is not the first time that this problem has occurred. In the 1930s mass unemployment was accompanied by the major political upheavals associated with Fascism and Communism. The aim of both social democratic and conservative governments in the advanced industrialized countries has been to try to negotiate this recurrence of mass unemployment without a return to those political turmoils.

In most of the Western industrialized countries, unemployment is not yet such a serious problem as it was at the lowest depths of the Depression. Figure 1.1 compares unemployment rates in the United States in the 1930s with those of recent years.[1] In Britain however, despite politicians' denials, the problem is actually worse than it was then. Unemployment has been rising steadily, and recently rapidly, towards the rates that prevailed briefly in the 1930s.[2] The difference, as figure 1.2 shows, is that all predictions indicate that it is likely to rise further still and surpass that record for the foreseeable future.[3]

In this book I shall be considering how unemployment is managed in the political process. In the first part I shall be looking at explanations of unemployment in economic theory, and how these have been employed in political rhetoric and ideology. In the second part I shall concentrate

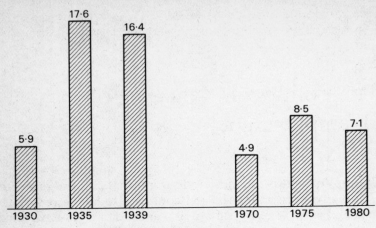

Figure 1.1   *Unemployment in the USA*
(as a percentage of the civilian workforce)

on Great Britain, and analyse how the very serious problem of long-term mass unemployment is being described and handled by politicians.

This involves the description of how national politicians handle the consequences of changes in an international economic system. It is a major thesis of this book that since the mid-1960s very important changes have been taking place in the overall structure and balance of the world capitalist system. In particular there has been a rapid emergence of

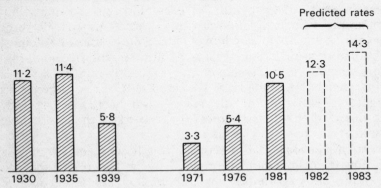

Figure 1.2   *Unemployment in the UK*
(as a percentage of the civilian workforce)

certain previously underdeveloped countries as centres for industrial production, and a slowing down of the rate of growth of industrial output in the advanced industrialized countries. This in turn has led to an increase in industrial employment in the underdeveloped world and a decline in industrial employment in the developed countries.

For many years after this process began to occur, it remained largely unnoticed, or its significance was denied. On the whole it has only been Marxist commentators who have tried to analyse international capitalism as a system, and construct a theory about the relationships between the different parts of that system. Among Marxists, the industrialization of parts of the Third World, which began to become increasingly evident in the early 1970s, provoked a furious debate. Although Marx himself had anticipated this development, most post-war Marxist theorists had emphasized the continued economic dependence of the underdeveloped countries in the post-colonial era – a view largely shared by Liberal and social democratic writers and politicians. But it was almost exclusively in Marxist circles that the possibility of a major shift in the balance of international production was discussed.

Rising unemployment in the advanced industrialized countries has begun to change this. Faced with continuing lower rates of economic growth and higher unemployment rates, national politicians in the developed world have been forced to consider the wider implications of the changes taking place. Hence analyses in terms of world economic developments have become more common, and politicians of all parties have ranged more widely in their thinking about the implications of change.

However, this thinking has continued to be done within the frameworks of established political and economic ortho-doxies. I shall argue that neither Keynesian nor monetarist analyses of national or international developments are in any way adequate as explanations of recent events or guides to future action.

Only in Britain has the scale of unemployment, and its continued growth, provoked a debate which has gradually become more and more fundamental in its questioning of the direction of world capitalist development. Suddenly it is becoming possible for serious-minded people in the Labour Party and in the academic establishment to ask whether it is in Britain's interest to continue to participate in the institutions of the international capitalist system. Since rising unemployment has been the biggest single factor in bringing about this change of hearts and minds, it seems very important to examine the origins of unemployment in the advanced countries of the capitalist world economy.

THE ARGUMENT OF THIS BOOK

Although much of the analysis in Part One is complex, the essential argument of this book is simple. It describes why mass unemployment has occurred, why it is certain to continue, particularly in Britain, and why politicians are so unwilling to face up to both its origins and its consequences.

The origins of unemployment in the advanced industrialized countries of the capitalist world can be traced to the period 1965–75. During this decade there began to occur in the industrial sector of these economies a phenomenon that had previously been confined to certain backward, rural regions and sectors of production. The industrial workforce began to decline. As industrial employment fell, unemployment rose. The connection between the two processes was clear, since the rise in unemployment in each county coincided with the fall in the number of industrial jobs.

No subject is less clearly explained or understood than the connections between this process and the introduction of new technology. It is generally supposed that some quality of the new technology 'caused' automation, i.e. that because new processes used automatically or electronically controlled devices they led to diminished employment. As I shall show in chapter 5, this idea is quite wrong. 'Automation', in the sense of the displacement of workers by machines, has occurred at various times in various industries, but particularly in agriculture, ever since the Industrial Revolution. The fact that the introduction of new technology resulted in the redundancy of industrial workers had nothing to do with the specific qualities of that technology. Steam looms and horse-drawn threshing machines had equally caused redundancy in the nineteenth century. Electronic technology brought increased employment in other parts of the world.

What was new about the process of automation that occurred in the advanced industrialized countries of the capitalist world from the mid-1960s onwards was that it took place in a sector of the economy in which employment and output had previously been expanding rapidly – the industrial sector. Previous examples of automation had occurred in stagnating or declining industries (like coalmining in the 1930s) or in farming. Now manufacturing and other growth areas of industry began to experience automation – i.e. to reduce their industrial workforce, which had been expanding steadily for over a century. Previous contractions in the total industrial workforce had been extremely brief, and confined to periods of acute recession. In Britain and Germany, industrial employment declined for 15 years after 1966, even when industrial output was increasing (in the case of Germany, increasing quite rapidly).

The examples of Britain and Germany indicate that automation is not a homogeneous process. There are several different kinds of automation, as I shall explain in chapters 5 and 6. The less common kind is the one that was achieved in Germany. There, industrial production went on expanding after the workforce began to decline. New technology was able to raise the productivity of industrial labour (i.e. output per man-hour) even more rapidly than it increased industrial output. As a result, although fewer workers were employed in the high-wage sector of the German economy, the real living standards of the German working class did not decline significantly during the period of automation.

In Britain, however, automation was associated with stagnant or declining industrial output in the 1970s. In the final quarter of 1980, industrial output (excluding North Sea oil and natural gas) was 10 per cent lower than it had been in 1970. But the industrial workforce was over 20 per cent less than it had been in 1970. Thus, the average living standards of the working class fell during this period, and unemployment reached much higher levels than it had in Germany.

Indeed, the fate of the British economy during this period serves as an example of what can happen to an industrialized nation in which automation is not accompanied by steady growth of industrial production. The motive for automation is always the saving of labour costs – capital perceives wages as rising unduly, sees its rate of profit falling, and can only increase profits by saving labour costs. This may be effective for each firm or industry, but if it occurs simultaneously across the whole industrial sector, industry ceases to distribute sufficient income to maintain demand for its products. Hence it is extremely important for capital to keep up sales of its products during automation, and home demand for industrially produced commodities is constantly threatened by a falling volume of industrial wages – as happened in Britain. The overall growth of industrial production in the major industrialized countries in the 1970s was very slow by the standards of the previous two decades.

One way in which this potential fall in domestic demand can be combated is by increasing exports of industrial products. Germany and Japan were particularly successful in increasing their share of world trade in these commodities, while Britain and the United States were very unsuccessful, and experienced increased import-penetration of manufactured goods, which further depressed the demand for their own industrial products. The other way in which the effects of automation were offset by the advanced industrialized countries was through the rapid industrialization of certain previously backward and predominantly rural countries – Spain, Portugal, Greece and Turkey in the western hemisphere, Mexico and Brazil in the new world and Singapore, Hong Kong, the Philippines, Taiwan and South Korea in the east.

The countries were developed largely through multi-national corporations based in the advanced industrialized countries, and served the interests of capital there in two ways. Firstly, they allowed more labour intensive methods to be used in producing some manufactures, taking advantage of relatively cheaper labour power. Secondly, they allowed the development of an industrial proletariat in these countries, which provided another market for products of the advanced industrialized nations, offsetting the limitations imposed by automation.

In these ways, capital in the advanced nations was able to neutralize some of the potentially ill effects of automation and unemployment in its own domestic economies. However, Britain in particular was unable to do this effectively. British capital was unable to increase its (already high) investment in the industrializing countries to any significant extent until 1979, and its share of world trade continued to decline dramatically, while imports increasingly invaded its home market. Hence unemployment rose far more rapidly in Britain, and government policy since 1979 has merely exaggerated a long-standing trend.

The prospects of this trend being reversed under present trading conditions are negligible. Britain's share of world trade has been declining since 1870 – recent events have simply accelerated the decline. Further automation will simply increase the burden of unemployment (in taxation and social security contributions) and reinforce the long-term tendency for working-class incomes to decline and demand for industrial products to fall. The rate of profit on home investments is too low to encourage the sort of expansion that would produce increased industrial employment.

This explains why even sober commentators are predicting unemployment of over 4 million in 1983, as industrial automation continues while industrial production remains stagnant. The simple fact is that the British economy is doomed to be trapped in this vicious circle for as far ahead as can be seen. Britain's function for international capital will largely be as a market for the products of richer countries with higher rates of labour productivity, and for the products of the newly industrializing countries, with lower labour costs. Britain will come to serve the purpose of an 'internal colony', for the consumption of surplus production by overseas industry.

This prospect is far too stark, bleak and clear to be presented to the British people. This is why no political party in Britain has addressed itself directly to the twin problems of falling industrial employment and rising unemployment. As I shall show in the second part of this book, they have accounted for unemployment in terms of traditional Keynesian and monetarist economic theories which cannot explain its emergence.

It also explains why even moderate and reformist figures on the left in British politics have recently been identifying themselves with what until recently would have seemed very extreme measures. As the Labour movement generally comes to recognize the symptoms of this problem, there is mounting pressure from trade unionists for a massive programme of public investment and for protective tariffs on industrially produced goods. But the political implications of such a radical programme are immense. British industry could not be protected without breaking the rules not only of the European Economic Community, but also of the General Agreement on Tariffs and Trade. Up to now, membership of these two important capitalist clubs has been seen as a badge not only of economic prosperity but also of political participation in the power structure of the Western world. The notion of pulling out of these organizations implies a form of non-aligned political position hitherto unimagined outside 'extreme' left-wing circles.

The purpose of this book is to show that such discussion does not stem from the political fantasies of certain left-wing figures, but is based on the economic realities of Britain's present situation in the capitalist world economy. Indeed, I shall argue that the radicals have not yet gone far enough in questioning the direction of change.

DEVELOPMENTS IN THE BRITISH LABOUR MOVEMENT

In the second part of the book, after reviewing briefly the confusions and contradictions in the Conservative Party over unemployment, and the Liberal–SDP position, I shall concentrate in detail on the response of the British Labour movement. In particular, I shall consider the new left-wing analysis of developments in world capitalism and recent attempts to justify Keynesian approaches to public spending.

According to the view expounded by Tony Benn, and based

on the views of the Cambridge Keynesians, Britain's economic problems stem largely from the emergence of a form of international capitalism which is highly resistant to national economic management. Multinational corporations, deriving originally from America, but setting a pattern increasingly followed by the rest of the developed world, have pursued their interests in a way that has cut across the needs of nation states. In foreign exchange markets, in international capital movements, in decisions about investment and production levels, they have defied the policies of national governments. Benn and his followers have described the result as 'anarchy'. Benn has even contrasted the present situation with the 1930s by saying that 'in this slump we have a government that no longer has a patriotic element in its capitalism'.[4]

The Cambridge school are therefore able to argue that Keynesian measures would be successful if political steps were first taken to control international movements of currency and capital, and to regulate trade and production. Benn claims that capital could thus be redirected towards national interests – that it could be 'nationalized' in a number of senses, in which state ownership would merely be a last resort.

Unfortunately, this analysis concentrates on the institutional structure of international capitalism at the expense of studying the logic of the particular way it has developed. It makes no serious attempt to consider why international capital has chosen to follow certain pathways and to neglect others. It gives no account of why so much production has been shifted away, not only from Britain but from the whole advanced industrial world. It develops no convincing model of the relationship between the developed, the developing and the underdeveloped nations. If international capital is seen as merely 'anarchic', rather than as pursuing a certain logic in its development, any attempt to harness it to socialist purposes seems highly speculative.

Furthermore, the notion that increased public investment will give rise to higher employment is seldom accompanied by analysis or quantification. While some public spending would clearly provide new jobs (mainly in housebuilding and other construction) modernization of the railways and other public utilities could well cause a net loss of jobs in the long run.

There is evidence from many advanced industrialized countries of increased investment leading to reduced employment.

But above all, Benn's programme is based on a premise of faster economic growth. It postulates that a combination of controls over international companies, import tariffs and increased state spending will lead to the rapid expansion of national income which has been awaited for so many years. It is essentially Keynesian in its optimism about the possibility of national government stage-managing the expansion of a mixed economy, given the proper policies.

Every British government since Harold Wilson's of 1964 has made the mistake of assuming that, given the right institutional framework, rapid economic growth could be achieved. Benn and his followers are no different from all the others in this. They are more radical about the means, but not about the ends of economic policy. Thus Labour's 'alternative economic strategy' has many of the weaknesses of previous programmes.

Since 1964 every British government has been forced to retract its promises on economic growth, and along with these on most issues of social policy. Every government has ascribed its failure to some new international crisis or world event. None has been willing to accept the historical evidence that Britain is unlikely to achieve rapid economic growth again, whatever the institutional framework.

Ever since 1918 the rank order of the major industrialized countries for growth of national income has been remarkably consistent. Britain has always been bottom of the league table, except in the 1930s, when the United States and France suffered long-term recessions. In the later 1970s not even the most successful of the major industrialized countries achieved growth rates of more than half their rates in the 1960s, and in this Britain was no exception. While recent Conservative policies have unquestionably contributed to rapid recession, there is no evidence to suggest that any other policies could have achieved rapid expansion.

Most significantly, since 1966 the decline in employment in British industry has been very marked, even when industrial output was growing. This above all has been the factor which successive governments failed to take into account in their calculations of economic and social policy. Unless Labour's policy-makers recognize this phenomenon – which cannot be accounted for in terms of Keynesian economic theory – they are very likely to make the same mistakes, and suffer similar consequences.

A declaration of national independence over economic management is, in socialist terms, a necessary step in the process of political change; so is increased public spending. But as means to faster economic growth they are uncertain weapons, and as means to increased employment even more uncertain.

The major weakness of the Keynesian system was that it was based on the notion of management of a national economy, and took only secondary account of international considerations. For the two decades after the war, this analysis seemed more than adequate. It appeared to offer governments all the tools they needed to promote economic growth. National economic growth become both the main criterion and the main focus of political decision-making. When national economic management appeared to falter, international factors were brought in to explain failure. Keynesian theory can neither explain the relative success of some of the newly industrializing countries, nor the relative stagnation of the advanced ones, because it has no systematic way of looking at international capitalist development.

Meanwhile, there has been renewed interest in Marxist economics. A serious attempt has been made by Marxists both to take account of recent developments in the capitalist world economy, and to quantify and tighten up their analysis of national economies. Thus Marxist economists increasingly provide a challenge to the orthodox intellectual systems on which the main political parties of the capitalist world base their appeals. Throughout this book I have tried to evaluate and criticize the contribution of Marxist theory to the problems of unemployment in the industrialized world.

My conclusion, which is argued at length in the final chapter, is that the British working class has little choice but to accept the bleak consequences of being part of the inter- national capitalist system, unless it is willing to reject capitalism altogether. In other words, I consider that Benn and his followers are unduly optimistic in their hopes that they can steer a mixed economy in the direction of socialism. In fact, a growing section of the British Labour movement is already coming to that conclusion. The only theoretical framework that is at present available to them in which to formulate their analysis is a Marxist one. If they reach Marxist conclusions, this will be partly because the analyses offered them by all the respectable political leaders, including Benn, have proved hollow.

REFERENCES

1   William Beveridge, *Full Employment in a Free Society*, Allen and Unwin, 1944, p. 107, and OECD, *Main Economic Indicators*, 1972—81.
2   C. H. Feinstein, *Statistical Tables of National Income, Ependiture and Output of the UK, 1855–1965*, Cambridge University Press, 1972, and OECD, *Main Economic Indicators*. The considerably higher unemployment rates often quoted for the 1930s reflect percentages of the *insured* workforce.
3   Paul Cockle, Nigel Morgan and Brian Reading, 'Running out of time', ITEM Forecast, *Guardian*, 4 August 1981.
4   'How Benn would liberate Britain, the last colony', interview with Tony Benn by Eric Hobsbawm, *Guardian*, 29 September 1980. See also Tony Benn, 'Britain as a colony', *New Socialist*, September–October 1981, pp. 58–62.

2

Unemployment as Underutilization of Resources

No economic theory can have achieved such rapid and wide-spread political acceptance as Keynes' 'General Theory' did in the ten years after its publication. Equally, no economic theory can have been so widely and suddenly rejected as a guide to policy as that same theory was in the mid-1970s.

Keynes' theory was a product of the 1930s. It started with an explanation of mass unemployment in the industrialized world and developed into an account of the dynamics of a national economy. But its political success was a product of wartime and post-war conditions. By the time Keynes' theories began to be used in economic policy, unemployment was already far below its 1930s level. Without the war and the post-war boom it is highly improbable that his ideas would have been so quickly adopted.

The aspect of his system – or rather that developed by his followers – which most appealed to post-war governments was his emphasis on the management of aggregate demand. This suggested a positive role for government in the promotion of economic growth and – often somewhat incidentally – full employment. The great attraction of Keynesian theory was not so much that it seemed to provide a formula for the avoidance of cyclical slumps; it was that it seemed to suggest a way in which resources could be most efficiently brought to bear on the task of sustained expansion. According to Keynes, unemployment signified the wasteful underutiliza-tion of potentially productive resources.

His *General Theory,* published in 1936, started with an attack on the classical theory, which explained away all unem-ployment as either 'frictional' (short-term changes in the type of demand for labour) or 'voluntary' (unwillingness of workers to accept jobs at the wage-level offered). He agreed that it was possible, and often likely, that a national economy might reach an equilibrium below the level of full employment because of 'an insufficiency of effective demand'. This was because there was a constant danger that the total sum of consumption plus investment would fall short of the levels required to provide jobs for all. In particular, investment tended to fall away if the rate of profit declined. Thus, 'If the propensity to consume and the rate of new investment result in deficient effective demand, the actual level of employment will fall short of the supply of labour potentially available at the existing real wage.'[1]

Keynes also offered an explanation, albeit a rather simple one, as to why recessions were more likely to occur in rich countries than in poor ones; and hence, by implication, why more and more serious recessions were characteristic of the advance of capitalist development and industrialization.

> . . . the richer the community, the wider will tend to be the gap between its actual and its potential production; and therefore the more obvious and outrageous the defects of the economic system. For a poor community will be prone to consume by far the greater part of its output, so that a very modest measure of investment will be sufficient to provide full employment; whereas a wealthier community will have to discover much ampler opportunities for investment if the saving propensities of its wealthier members are to be compatible with the employment of its poorer members.[2]

Yet the eclipse of Keynesian theory as a political force coincided precisely with the reappearance of mass unemployment in the advanced industrialized countries. At the very moment when millions of industrial workers became redundant, the major capitalist nations decided virtually unanimously that this phenomenon could not be interpreted or handled as a failure of effective demand. It was not until 1981 that neo-Keynesianism re-emerged as politically significant, with Mitterrand's successful campaign to the French presidency, and in the Labour Party's programme in Britain.

In this chapter I shall trace the rise and fall of Keynesian accounts of unemployment and economic management, and consider their relevance for recent changes in the capitalist world economy.

KEYNESIANISM AND SOCIAL DEMOCRACY

The Great Depression of the early 1930s produced levels of unemployment that threatened the credibility of economists and politicians alike. In particular, mass unemployment discredited the orthodox economic theorists of the capitalist world, and the politicians of the centre parties. What Keynes called the 'classical school' of economists could not account for a recession that was so deep, so long-lasting and caused such massive human misery – or rather, their attempted explanations had a hollow ring. As technical political solutions seemed increasingly inadequate, political action – on the left and the right – prescribed more drastic remedies.

Even lifelong gradualist reformers saw the emergence of mass unemployment as a turning point in the viability of Western democratic capitalism. Although Britain and the United States avoided fascist coups and communist revolutions, leading political and economic thinkers lost faith in the technicalities of reform. Beatrice Webb, looking back in the early 1940s on five decades of Fabian endeavour, wrote:

> Confronted with this dismal tragedy of mass unemployment, . . . it is futile to suggest that . . . [our proposals for reform], even if fully implemented, would or could prevent mass destitution of the able-bodied. . . . Where we went hopelessly wrong was in ignoring Karl Marx's forecast of the eventual breakdown of the capitalist system. . . .[3]

Keynes' theory simultaneously rescued academic economics from this low ebb and restored the credibility of political parties of the centre. Whereas the Depression had made such governments seem impotent, Keynes appeared to give them new powers. But at the same time he seemed to show that the basic fault that caused mass unemployment was not in capitalism itself, still less in democracy, but rather in a technical issue concerned with aggregate levels of consumption, saving and investment.

Whether or not he fully intended this, Keynes' greatest contribution to economic policy was the notion that demand could be managed by government, and that this in turn meant that the economy as a whole could be managed. Before Keynes, the dominant orthodoxy suggested that economic events were ruled by the 'invisible hand' of laws, such as the law of supply and demand, and that the main role of government was to ensure free competition, and allow market forces to take their course. Confidence in a benevolent intelligence guiding the 'invisible hand' was greatly shaken by mass unemployment; thus the news that government itself could provide such an intelligence was very welcome to those who hoped that Western countries could gradually adapt to change, rather than be embroiled in the politics of class conflict.

In Britain, plans for full employment policies began to be made during the war. Lord Beveridge drew heavily on Keynes' theories in his report, *Full Employment in a Free Society*, in which he sought to show that such policies were consistent with 'the proviso that all essential citizen liberties are preserved. . . . The proviso excludes the totalitarian solution of full employment in a society completely planned and regimented by an irremovable dictator.' But he insisted that the state must accept responsibility for ensuring sufficient aggregate demand for the number of vacant jobs always to be as high as, or higher than, the number of people looking for jobs.

> No-one else has the requisite powers. . . . It must be the function of the state in future to ensure adequate total outlay and by consequence to protect its citizens against mass unemployment, as definitely as it is now the function of the state to defend the citizens against attack from abroad and against robbery and violence at home.[4]

The war and its aftermath provided many of the institutional frameworks for Keynesian policies. Wartime planning and controls, post-war reconstruction all required a more active role for the state. Fear of unrest and agitation, such as followed the First World War, contributed to a commitment to full employment, at least as an aim of economic policy. As the post-war boom continued in the late 1950s, this commitment gradually extended into an expectation of sustained economic growth. For if unemployment was essentially an avoidable underutilization of resources, this meant that each increase in the population, and each technological improvement in methods of production, could result in higher output of goods and services, and increases in productivity (output per person employed). Not only could governments control levels of employment; they could also predict and plan levels of growth of national income.

France was perhaps the leading exponent of economic planning in the 1950s, and the success of the French economy served as an advertisement for this method. In Britain both Conservative and Labour governments came to believe in the 1960s that faster and more sustained growth could be achieved by planning and co-operation between the state and private industry. The notion of economic management, in which a well-informed technocratic government played a leading role in smoothing the path to national prosperity, fitted the social democratic politics that were the predominant mode in Europe in this period. The Kennedy and Johnson administrations in the United States adopted a similar philosophy and style.

ECONOMIC MANAGEMENT AND GROWTH

In fact, I would argue that the capacity of governments to manage their economies was greatly over-estimated during this period. National incomes grew rapidly during these post-war boom years as world trade expanded, but this had little to do with government policies. Neither changes of government nor the differences between the regimes in different countries appeared to have much influence on rates of growth.

Indeed, if we compare the annual rates of growth in Gross National Product of the major industrialized nations in two

very different eras – the 1920s and the post-war period – a
remarkable consistency in the rank order of growth rates
becomes apparent (see table 2.1).[5] Two points about this
table stand out. The first is that the rank order of the nations is
almost identical in the two periods; the second is that, with the
exception of Japan's improved growth rate and the USA's
slight deterioration, the rates are very similar – in the cases of
Germany and Britain identical. This suggests that there are
far greater consistencies and continuities in comparative
growth rates than has been generally recognized.

Of course, the high growth rates of the 1920s were achieved
without the assistance of demand management or economic
planning, concepts that had not at the time been invented.
They were achieved in an era when the predominant
economic orthodoxy that guided governments was what today
would be called monetarism, and what Keynes called the
'classical theory'. The same consistency in growth rates can be
found by comparing the rates of some smaller industrialized
nations during the same two periods (see table 2.2).[6] The only
major exception to this consistency was Italy, whose growth
rate in the 1920s was only 2.3 per cent, but which achieved a
rate of 5.1 per cent in the period 1951–73.

Table 2.3 illustrates the way in which the rank order of
growth rates of the major industrialized countries remained
similar after 1973, even though growth slowed in most
countries to about half its previous rate of increase.[7]

What these figures suggest is a 'historical' rank order of

Table 2.1   *Average annual growth rates
of GNP of major industrialized countries
(per cent)*

	1922–29	1951–73
Japan	6.5	9.5
France	5.8	5.0
Germany	5.7	5.7
USA	4.8	3.7
UK	2.7	2.7

Table 2.2   *Average annual growth rates of GNP of smaller industrialized countries (per cent)*

	1922–29	1951–73
Canada	5.1	4.6
Denmark	3.6	4.2
Netherlands	4.0	5.0
Norway	3.9	4.2

rates of economic growth for different nations at any given rate of expansion of world trade. They suggest, for instance, that Britain can expect its rate of growth to be the slowest among the industrialized nations, just as surely as Japan can expect its rate to be the fastest. The historical reasons for these relative rates since the First World War will be discussed in later sections of this book. My main point here is that they have very little to do with economic management, and can be traced back to the pre-Keynesian era.

It is, of course, true that growth rates in the 1930s were not only much lower than in the 1920s, but also far more variable. France suffered a decline in national income of about 2 per cent per year in that decade, and the United States' economy was virtually stagnant. By contrast, Italy, Germany and Japan, all applying totalitarian versions of economic planning, achieved growth rates of half that of the previous

Table 2.3   *Average annual growth rate of GNP in the 1970s (per cent)*

	1951–73	1973–79
Japan	9.5	4.1
Italy	5.1	4.0
France	5.0	3.0
Germany	5.8	2.3
USA	3.7	2.4
UK	2.7	1.0

decade, or more. Clearly government policies can make recessions worse, as the present British government is illustrat-
ing, and there is evidence that they can also make them rather
less bad. There is much less evidence that governments can
make any long-term improvements in growth rates – that they
can speed up growth.

It was greatly in the interests of social democratic governments in this era to exaggerate their control over national
economic growth. Appealing as they did to a national
harmony of interests, and emphasizing a technical and man-
agerial style of government, they were able to play down the
significance of class conflict. Social policy enabled them to
provide some compensation to those excluded from growing
prosperity, while at the other end of the scale, progressive
taxation was justified in Keynesian terms as well as by notions
of social justice. Without any radical redistribution of income,
they could claim a key role in simultaneously managing the
increase in national income and ensuring that all classes
shared proportionately in the fruits of growth. Economic and
political stability were both founded on a consensus of the
social democratic centre.

SOCIAL DEMOCRACY AND UNEMPLOYMENT

Social democratic governments also exaggerated their control
over levels of unemployment. Just as there are countries
which historically have had high rates of economic growth, so
there are countries which historically have had high rates of
unemployment, even in times of relative prosperity. It is
important to note at this stage that there is no close correlation between rapid growth and low unemployment. Examples
of the industrialized countries which historically have had
high rates of unemployment are the United States, Italy,
Canada, Ireland and Denmark. Of these, Italy, Canada,
Denmark and recently Ireland have had high rates of growth.
Until recently, Britain has had one of the lowest rates of
economic growth and also one of the lowest rates of
unemployment.

If we compare the rates of growth of the OECD (i.e.

relatively developed capitalist) countries in the whole post-war era, the closest correlation between any one factor and economic growth is a purely structural, developmental one. It is the proportion of the active population still engaged in agriculture at the start of the period in question. In my book *Automatic Poverty*, I argued that this was because the situation of a rapid increase in industrial output and employment, and a rapid decline in agricultural employment, is the ideal recipe for fast expansion of national income.[8] This whole issue will be discussed at greater length in chapters 4, 5 and 6. The figures that illustrate this close correlation are shown in table 2.4.[9]

Table 2.4   *Growth rates and employment in agriculture (per cent)*

	Annual average rate of growth of GNP, 1960–73	Percentage of civilian workforce employed in agriculture, 1960
Japan	10.4	30.2
Italy	5.2	32.8
France	5.7	22.4
West Germany	4.6	14.0
USA	4.2	8.3
UK	3.0	4.2

	Annual average rate of growth of GNP, 1965–73	Percentage of civilian workforce employed in agriculture, 1965
Turkey	6.9	74.7
Greece	7.8	50.1
Portugal	6.7	35.5
Spain	6.8	33.6
Ireland	4.7	32.0
OECD (average)	4.8	32.6

For the purposes of this section, it is sufficient to note that the transition from a predominantly rural to a predominantly urban, industrialized economy is often but not always accompanied by relatively high levels of unemployment. This was true of Britain during much of the nineteenth century.

If it is true, as I shall suggest, that this transition provides the optimum conditions for economic growth, then this tends to undermine the importance of Keynesian demand management. It suggests that structural features of the national economy are more important than government policies in determining rates of economic growth. It also suggests that growth is often faster under conditions of less than full employment, if these other structural conditions obtain, than under conditions of full employment. Thus although unemployment represents unused resources, this does not necessarily imply an impaired rate of growth.

The countries that continued to have rather high rates of unemployment even during the post-war boom experienced a reduction or stabilization in unemployment rates in the 1960s and early 1970s compared with the 1950s. However, their unemployment rates rose rapidly in the mid and late 1970s, as is shown in figure 2.1.[10] (The data shown there are derived from OECD statistics, which are supposed to be broadly comparable.) Those countries that had lower unemployment rates in the 1950s and early 1960s began to experience gradually increasing rates of unemployment in the late 1960s, and subsequently rapid rises in their unemployment rates in the late 1970s, as is shown in figure 2.2.[11]

The real tests of Keynesian theories of economic management came, first when the United States, with its historically high rate of unemployment, tried to reduce this in the 1960s; and secondly, when Britain, whose rates were rising from the mid-1960s onwards, tried to curb this rise. If theories of demand management worked, and if unemployment represented wastefully underutilized productive resources, then governments should have been able to reduce or contain unemployment rates in these circumstances, and also to improve their rates of economic growth.

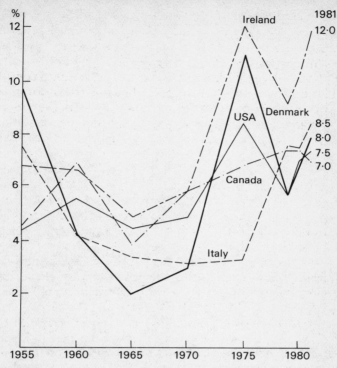

Figure 2.1   *Unemployment rates for countries with
relatively high post-war unemployment
(as a percentage of civilian workforce)*

THE FIRST TEST: THE UNITED STATES
IN THE 1960s

The persistence of high rates of unemployment and of widespread poverty in the United States in the early 1960s led the
Kennedy administration to adopt programmes based specifically on Keynesian economic theory. The government
sought to improve long-term rates of growth and to launch
anti-poverty policies simultaneously by raising public spending and by other measures to increase aggregate demand.

In fact, both poverty and unemployment in the United
States had historically been concentrated (along with every

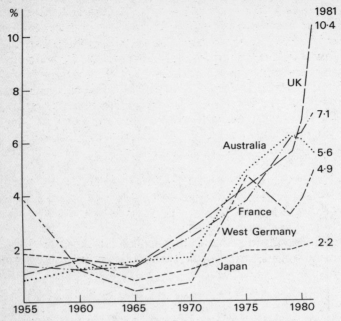

Figure 2.2   *Unemployment rates for countries with
low post-war unemployment
(as a percentage of civilian workforce)*

other social problem and indicator of social deprivation) in
certain social groups – black people, recent immigrants from
South and Central America, the unskilled, the under-
educated, the young and the old. In an economy with wide
differentials of earnings, such people, if they got work at all,
tended to be in short-term jobs, with low wages. They were
unlikely to belong to trade unions, or to have access to permanent jobs with prospects of promotion. Ample research had
shown that these inequalities were structural features of the
American social and economic system.

Yet the Kennedy and Johnson administrations attempted
to use macro-economic measures to increase economic activity, and draw these groups more fully into the employment
market. The theory behind this policy was that there was a

potential 'trade-off' between inflation and unemployment. This notion was not derived from Keynes himself. The British economist Professor A. W. Phillips had drawn attention in 1958 to the historical fact that inflation tended to be associated with low levels of unemployment. He set out the relationship between unemployment and inflation geometrically in his celebrated 'Phillips curve', plotting the level of unemployment on one axis, and the rate of change of wages over time on the other, showing that the more rapidly wages rose through increased demand, the less unemployment there would be. The Phillips curve was quickly accepted as a basis for economic policy.[12]

The deliberate creation by government of a measure of inflation in the American economy for purposes which could be interpreted as social policy (though it equally served economic policy ends) caused bitter controversy among academic economists and politicians. It gave rise to the Keynesian–monetarist conflict which has polarized economic policy in the capitalist world ever since. Monetarist criticisms of this policy will be discussed in detail in the next chapter. For the purposes of this section, my aim is to show that the policy did not work as the Phillips curve suggested it should, and that the reasons for this were structural to the United States economy.

The policies were intended to boost the rate of growth of national income as much as they were designed to increase the income of disadvantaged groups. The Kennedy adminstration took a number of Keynesian economists to Washington as advisers, and this group at once attracted the hostility and suspicion of the financial establishment and business world. Kennedy's measures were strongly resisted by Congress and many interest groups, and it was not until the Johnson administration that many of the main measures of the new programme were adopted. One of the new economic advisers, James Tobin, wrote in defence of the Kennedy approach in 1963:

> In January 1962 the President proposed three measures to reinforce the federal government's arsenal of anti-recession weapons. . . . None of these proposals involves

new government controls over individuals or businesses; none of them thrusts the government into new areas of activity. . . . the Kennedy Administration explicitly aims at a higher growth rate – specifically to reach 4½ per cent per year in the '60's, compared to the 2½ per cent realised in the years 1953–60. . . . All that the growth orientation implies is a somewhat different emphasis in the use of traditional instruments of policy – the budget, the tax structure, and monetary control. At the same time, more explicit long-range economic planning, both public and private, may help promote economic growth.[13]

Like other Keynesian economists, Tobin argued that an unemployment rate of over 5 per cent represented a level of economic activity leading to well below potential industrial output and national income. As the new policies began to be implemented, the first results were encouraging. Between 1962 and 1966, GNP at constant prices grew by 24.2 per cent, an annual average of nearly 6 per cent, which, with the steady growth of the US population, represented an average annual increase of GNP per head of 4.2 per cent. In the same period, unemployment as a percentage of the civilian workforce fell from 5.6 per cent to 3.8 per cent. The general rise in consumer prices during these years was 7.1 per cent, an average of only 1.7 per cent a year.[14] The new policies seemed to be working; unemployment was reduced without an unacceptable increase in the rate of inflation.

However, between 1966 and 1970, all these encouraging signs had disappeared. In these four years, the average rate of growth of GNP was only 2.4 per cent. GNP per head of population increased by a mere 1.4 per cent, and allowing for increases in taxation was virtually static. Unemployment, which had fallen to 3.5 per cent in 1969, rose again to 4.9 per cent in 1970, and to 5.9 per cent the following year. Consumer prices increased by 19.5 per cent between 1966 and 1970, an annual average of 4.6 per cent. A great many of the difficulties of the United States economy could be attributed to the costs of the Vietnam War; many others could be blamed on the economic policies of the Nixon administration, which took office in 1969. But it was largely Keynesian methods that were discredited by these setbacks.

The American experience of the 1960s was a severe test of Keynesian economic management, but one which the leading Democrats had sought. Keynesian economists and their political adherents had been highly critical of the way in which the economy had been run under the Eisenhower administration. The USA had a high historical unemployment rate, and they suggested that government intervention could, with only mildly inflationary policies, reduce this to a lower long-term rate. The USA had also entered, after the Second World War, a stage of historically slower growth of national income (as Britain did after the First World War). They also claimed that they could alter this trend.

The major reason for this slower rate of growth was the decline in the United States' share of world trade. Figure 2.3 illustrates the falling percentage share of the United States (and Britain) of the volume of manufactured exports, compared with the shares of other industrial countries.[15] It shows that the United States' share of world exports of manufactures was falling rapidly in the 1950s, and was a major factor in the slowing of economic growth (the same factor that caused the decline of the British growth rate in the 1920s). This fall in the share of exports did *not* increase in the 1960s when Keynesian policies were applied; in fact the rate of decline slowed down in the early part of that decade, and even in the late 1960s was not as rapid as in the late 1950s. Even so, Keynesian policies could not reverse this tendency, which was the chief cause of slower growth.

It is important to note that this decline in the United States' share of world trade cannot be attributed either to domestic inflation or to rising relative labour costs (stimulated by government monetary policy). Figure 2.4 illustrates the dramatic fall in relative labour costs in the United States in the 1960s, compared with most of its competitors, and particularly West Germany.[16] What was illustrated in the United States in the 1960s, therefore, was that Keynesian demand management could not offset structural factors, such as inequalities of wages and job opportunities and changes in the pattern of world trade. Furthermore, opposition to the policies indicated that business interests and the financial establishment preferred government to run the economy with stricter monetary controls, less state intervention in the market, less provision for the relief of poverty, and higher rates of unemployment. In other words, the business and financial sectors believed that the persistence of unemployment and poverty were not merely impervious to Keynesian policies, but also served their long-term interests.

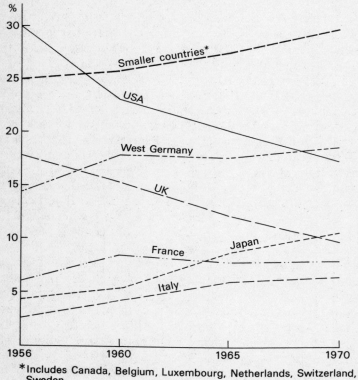

*Includes Canada, Belgium, Luxembourg, Netherlands, Switzerland, Sweden.

Figure 2.3   *Percentage shares of the volume of manufactured exports from industrial countries*

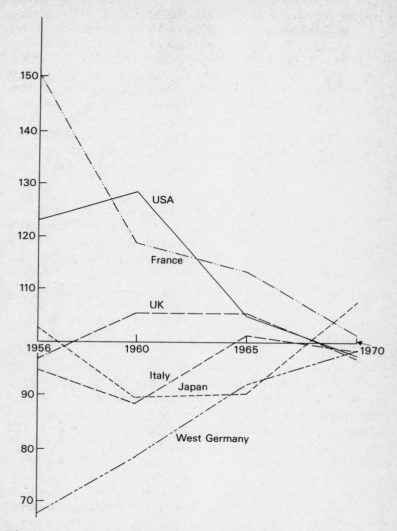

Figure 2.4 *Indices of relative unit labour costs of six large exporting countries*

THE SECOND TEST: BRITAIN IN THE
EARLY 1970s

A different kind of test of Keynesian principles of economic management was provided by Britain in the early 1970s. A Conservative government came to power in 1970 with a firm commitment to reducing the role of government in economic and social planning. In its election manifesto the Conservative Party argued that the Labour governments of the 1960s had failed in their attempts to use such interventions to promote growth. What was needed was a return to the laws of the market.

> Under Labour, there has been too much government interference in the day-to-day workings of industry and local government. There has been too much government: there will be less. . . . Our aim is to identify and remove obstacles that prevent effective competition and restrict initiative. . . . The bureaucratic burden imposed upon industry by government departments, agencies and boards has steadily increased in recent years. We will see that it is reduced.[17]

When the Conservative government came to power, the unemployment rate stood at 2.7 per cent of the civilian working population. Eighteen months later it had risen to nearly 4 per cent, with almost a million out of work. This had occurred despite several conventional attempts to produce an expansion of economic activity by fiscal and monetary measures – cuts in income tax, in purchase tax, and in the bank rate. At this point the government drastically revised its economic strategy, and increased its public spending plans. Government expenditure as a proportion of GDP increased from 51 per cent to 58 per cent between 1970 and 1974. Much of this increase was on social services, despite specific pledges at the election to control spending in this sector. However, there was also a considerable rise in government aid to industry under the Conservative government.

The problem that the Conservative government under

Edward Heath attempted to tackle by these Keynesian methods was one of slow growth of industrial production and gradually rising unemployment. Between 1966 and 1972, output of production industries (manufacturing, construction, mining and energy) increased by only 13 per cent, an annual average of 2.2 per cent. But employment in those industries declined by 14 per cent. In my recent book, *Automatic Poverty*, I argued that this was because industrialists began to use new methods of production to save labour costs rather than to increase output during this period. As this trend began to develop more rapidly from 1970 to 1972, the government attempted to stimulate increased industrial production by raising demand in the economy through rapid rises in public spending.

According to Keynesian theory, this policy should have been reasonably successful (subject to there being sufficient productive capacity available, or a sufficient amount of new industrial investment). The availability of a pool of unused potential industrial labour should have allowed a fairly rapid increase in production, and thus a simultaneous improvement in the rate of economic growth and lowering of the unemployment rates.

In fact, industrial production was slow to respond to the increase in aggregate demand. It did rise by 7.5 per cent between 1972 and 1973, but imports of manufactured goods were rising much more rapidly. Between 1969 and 1974, manufactured imports as a percentage of the UK domestic market increased from 10.2 per cent of the market to 16.7 per cent. This represented a rise in manufactured imports of 64 per cent. In the same period, West Germany (for example) had a fall of 12 per cent in its imports of manufactured goods.

This experience in Britain in the early 1970s suggests that under certain circumstances, attempts to stimulate production by increasing demand are likely to fail. Rising unemployment rates and falling employment in productive industry, which characterized the British economy in this period, were not indicative of artificially restrained output, resulting from deliberately dampened home demand (as the Keynesians suggested). They indicated instead that industrial decision-makers were anticipating a certain level of demand for their products and profitability of their firms, and were unwilling to alter their expectations as a result of increased aggregate demand in the economy as a whole.

When these long-term expectations about demand for products and profitability of enterprises are determining investment and output decisions, it appears that increases in the money supply and in public spending simply lead to higher imports and increased spending on speculation. Under the Conservative government, money intended for industrial investment was diverted into property speculation, with the result that the price of land and property rose very rapidly. Industrial profits actually *fell* considerably under the Conservative government – a fact that helps explain the rapid change in policies by the Conservative Party after its election defeats of 1974.

The fact is that industrial decision-makers base long-term investment decisions on historical rates of growth and profits, and are unwilling to change their long-term plans in line with short-term changes in government spending policies. The historical rate of growth of the British economy was relatively slow even during the post-war boom, and began to slow down even more after 1966, despite the Labour government's efforts to achieve long-term, planned growth. The experience of the Heath Conservative government merely underlined what became increasingly obvious in the 1970s. As a report by the Economist Intelligence Unit observed:

> . . . the general instability of the world economy, both stemming from and reinforced by uncertainty as to the availability of markets and of the value of currencies, means that any revival of productive activity through official attempts to stimulate demand is (a) harder to achieve (i.e. it requires a greater degree of deficit financing than in the past to achieve the same increase in activity), and (b) more likely to stimulate speculative than productive investment, which itself only reinforces inflationary pressures by pushing up the prices of raw materials and other factors of production into which speculative money is switched, as soon as there appears to be any sign of revival in growth.[18]

Thus the *ad hoc* British experiment in Keynesianism produced a very high rate of inflation (running at an annual rate of 16 per cent by 1974) for a rather modest rate of growth. It also had less than dramatic effects on unemployment, which fell from over 900,000 in early 1972 to 575,000 in mid-1973, but rose again to 866,000 in 1975. As in the United States during the previous decade, this failure played right into the hands of monetarist and conservative critics, who had been predicting that inflation was cumulative under such methods of demand management.

The structural problems of the British economy were rather different from those of the American, but one major factor – their declining share of world trade – was common to both. These experiments indicated that demand management on its own could not counter a fall in international competitiveness, historically high rates of unemployment, nor the tendency for industrialists to use new investment to save labour – the 'Ricardo phenomenon' which I identified in *Automatic Poverty*.

THE ECLIPSE OF KEYNESIAN ECONOMIC POLICY

With the Middle East War and the oil price crisis of 1973–74, the advanced industrialized countries faced a recession, accompanied by the re-emergence of mass unemployment among industrial workers. Some social democratic leaders, including Harold Wilson (see chapter 4, p. 57), agreed that governments could spend their way out of this situation, provided they all adopted similar policies, in spite of adverse trade balances with the OPEC countries.

Yet the rejection of Keynesian arguments for such an approach was emphatic and, within two years, virtually unanimous among the advanced capitalist nations. The Secretary-General of the OECD (representing the most developed 24 countries of the capitalist world) made clear the basis of this rejection in a speech in 1977.

. . . it is important to distinguish conceptually, though it may be difficult statistically, between two kinds of

unemployment. *First,* and the more important quantita-
tively, there is the cyclical (or conjunctural) kind, stemming from the deep world-wide recession of 1974–75,
and the fact that a prudent non-inflationary recovery
from that recession will necessarily be a slow process
lasting several years. . . .

Second . . . there are other forms of unemployment –
long-term structural unemployment – calling for policies
other than demand-management. . . . The [OECD]
strategy held, and holds, that a too-rapid increase in
demand would lead to only short-lived employment
gains, since the resulting inflation would soon touch off a
new recession and lead to increased rather than
decreased unemployment.[19]

The 'structural problems' mentioned by the Secretary-
General remained extremely shadowy; they defied either
economic analysis or political solution. But the consensus of
opinion among governments of the advanced capitalist world
was that they were unresponsive to Keynesian measures
alone.

The first factor, noted by economists in all the European
countries and in Britain, was a tendency from 1965 onwards
for the rate of increase of industrial employment to decline. In
Britain and West Germany the number of industrial jobs
actually fell, but in several other countries the total number of
man-hours worked in industry declined, even where the
number of jobs continued to increase slowly.[20] While dis-
agreeing about the causes of this, economists noted that in the
mid-1960s there had been a shift in the relative use of capital
and labour in the advanced industrialized countries, and a
tendency for capital to be substituted for labour. Research
studies in Italy and France suggested that government-
supported investment was being used to save labour costs,
and not increase employment.[21]

This in turn was connected with a second factor. As a result
of the high capital intensity of much new industry, new
factories had become very expensive to set up, and a great
deal of expenditure produced very few jobs. Where new
capital-intensive industry was growing, and old-fashioned

labour-intensive factories closing, this investment might well, while increasing output, still result in a net loss of jobs.

All this suggested that, at the lower level of growth of world production that prevailed in the late 1970s, the industrial sectors of the advanced capitalist countries could not provide increased employment opportunities. But employment in other sectors of these economies might be increased more readily by government action – for example, in the public sector, and especially in the social services. The problem here was that although there was always work to be done, rates of pay tended to be very low. The new incomes provided did not compensate for the loss of better-paid industrial jobs. This could cause governments problems – for example, the 'winter of discontent' in Britain in 1979, when public sector workers rebelled against pay restraint.

Keynesian theory provided no indications of how to deal with any of these problems. But nor did any other orthodox economic theory. Into this theoretical vacuum stepped monetarism, which dismissed the whole notion that unemployment necessarily implied underutilized resources. The political right was quick to take advantage of the opportunity provided by the eclipse of Keynesian economic management; it simply argued that full employment was an unrealistic goal.

Mass unemployment had reduced social democratic governments to a similar state of impotence in the late 1970s to that which it produced in similar governments in the 1920s and 1930s. Their failure was all the more ignominious because of the exaggerated claims they had made for their techniques of economic management. In the last resort, social democratic governments could do little or nothing about the 'structural' features of unemployment because these represented new developments in capitalism. Having ridden largely passively on capitalism's back for 30 years, they could do little but allow themselves to be carried off in its new directions.

KEYNESIANISM REBORN

With Mitterrand's campaign for the French presidency and the new programme of the British Labour opposition, Keynesian policies for economic expansion re-emerged in 1981. It is too early, at the time of writing, to judge Mitterrand's commitment to the Keynesian approach. In the case of the British Labour Party, an attempt has been made to try to counter another important weakness of the Keynesian analysis.

I have already suggested in this chapter that the major factor in the failure of American and British attempts to reduce unemployment and increase the rate of economic growth was their tendency towards a falling share of world trade, especially in manufactured exports, and a rising proportion of imports. Tony Benn and his followers have argued that this can only be countered in Britain by import controls and tariffs, and that the use of these tools of economic management are a necessary part of successful Keynesian policies in such circumstances.

It is true that Keynes was not opposed in principle to protectionism. In his *General Theory* he pointed out 'an element of scientific truth' in the notion of using import controls and tariffs to restore a favourable balance of trade.

> When a country is growing in wealth somewhat rapidly, the further progress of this happy state of affairs is liable to be interrupted, in conditions of *laissez-faire*, by the insufficiency of the inducements to new investment. . . . In conditions in which the quantity of aggregate investment is determined by the profit motive alone, the opportunities for home investment will be governed, in the long run, by the domestic rate of interest, whilst the volume of foreign investment is necessarily determined by the size of the favourable balance of trade. Thus, in a society where there is no question of direct investment under the aegis of public authority, the economic objects, with which it is reasonable for the government to be preoccupied, are the domestic rate of interest and the balance of trade.[22]

Keynes went on to examine in some detail the mercantilist theories of protectionism which prevailed before Adam Smith. In other words, his purpose was not to justify tariffs in modern economic management, but to complete his discrediting of classical economic theory by showing that one of its central tenets, free trade, was not a universally valid principle, even though it had been appropriate in nineteenth-century conditions. He tried to show that the mercantilists were justified in their doctrines under very early capitalism. If there is an inference to draw from this in terms of modern applications, it would probably apply to young, newly industrializing economies.

Furthermore, Keynes issued numerous caveats about his justification of protectionism. He warned that 'the advantages claimed are avowedly national advantages, and are unlikely to benefit the world as a whole.'[23] He suggested that it was less likely to be successful for a large country with a major share in world trade than for a small one. He pointed out that it was only likely to succeed if the money supply was rigidly controlled, and domestic costs firmly kept down, as inflation could quickly transform potential expansion into persistent recession.[24] He concluded:

> For this and other reasons the reader must not reach a premature conclusion as to the *practical* policy to which our argument leads up. There are strong presumptions of a general character against trade restrictions unless they can be justified on special grounds. The advantages of the international division of labour are real and substantial, even though the classical school greatly overstressed them. The fact that the advantages which our own country gains from a favourable balance is liable to involve an equal disadvantage to some other country . . . means not only that greater moderation is necessary, . . . but also that an immoderate policy may lead to a senseless international competition for a favourable balance which injures all alike.[25]

My own purpose in recording these observations by Keynes is not to attack protectionism, but to point out that it was never an important feature of his system. He was essentially an economist who believed that national economic policies could produce an efficient enough use of national resources to ensure a rapid rate of growth of world trade; and that expanding international trade, including foreign investment, was the best way of maximizing national prosperity. This is clearly shown in the following passage:

> It is the policy of an autonomous rate of interest, un-impeded by international preoccupations, and of a national investment programme directed to an optimum level of domestic employment which is twice blessed in the sense that it helps ourselves and our neighbours at the same time. And it is the simultaneous pursuit of these policies by all countries together which is capable of restoring economic health and strength internationally, whether we measure it by the level of domestic employment or by the volume of international trade.[26]

In other words, the Cambridge group whose theories inspire Benn and his followers are in an important sense Keynesian revisionists, and the onus is very heavily on them to show how their doctrines represent an improvement on those of their avowed master. I shall consider this question in chapter 4.

REFERENCES

1   J. M. Keynes, *The General Theory of Employment, Interest and Money*, Macmillan, 1936 (1957 edn), p. 30.
2   Ibid, p. 31.
3   Beatrice Webb, *Our Partnership*, Longman, 1948, pp. 487–8.
4   William Beveridge, *Full Employment in a Free Society*, Allen and Unwin, 1944, pp. 21, 29.
5   J. Cornwell, *Modern Capitalism, its Growth and Transformation*, Martin Robertson, 1977.
6   Ibid.
7   OECD, *Main Economic Indicators*, 1970–81.
8   Bill Jordan, *Automatic Poverty*, Routledge and Kegan Paul, 1981.
9   OECD, *Main Economic Indicators*, 1974, and OECD, *Labour Force Statistics*, 1958–1969.
10   OECD, *Main Economic Indicators*, 1955–81.
11   Ibid.

12 A. W. Phillips, 'The relation between unemployment and the rate of change of money wage rates in the United Kingdom, 1861–1957', *Economica*, November 1958, pp. 283–99.

13 James Tobin, 'How planned is our economy?', *New York Times Magazine*, 13 October 1963. Republished in *National Economic Policy*, Yale University Press, 1966, pp. 10–11.

14 OECD, *Main Economic Indicators*.

15 M. Fetherston, B. Moore and J. Rhodes, 'Manufacturing export shares and cost competitiveness of advanced industrialised countries', in Cambridge Department of Applied Economics, *Cambridge Economic Policy Review*, March 1977, no. 3, Gower Press, table 6.1, p. 63.

16 Ibid., table 6.2.

17 F. W. S. Craig (ed.), *British Election Manifestos 1900–1974*, Macmillan, 1975, pp. 330–2.

18 H. Shutt, *The Jobs Crisis*: *Increasing Unemployment in the Developed World*, Economist Intelligence Unit, Special Report no. 85, 1980 (price £30, pp. 78), pp. 50–1.

19 OECD, *Structural Determinants of Employment and Unemployment* vol. 1, Experts' Meeting, Paris, 7–11 March 1977, pp. 3–4.

20 Ibid., p. 84.

21 Ibid., p. 72.

22 Keynes, *General Theory*, p. 335.

23 Ibid.

24 Ibid., pp. 337–8.

25 Ibid., pp. 338–9.

26 Ibid., p. 349.

3

Unemployment as Misallocation of Labour

Although the political economy of free market capitalism has had a long history, there is a peculiar sense in which this political and economic tradition is now associated with a reaction against Keynesian policies and social democratic governments. The monetarist critique has been strongest in the English-speaking countries precisely because it was in the United States and Britain that Keynesian policies were tested and found wanting. Margaret Thatcher and Ronald Reagan both declared 'war on inflation', and fought successful election campaigns based on cuts in public spending and a return to free market principles.

The monetarist explanation of high rates of unemployment depends entirely on the notion of a long period during which productive resources have been misallocated because of government policy. The explanation of unemployment is secondary to the explanation of inflation. The sole cause of inflation, according to the monetarists, has been the tendency of government to allow the supply of money to grow more quickly that the output of goods and services. Governments' desire to prevent or reduce unemployment has certainly been one reason for this tendency, but the main explanation for unemployment is as a consequence rather than a cause of monetary policy.

According to the theory, all the mechanisms of the market, upon which the healthy functioning of economic life depends, have been continuously weakened by the monetary policies of most Western governments since the war. Gradually government intervention, planning and direction have replaced the movement of prices and wages as the major influence on these economies. As a result, labour has become maldistributed between industries, with government-induced inflation allowing many undertakings to survive which would have been unprofitable under normal market conditions.

Thus monetary expansion only succeeds in creating a sector of employment which depends on still further inflation to continue in existence. What is prevented by such policies is precisely the adjustment of the distribution of the labour force and the structure of wages to continuous changes in the direction of demand which is necessary for high and stable employment.

The veteran Austrian economist F. A. Hayek summed up the monetarist position in 1972 thus:

> The illusion that maladjustments in the allocation of resources and of *relative* prices can be cured by manipulation of the *total* quantity of money is at the root of most of our difficulties. Such a use of monetary policy is more likely to aggravate than to reduce these maladjustments. Monetary policy can at most temporarily, but never in the long run, relieve us of the necessity to make changes in the use of resources required by changes in the real factors. It ought to aim at assisting this adjustment, not delaying it.[1]

The logic of monetarism thus stands the Keynesian revolution on its head. It reasserts the benevolence of the 'invisible hand' of market forces, and castigates the all-too-visible hand of government intervention as the cause of both unemployment and inflation. Its strength, both as a theory and as a political force, depended heavily on its criticisms of the failures of Keynesian methods and social democratic policies.

In this chapter I shall show how the monetarist critique developed, and how it was adapted to fit the political needs of the right-wing politicians in the United States and Britain. But I shall also show that once the impetus of its onslaught on Keynesian failures has been spent, the theory has very little to say about long-term structural features of unemployment in the Western developed world.

THE ORIGINS OF MONETARISM

Monetarism is no more or less than a revival of the doctrines of the 'classical school', which Keynes seemed finally to have discredited in the 1930s. It owed its successful reappearance to the increasing evidence of failures in the policies of social democratic governments. But before this evidence became clear, Keynesian economic management had already received a setback with the election of Richard Nixon to the American presidency.

Nixon did not put forward a coherent critique of his predecessors' policies. In the build-up to the American presidential election of 1968, opposition to the Johnson administration centred on its increased provision for social welfare expenditure, its budget deficits and its tolerance of high rates of inflation. These discontents were fuelled by academic criticisms of economic policy under Johnson, but when Nixon came to power he had no clear alternative economic strategy. His main economic advisers were not of the new monetarist school, and many of his subsequent policies were quite at odds with monetarist advice. Thus, although monetarist criticisms of the Johnson administration may have contributed to Nixon's victory, monetarism was not directly implicated in the failure of Nixon's economic policies.

One of the clearest statements of the new monetarist philosophy was made by Milton Friedman in his presidential address to the American Economic Association in December 1967. In his lecture on 'The Role of Monetary Policy', he attacked the theory that there was a 'trade off' between inflation and unemployment, and the policies derived from it. He argued that in originating the theory of the 'trade off', Phillips had confused rises in money wages with rises in real wages. Increases in money wages could only reduce unemployment in so far as they were unanticipated. In an inflationary situation, employers and employees would anticipate future likely inflation rates, so that the 'Phillips curve' would in fact be a vertical line in the long run, with the result that unemployment would stay the same at any rate of inflation.

Friedman's analysis suggested that the only stable

equilibrium between wages and unemployment occurred at the point where aggregate demand and supply in the economy were in balance, so that there was neither upward nor downward pressure on the rate of inflation. This point would indicate the 'natural rate' of unemployment, a rate determined by factors quite other than government management of the economy. According to Friedman:

> The 'natural rate of unemployment' . . . is the level that . . . [reflects] the structural characteristics of the labour and commodity markets, including market imperfections, . . . the cost of gathering information about job vacancies and labour availabilities, the costs of mobility and so on.[2]

The role of monetary policy was to ensure that the supply of money corresponded with the output of goods and services. The 'natural rate of unemployment' could be changed, by policies that directly affected conditions in the labour market – skills training, mobility subsidies, and so on – but not by increasing aggregate demand.[2]

At this stage in the development of the monetarist thesis, the emphasis was thus still on the folly of trying to reduce unemployment below the 'natural rate', rather than on the tendency of inflationary policies to produce higher rates of unemployment in the long term. In his presidential campaign, Nixon attacked his predecessors' record on inflation much more in terms of its effect on individual freedom than its implications for full employment.

> Inflation penalizes thrift and encourages speculation. Because it is a national and perverse force – dramatically affecting individuals but beyond their power to influence – inflation is a source of frustration for all who lack great economic powers.[3]

In office, Nixon's economic policies were pragmatic and spectacularly unsuccessful. He managed to attract almost equally strong condemnation from Galbraith, the leading Keynesian economist, and Friedman, the leading monetarist.

For the first two years of his presidency he combined a considerably larger budget deficit (as a result of the growing costs of the Vietnam war) with tight monetary control – so tight that even Friedman (through his column in *Newsweek*) begged him to increase the money supply. The result was a combination of rapidly rising unemployment and accelerating inflation in 1970–71. Having rejected Johnson's incomes and prices 'guideposts', Nixon imposed in August 1971 a statutory wages and prices freeze, to the fury of the monetarists. But in 1973 he dismantled this sytem, so that even before the Middle East War of that November, inflation was again rampant (wholesale prices were rising at an annual rate of 18 per cent). By 1974 the unemployment rate was 7.1 per cent of the civilian labour force.

Yet because Nixon briefly followed Galbraith's advice on imposing prices and incomes controls, it was possible for the monetarists to blame these disasters mainly on a combination of Nixon's policies in this period (1971–72) and the oil price crisis. Monetarism emerged remarkably unscathed from the Nixon episode.

MONETARISM AND THE BRITISH
CONSERVATIVE PARTY

As monetarist theory developed in the early 1970s, the British Conservative Party represented a challenging target for its influence. On the one hand, monetarist thinking had influenced the Selsdon Conference, which gave rise to the Conservative election manifesto of 1970, and there were still a number of leading backbench Conservatives who held strongly monetarist views. On the other hand, the Conservative government of 1970–74 had committed itself to rapid expansion of the money supply and of public spending.

Following the oil price crisis and the defeat of the Conservatives in the 1974 election, the monetarists argued forcefully that rates of inflation in Britain were already far too high, and accelerating. In September 1974 Milton Friedman came to London and delivered an updated version of his 1967 lecture, incorporating the new notion that the effects of expansionist monetary policy were cumulative.

The only way unemployment can be kept below the 'natural rate' is by an *ever-accelerating* inflation, which always keeps current inflation ahead of anticipated inflation. Any resemblance between that analysis and what you in Britain have been observing is not coincidental: what recent British governments have tried to do is to keep unemployment below the natural rate, and to do so they have had to accelerate the rate of inflation – from 3.9 per cent in 1964 to 16.0 per cent in 1974, according to official statistics. . . . the higher the rate of inflation, the more widespread is likely to be the government interference in the market. In effect, such interference is equivalent to increasing the amount of frictions and obstacles in the labour market, and therefore does tend to create a higher level of unemployment. . . . Given the way in which the political and economic structure will adapt itself to different rates of inflation, *if you continue to let inflation accelerate you are going to have higher unemployment either way.* So you only have a choice about which way you want unemployment to come. Do you want it to come while you are getting sicker, or do you want it to come while you are getting better?[4]

The same month, Sir Keith Joseph made a speech on unemployment and economic policy which marked the beginning of the conversion of the Conservative Party to monetarism, and the ousting of Edward Heath. Arguing that unemployment statistics were misleading, and largely reflected people changing jobs and the voluntarily unemployed, he claimed:

The effect of over-reacting to temporary recessions has been to push up inflation to even higher levels, not to help the unemployed, but to increase their numbers. . . . If policies are to be judged by the criterion of the greatest good of the greatest number, then excessive expansion of the money supply has been found wholly wanting, in practice and theory alike. . . . The monetarist thesis has been caricatured as implying that if we get the flow of money spending right, everything will be right. This is not – repeat not – my belief. What I believe is that if we

get the money supply wrong – too high or too low –
nothing will come right. Monetary control is a pre-
essential for everything else we need and want to do; an
opportunity to tackle the real problems – labour
shortage in one place, unemployment in another; . . .
inefficiencies, frictions and distortions; hard-core unemployment; the hundreds of thousands who need training
or retraining or persuading to move if they are to have
steady, satisfactory jobs; unstable world prices. There is
no magic cure for these problems; we have to cope with
them as best we can.[5]

As the new philosophy developed in the Conservative
Party, explanations of the long-term distortions in the allocation of resources in Britain were made in terms of excessive
state intervention. Ever since the war, governments had
pursued policies that affected the balance between public
and private sectors, between consumption and investment,
between profitable and tax-supported enterprises. In another
speech in 1976, entitled 'Monetarism in Not Enough', Sir
Keith Joseph dwelt on the discouragement of the manufacturing sector.

Normally in a balanced economy we need not worry
about the direction of enterprise . . . because the advantages and disadvantages are market questions and
enterprise will go where there is a demand for it. But the
choice is no longer balanced: legislation, taxation, inflation, union attitudes, all make employment of labour
and the risks of manufacture more and more disproportionate to the potential rewards. So the balance has
been shifted sharply in favour of service activity – and the
consequent loss of manufacturing enterprise narrows the
base on which all depends.[6]

That there were sufficient potentially profitable enterprises
to absorb the labour available in the economy was largely a
matter of faith. The new theories were acknowledged by one
of their most distinguished proponents to be untestable.
Hayek argued that there could be no tests of hypotheses about

intrinsically complex human phenomena. Successive Keynesian measures had distorted the whole system of prices and wages. 'And it can be corrected only by a change in these relations, that is, by the establishment in each sector of the economy of those prices and wages at which supply will equal demand.'[7] He claimed that the process had been going on for so long that it was impossible to know exactly where the most important over-developments had taken place, and that this would have to be investigated separately for each country. Furthermore, 'the places where misplaced and consequently now *displaced* workers can now find lasting employment can be discovered only by letting the market operate freely'.[8]

'TOO FEW PRODUCERS'

Following the oil price crisis of 1973–74, the rates of growth of all the Western industrialized countries slowed to roughly half their average rate during the previous 20 years. The crisis was used to justify higher rates of unemployment, and the adoption of measures of economic policy that concentrated on attempts to restore the profitability of private industry. Those social democratic governments that were in power pursued similar policy aims.

As I have already suggested in the cases of the United States and Britain, a tendency for rates of growth to slow down was already apparent from the mid-1960s onwards. The same tendency was also emerging in the other Western industrialized countries at the time, as I shall argue in subsequent chapters.

For the monetarists and their Conservative followers, the slowing down of growth and the rise in unemployment were seized upon as evidence for their thesis on the long-term consequences of government intervention. Above all, they argued that the direction of change should be towards a return to the free market, and away from state action and state control – a strengthening of the private sector at the expense of the public sector.

In Britain one of the influential statements by economists of the dangers of the growth of the public sector was the book by

Robert Bacon and Walter Eltis, first published in 1976, and entitled *Britain's Economic Problem: Too Few Producers*. Its analysis was not made in doctrinaire monetarist terms, and it was aimed as much at the Labour government as at the Conservative opposition. Indeed, it put forward a way of thinking about the British economy (based on rather specious comparisons with other economies) which was rapidly becoming the orthodoxy of the Labour government.

Bacon and Eltis argued that successive governments of both parties had eroded the profitability of British industry by imposing prices and incomes controls. But above all governments had been guilty of using up national resources by the rapid expansion of the public sector.

> . . . successive governments have allowed large numbers of workers to move out of industry and into various service occupations, where they still consume and invest industrial products, but produce none themselves. . . . the proportion of the nation's labour force that has been producing marketed output has been falling year by year; at the same time those who have had to rely on others to produce marketed output for them, civil servants, social workers and most teachers and medical workers, have been increasingly numerous, and have had to satisfy their requirements by consuming goods and services that diminishing numbers of market sector workers are producing.[9]

Bacon and Eltis were expressing views that largely reflected what was already government policy by 1976. Having been elected on what it called its 'socialist programme' in 1974, the Labour government rapidly shifted its gound in the second half of 1975, and declared itself intent upon restoring the private sector. In a speech in February 1976, the Chancellor of the Exchequer, Denis Healey, declared that:

> The TUC and the Labour Party are united in believing that the steady contraction in our manufacturing industry is the main reason for our disappointing economic performance since the war. This contraction must be halted and reversed. But we cannot reverse the trend if

we plan to take more resources into the public services. . . . In recent years our competitors have increased the manpower in their manufacturing industry; we have seen a massive shift of manpower out of manufacturing into public services. . . . We cannot afford to continue eroding the foundation of our prosperity in this way.[10]

In much the same vein, the Prime Minister, James Callaghan, spoke in the House of Commons on 27 April of the same year. 'It is important that productive jobs should be created and that we should rely on investments on which a successful return can be expected. That is the way to achieve more employment rather than by transferring more and more jobs to the public sector.'

Cuts in public expenditure held down the numbers employed by central and local government between 1975 and 1979, as can be seen from table 3.1.[11] In fact, however, service employment in the private sector went on increasing during the same period. This was particularly the case in financial and professional services, in miscellaneous services and in catering. This can be contrasted with the continued decline in the same period in the numbers employed in the production industries. As the table shows, depite the efforts of the Labour government the slight increase in this type of employment in 1976–77 was not sustained.

Table 3.1   *Numbers employed in different sectors in the UK (thousands)*

	1975	1976	1977	1978	1979
Local government	996	958	944	952	968
Central government	612	623	621	616	612
Financial,business, professional and scientific services	4,552	4,647	4,674	4,720	4,797
Miscellaneous services	1,341	1,412	1,441	1,474	1,506
Catering	816	840	853	880	912
Production industries	9,509	9,256	9,259	9,191	9,138

The change in the proportion of industrial to other forms of employment was not a uniquely British phenomenon. In spite of Bacon and Eltis' rhetoric, Britain merely experienced a rather exaggerated form of a change that affected all the major OECD countries in the 1960s and 1970s. Furthermore, similar attempts made by the other countries to control public spending and strengthen the private sector after 1973 were hardly more successful than Britain's. The figures in table 3.2 show the changes between 1962 and 1980, by which time Britain had a Conservative government, even more committed to an attempt at cutting the public sector and strengthening industry.[12]

The trend in these figures emerges more clearly when they are expressed as percentages of the total labour force in the six countries (see table 3.3). (The missing percentage represents the proportion employed in agriculture in each country.)[13] From this table it is clear that the proportion of the labour force employed in productive industry has declined in every one of the six major Western industrialized nations since 1973 – even in Japan. In Italy, the percentage decline was even larger than in Britain. Similarly, in every country the percentage employed in other (mainly service) jobs has increased

Table 3.2 *Numbers employed in industry (thousands)*

		1962	1973	1978	1980
UK	Industry	11,945	10,487	9,698	9,068
	Other	11,885	13,432	14,204	14,350
W. Germany	Industry	13,062	12,973	11,112	11,322
	Other	9,920	11,275	11,980	12,444
France	Industry	7,244	8,243	7,790	7,639
	Other	7,692	10,151	11,396	11,602
Italy	Industry	7,842	8,051	7,633	7,766
	Other	6,192	7,067	9,321	10,086
USA	Industry	22,173	26,745	29,427	29,567
	Other	39,585	52,212	61,445	64,771
Japan	Industry	14,210	19,470	18,930	19,750
	Other	18,680	25,830	28,820	30,283

Table 3.3   *Percentage of total labour force employed in industry*

		1962	1973	1978	1980
UK	Industry	48.2	42.6	39.5	37.7
	Other	48.0	54.5	57.9	59.6
W. Germany	Industry	49.7	49.5	45.0	44.9
	Other	37.7	43.0	48.5	49.3
France	Industry	38.5	39.3	36.9	36.4
	Other	40.9	48.4	54.0	54.9
Italy	Industry	39.5	44.0	38.1	37.3
	Other	31.2	38.6	46.5	48.4
USA	Industry	31.7	33.2	31.2	30.2
	Other	64.2	59.3	65.1	66.3
Japan	Industry	31.2	37.2	35.0	35.6
	Other	41.0	49.4	53.1	54.6

since 1973. The percentage increase in Britain between 1973 and 1980 was the lowest of all the six countries.

The highest proportions of industrial employment achieved in any of these countries during the whole period 1962–80 were in West Germany and Britain (49.7 per cent and 48.2 per cent respectively) in 1962. In 1980, only West Germany had over 40 per cent of its labour force in industrial employment. Only Japan of all the six major industrialized countries had a higher proportion of industrial workers in 1980 than it had had in 1962. The pattern of the proportions between the two sectors is fairly similar between the six countries, with only Germany and Italy having proportions of non-industrial employment less than 50 per cent.

On the other hand, industrial employment increased as a proportion of all employment in each of the six countries between 1962 and 1973, with the exception of West Germany, where it declined very slightly, and Great Britain, where it declined much more. This is paradoxical, since it was precisely in this period that governments generally were following the interventionist, inflationary, Keynesian policies of which the monetarists complain. If misallocation of labour was occurring throughout this period, it seems remarkable that industrial employment was able to grow as a proportion of all employment then, whereas during the following period (1973–80), when monetarist policies were more generally adopted, industrial employment universally fell as a proportion of all employment.

The obvious conclusion to draw from this is that monetarist restrictions can slow down or reverse the tendency of service and public sector employment to grow, but they have an even more negative effect on employment in the industrial and private sectors, especially in manufacturing industry. This has been vividly illustrated in Britain during the Conservative government's spell in office.

Figure 3.1 illustrates the decline in employment in British manufacturing industry since 1970. It shows how rapid the fall was in 1980, when the Conservatives' economic measures began to take effect.[14] It also illustrates how difficult it would be to reverse the downward trend of employment in this sector. In only two years, 1972–73 and 1976–77, was there an increase in employment in manufacturing industry. The rapid expansion attempted by the Heath government increased employment by only 0.5 per cent. Even if the Conservative government attempted another such expansion, it is unlikely it would do any better. In fact, numbers employed in manufacturing were still falling rapidly in 1981.

LONG-TERM CHANGES

In monetarist theory, there is a price for every commodity and a wage for every potential employee which will evolve through the mechanisms of demand or supply if the market is left free to reveal them. Unemployment is merely an expression of the time it takes for people to accept these revelations.

If the theory was carried to its logical conclusion, even in times of rapid economic growth, firms, industries, regions and even nations that were relatively uncompetitive in their productive methods would suffer loss of income. The result would be that unemployment would occur, wages would fall and standards of living decline until new industries were

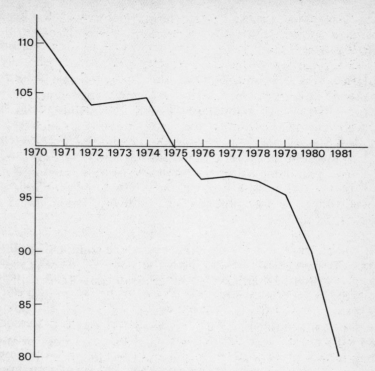

Figure 3.1 *Index of employed labour force in manufacturing industry (1975 = 100)*

established, or workers moved to other areas, regions or countries.

In times of stagnation or slow growth of world trade, there would be far more widespread redundancies and a general fall in the levels of wages and living standards. Although there might be a few districts in which employment was increasing, and wages rising, there would be no widespread opportunities for labour to move about in search of higher standards of living. The working population would be forced to endure a period – possibly prolonged – of reduced income.

This represents a return to the pre-war period. In order to justify the monetarist theory of unemployment, it is necessary to explain away the phenomena of the 1930s, since they cannot have been caused by Keynesian errors. This was precisely what Sir Keith Joseph tried to do in his lecture, 'Monetarism is Not Enough'.

> It is often forgotten that the thirties was a period of growth, expanding employment, rising living standards for a majority of manual workers. Our growth rate was higher in the 1930s than that of other countries such as the USA, Germany and France. We could not reach full employment because the world was in depression – indeed, the same constraint applies to us with even more force now that we are comparatively weaker economically than we were then – but relatively, Britain was successful.[15]

This extraordinary statement deserves some comment. In the whole period from 1929 to 1938 the numbers unemployed varied between 3,400,000 in 1932 (15.6 per cent of the civilian working population) and 1,776,000 in 1937 (7.8 per cent). In 1938 there were still over 2 million unemployed (9.3 per cent). Personal disposable income *per capita* fell from £91 in 1929 to £83 in 1932, and was still only £93 in 1936. The total amount paid in wages in manufacturing industry fell from £637.8 million in 1929 to £524.2 million in 1932, and was still only £607.3 million in 1935. The total amount paid in wages in mining and quarrying did not reach its 1929 level again until 1937. The numbers employed in manufacturing were still lower in 1935 than they had been in 1929, and still lower in mining in 1938 than they had been in 1929. The reason why Britain had a higher growth rate than the USA in the 1930s was that the US economy did not grow at all; as for France, its national income fell by an average of over 2 per cent per year. Germany's growth rate was in fact higher than Britain's.[16]

Recent calculations of population and employment rates have indicated the rates of growth that will be required to achieve 'full employment' levels by the mid-1990s. If technological changes produce improvements in productivity of the same order as prevailed in the years 1951–73, the growth rates required would be equivalent to an annual average rate of about 6 or 7 per cent for the OECD as a whole. For individual countries, the required rates would be as shown in table 3.4.[17] With the exception of France, all these required rates are faster than the average growth rates of these national economies during the boom years of 1951–73. In Britain's case, the rate required is faster than that achieved in any period since the First World War.

Table 3.4 *Estimated GDP growth rates required to restore full employment by 1994 (annual averages, per cent)*

Japan	10.0	France	5.5
W. Germany	6.2	USA	4.2
Italy	5.6	UK	3.2

In fact, a period of slow growth is widely predicted as likely for the next decade. If growth does not accelerate soon, the pool of unemployed, which already stands at over 25 million in the OECD countries, will go on growing larger, extending the period of time that would be required to achieve full employment, even when more rapid rates of growth returned.

This focuses attention on the world economy, for the rates of growth of individual countries depend on the rate at which world trade expands. Sir Keith Joseph explained the phenomenon of mass unemployment in the 1930s in terms of a 'world depression' – a notion that begs every possible question. Since it cannot have been the interventionism of governments that brought about that depression, what is the explanation for slow growth rates which recur every 50 years? The question can be answered only by examining the nature of capitalism as a world economic system. This is the subject of the next chapter.

REFERENCES

1   F. A. Hayek, *A Tiger by the Tail*, Institute of Economic Affairs, 1972, p. 118.
2   M. Friedman, 'The role of monetary policy', *American Economic Review*, vol. 58, no. 1, March 1968, p. 8.

3   Richard Nixon, CBS Radio broadcast, October 1968, quoted in R. Evans and R. Novak, *Nixon in the White House*, Davis-Poynter, 1972, p. 179.

4   M. Friedman, *Unemployment versus Inflation? An Evaluation of the Phillips Curve*, Institute of Economic Affairs, Occasional Paper 44, 1975, pp. 23, 32.

5   Sir Keith Joseph, speech at Preston, *The Times*, 6 September 1974.

6   Sir Keith Joseph, *Monetarism is Not Enough*, Centre for Policy Studies, 1976, pp. 12–13.

7   F. A. Hayek, *Full Employment at Any Price?* Institute of Economic Affairs, Occasional Paper 45, 1975, p. 19.

8   Ibid., p. 45.

9   R. Bacon and W. Eltis, *Britain's Economic Problem: Too Few Producers* (1976) 2nd edn, Macmillan, 1978, pp. 24, 28.

10 Denis Healey, speech on the economy, *The Times*, 26 February 1976.

11 Central Statistical Office, *Annual Abstract of Statistics, 1981*, HMSO, 1981, table 6.1.

12 OECD, *Labour Force Statistics, 1962–1973*, and *1967–1978*, quarterly supplement, 1981.

13 Ibid.

14 Department of Employment, *British Labour Statistics, Year Book 1976*, HMSO, 1978, table 156; and *Employment Gazette*, vol. 89, no. 4, April 1981, table 1.8.

15 Joseph, *Monetarism is Not Enough*, p. 8.

16 C. H. Feinstein, *Statistical Tables of National Income, Expenditure and Output of the UK, 1855–1965*, Cambridge University Press, 1972, tables 57, 10, 22, 59.

17 H. Shutt, *The Jobs Crisis; Increasing Unemployment in the Developed World*, Economist Intelligence Unit, Special Report no. 85, 1980, p. 63.

4

Unemployment as a Product of World Recession

No economist or politician could doubt that something important happened to the capitalist world economy in the 1970s. Clearly that decade marked the end of the post-war boom, and the beginning of a far more difficult period in the economic development of the whole 'western' world. However, there is a great deal of dispute about exactly what did go wrong with the international capitalist system at this point. This dispute is highly relevant to the political explication of mass unemployment, and hence also to political action (or inaction) in response to its re-emergence.

One key issue in this dispute is the significance of the oil price crisis of 1973–74. Both conservative and social democratic governments suggested that it was the major cause of a 'world recession'. They claimed that the increased cost of oil and the unfavourable trade balances of the non-OPEC countries caused an abrupt end to previously healthy rates of growth. In particular, social democratic governments blamed this factor above all else for mass unemployment and the limitations of Keynesian measures. They identified increased oil prices as of prime significance both as a cause of inflation and as a factor that contributed to the deflationary policies of the leading western governments. For instance, Harold Wilson wrote in his memoirs:

> The staggering increase in oil prices which was the prompt Arab response to the Yom Kippur war had forced inflation on the world; on the advanced industrial world, on the Third World, and on the starving Fourth World. Only those developing countries with oil re-

sources such as Nigeria or with raw materials such as tin, phosphates and bauxite sharing in the commodity boom, grew richer: others grew immensely poorer. . . . And few statesmen with perception could brush aside the certainty that in the wake of inflation lay unemployment. There were warnings such as those summarized in Harold Lever's analysis that a massive surplus on the part of the oil-producing countries should not be regarded as a signal for deflation in the importing countries. But wherever the representatives of the developed countries met, in the EEC, in the IMF, at the conference of the World Bank – less so in the OECD – or the monthly meetings of the US–European Central Bankers at Basle, the emphasis was on deflation. When the strong, such as the United States – as they then were – and West Germany, showed no inclination to pursue policies of expansion, the weak were in no position to argue. Deflation ruled. The disciples of Keynes and Galbraith sang small, those of Friedman, and especially the master himself, were canonized. Even two and three years later the surplus countries, such as Japan and Germany, with a better record on anti-inflationary policies than their partners, were still resisting the call to give a lead to economic expansion, because they feared that such obvious boldness would lead to internal inflation. For the rest, including the weaker EEC countries, it was clear that inflation itself, not to mention counter-inflationary measures, appropriate or inappropriate, would lead speedily to widespread unemployment.[1]

It is certainly possible to produce statistics that show a marked discontinuity in the growth of the capitalist world economy after 1974, and which therefore suggest that the oil price crisis marked a crucial turning point. But it is equally possible to show that the economies of most of the advanced capitalist countries were already growing more slowly from the mid-1960s onwards. Furthermore, it can also be shown that Harold Wilson was fundamentally misleading in his suggestion that the 'developing' countries suffered disproportionately from the world recession. Quite the opposite was

the case. Both immediately before the oil price crisis and after
it, the total GNP of the developing nations of the capitalist
world grew more rapidly than that of the advanced countries.

SLOWER GROWTH IN THE CAPITALIST WORLD ECONOMY

In order to understand these changes in the world economy in
the 1970s, we need to distinguish between various sectors of it.
In the first place, there is the distinction between the capitalist
'market economies' and the economies of the centrally planned (Eastern bloc) countries. The former comprise about 80
per cent of the whole world economy. The decline in the
growth rates of the capitalist world economy in 1974 was far
sharper than that of the centrally planned 'Marxian socialist'
economies. Up to 1974 the total GDP of both groups had been
growing at roughly similar rates. The capitalist world
economy had expanded by 93 per cent between 1960 and
1973, and the Marxian socialist group (excluding China and
the newer members of that bloc) had expanded by 132 per
cent in the same period. Between 1973 and 1976 the capitalist
group grew by only 5 per cent, whereas the centrally planned
group grew by 17 per cent.[2]
Secondly, we need to distinguish between the growth rates
of the 'developed' nations, and those of the 'developing'
nations of the capitalist world. This distinction is made in the
statistics of the world economy compiled by the United
Nations, and it is implicit also in the quotation from Harold
Wilson above. In fact, I shall argue that this two-way division
of the world economy is increasingly misleading, whichever
particular allocation of countries is made between the two
categories. I shall suggest that at least three different
categories of economies in the capitalist world need to be
recognized to understand the developments of the 1970s.
Even so, a certain direction of change becomes clear by
examining the figures for the growth of the 'developed' and
'developing' economies of the capitalist world for the period
since 1960. The 'developed' economies (for the purposes of
UN statistics these are the countries of North America and

Europe, plus Australia, New Zealand, Japan, Israel and South Africa) produce over 80 per cent of the total GDP of the capitalist world. The pattern of their growth has been shown in figure 4.1. Expressed in this way, the 'developed' economies appear to have been growing at a fairly uniform rate (an annual average of about 5 per cent a year) right up until 1973, and since then to have grown much more slowly. On the other hand, the 'developing' economies (making up less than 20 per cent of the capitalist world market and comprising all of the countries of the Caribbean, Latin America, East and South-East Asia, the Middle East, Africa and

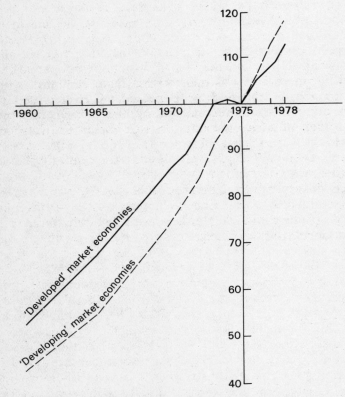

Figure 4.1 *Indices of GDP of 'developed' and 'developing' market economies (1975 = 100)*

Oceania, with above exceptions) had a different growth pattern. Their rate of growth accelerated from around 5 per cent a year between 1960 and 1965 to around 7 per cent a year between 1965 and 1970. Between 1970 and 1975 it was slightly faster still, and since 1975 it has still been above 6 per cent a year.[3]

We should not accept Harold Wilson's claim that the success of the underdeveloped countries was owing to the OPEC nations. The 13 OPEC countries produce only 3 per cent of the GNP of the whole world. Between 1960 and 1974 the growth rate of the OPEC group was already a very healthy average 9.6 per cent a year.[4] But the total GNP of the other 127 non-Marxian 'developing' countries was growing at an average annual rate of 5.3 per cent between 1960 and 1974 – higher than that of the advanced capitalist countries, even before the oil price crisis.[5] This is shown quite graphically if we compare the growth rates of certain regions of the capitalist world economy. In this comparison (table 4.1), we see that the economies of North America and the EEC were much more affected by the recession of 1973 to 1975 than were the economies of Africa (excluding South Africa) the Caribbean and Latin America, or East and South-East Asia (excluding Japan). The latter regions all comprise 'developing' countries which do not contribute very substantially to the world supply of oil.[6] It is quite clear from the table that the growth rate of the economies in the 'developing' regions of the capitalist world economy in the 1970s was much faster than that in the most 'developed' economies.

Table 4.1   *Indices of GDP by region (1975 = 100)*

	1970	1971	1972	1973	1974	1975	1976	1977	1978
North America	88	91	96	102	101	100	106	111	116
EEC	88	91	94	100	102	100	105	107	111
Africa (excluding South Africa)	79	83	86	91	97	100	108	114	119
Caribbean and Latin America	73	78	83	90	97	100	105	110	115
E and SE Asia	80	83	85	91	94	100	105	113	121

INDUSTRIAL PRODUCTION

However, even this does not clarify the most important change in the development of the capitalist world economy in this period. To see the underlying trend from 1965 onwards, it is necessary to focus on industrial production and particularly on manufacturing industry. The vast bulk of industrial production is carried out in the 'developed' capitalist countries, and particularly in the USA, the EEC and Japan. But industrial production has been growing much more rapidly in the 'developing' countries than in the advanced capitalist ones. Table 4.2 compares the growth of production in manufacturing industry between the regions examined above. The figures in brackets indicate the proportions of manufacturing output of the capitalist world economy produced in the respective regions.[7] The output of manufacturing industry thus grew much more quickly in these 'developing' regions from 1965 onwards than it did in the most 'developed' ones. Indeed from 1970 onwards there was relative stagnation in manufacturing output in the most 'developed' producers, and

Table 4.2   *Indices of manufacturing output by region (1975 = 100)*

	1965	1970	1971	1972	1973	1974	1975	1976	1977	1978
North America (31%)	83	93	95	103	112	109	100	109	116	123
EEC (34%)	69	91	93	97	104	106	100	107	110	111
Africa (excluding South Africa) (1.1%)	53	76	80	86	96	99	100	107	114	124
East and South-East Asia (excluding Japan) (3%)	51	71	75	81	90	94	100	111	120	133
Caribbean and Latin America (7.5%)	48	69	76	83	92	98	100	106	109	115

rapid growth in the 'developing' regions. In the case of North America, slower growth was evident from 1965 onwards.

This regional comparison masks the extremes of differentiation between the development of national economies. Figure 4.2 compares the oldest industrialized nation, Britain, with some rapidly industrializing economies in the 'developing' sector. Here the index uses 1970 as the year of comparison.[8]

On the basis of this comparison, I would suggest that the study of increasing unemployment in the capitalist world requires a rather different classification of the national

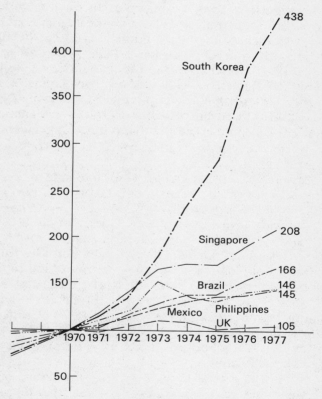

Figure 4.2   *Indices of manufacturing production (1970 = 100)*

economies of this system. We need to distinguish between the advanced industrialized nations (USA, all the EEC countries with the exception of Ireland, Japan and the 'white dominions' of the British Commonwealth) and a group of what I shall call 'industrializing' countries. In the latter category I would place some members of the OECD such as Turkey, Greece, Portugal, Spain and Ireland, all of which had higher growth rates in their industrial sectors than the advanced nations had in the 1970s. I would also include such 'developing' countries as Brazil, Mexico, Singapore, Taiwan, Hong Kong, the Philippines and South Korea.

The point about acknowledging such a category is not to try to make precise differentiation or exclusive lists of which countries are 'industrializing'. Any such category could also include a number of smaller nations, with equally rapidly expanding industrial sectors, such as Puerto Rico, Nicaragua and Panama. It is much more important to make a conceptual distinction between this group and two others. On the one hand, there is the OPEC group, which also has rapidly increasing industrial production, but which can attribute much of its growth to oil. On the other hand, there is the very large group of extremely poor nations, which are the truly 'underdeveloped' nations.

This last group is by no means simple to define, either. It is not easy to produce a homogeneous category of impoverished and stagnating Third World nations. This is because even these countries have experienced a degree both of economic growth and of industrialization during the post-war era. For instance, it is a surprising fact that in the period 1960 to 1974, the 25 most populous 'developing' countries of the capitalist world (including India, Bangladesh and Pakistan) had a higher annual average rate of growth of total GNP than the five major advanced capitalist countries (5.7 per cent compared with 5.3 per cent a year).[9]

However, it is also both true and very important that the 29 countries of the capitalist world with the lowest *per capita* incomes had the lowest rates of growth of national income during this same period. It is also significant that the rate of increase of population in the 'developing' countries (both the industrializing and the classic underdeveloped ones) is much higher than in the advanced industrialized countries. Between 1960 and 1974 the rate of growth of population in the non-OPEC developing countries was 2.5 per cent a year, compared with just over 1 per cent a year in the advanced industrialized countries.[10] As a result, the rate of growth of incomes per head has been slower in the developing countries than in the advanced ones. In the poorest of the underdeveloped countries, *per capita* incomes have hardly increased at all.

THE 'INDUSTRIALIZING' COUNTRIES

In proposing a cateogry of 'industrializing' countries for the purpose of this analysis, I am aware that I am including a very diverse selection in this group. Among them are some countries, such as Ireland and Spain, whose incomes per head of population are approaching those of the poorest of the advanced industrialized countries (Italy and Britain). At the other end of the scale, countries like South Korea and the Philippines have very low *per capita* incomes – as low as those of other nations that I have not included in this category.

Table 4.3 sets out the comparison between average incomes per head in some important 'industrializing' countries.[11] It shows the European industrializing countries have a far higher average standard of living than do most of the Asian or Latin American ones. Furthermore, the inequalities in incomes between different sectors of the population are very high in these poorer industrializing countries. For instance, in Brazil in 1970, the annual average *per capita* income of the poorest 40 per cent of the population was 97.5 US dollars, whereas the annual average for the richest 20 per cent was 1,200 US dollars. In Turkey in 1968, the poorest 40 per cent earned an average of 70 US dollars a year, the richest 20 per cent an average of 857 dollars. The equivalents in the Philippines in 1971 were 65 US dollars (poorest 40 per cent) and 642 dollars (richest 20 per cent).[12] In general, countries with an average *per capita* income of over 1,500 US dollars in 1975 had less unequal distribution than those with lower average incomes.[13]

Secondly, although all these countries had rapidly expanding industrial output from the mid-1960s onwards their combined contribution to the industrial production of the capitalist world is still extremely small. In all of them, industrial production is still a minor part of their output – in some cases tiny, relative to their production of foodstuffs and raw materials.

Table 4.3   *Average income per head in 'industrializing' countries*

Ireland	(1979)	2,827	(1975 US dollars per head)
Spain	(1979)	3,112	
Portugal	(1979)	1,805	
Greece	(1979)	2,683	
Turkey	(1979)	957	
Singapore	(1975)	2,279	
South Korea	(1977)	887	(1977 US dollars per head)
Mexico	(1977)	1,035	
Brazil	(1977)	1,365	
Philippines	(1977)	414	

My purpose in putting them in a single category is simply to draw attention to the existence of a sector of the capitalist world economy which began expanding more rapidly at the time when the advanced industrialized countries' growth began to slow down. Between 1945 and 1965, the rapid growth sector of the capitalist world economy was the advanced industrialized countries. From 1965 onwards the growth rates of the industrializing countries were consistently higher than those of the industrialized ones (see table 4.4).[14]

Thirdly, I do not wish to imply that the type of industrialization occurring in all these countries was similar. For instance, countries like South Korea and Taiwan have been developed mainly for labour-intensive methods of production, based on the use of cheap labour power; whereas a country like Spain has had a considerable development of more capital-intensive industry. Nor do I necessarily wish to imply that the younger industrializing nations, such as the two mentioned above, will

Table 4.4   *Average annual increase in GNP (per cent) at 1975 prices and exchange rates*

	1965–70	1970–73	1973–80
EEC	4.5	4.7	2.8
Ireland	4.5	5.0	3.2
Spain	6.5	7.7	3.0
Portugal	6.8	7.4	3.2
Turkey	7.0	7.0	5.7
Greece	7.3	8.4	3.6
Japan	12.1	9.0	4.1
Singapore	11.2	13.5	8.0 (1973–78)
South Korea	12.8	11.4	11.6 (1973–78)
Hong Kong	8.8	8.9	10.3 (1973–78)

develop from labour-intensive forms of production to capital-intensive ones; they may never do so. What all these countries have in common is that their industrial sectors have been growing rapidly relative to the other sectors of their economies.

Thus the concept of a world recession – used not only by Harold Wilson and Sir Keith Jospeh about the period 1974–76, but also increasingly frequently by political leaders of the advanced industrialized countries in the 1980s – oversimplifies the situation. The slower growth of the advanced industrialized countries was only partly reflected in the industrializing ones, many of which were still expanding their national incomes more rapidly in the 1970s than they had been in the immediate post-war period.

EFFECTS ON RATES OF UNEMPLOYMENT

Unemployment figures from the 'developing' countries are notoriously unreliable and are not strictly comparable with the figures issued by 'developed' countries. This is because by no means all the working population of such countries are employed in wage-earning jobs, and many peasant families work in occasional or part-time employment to supplement their farm incomes.

However, such figures as are available suggest that the trend of unemployment in the younger industrialized countries was downward in the 1970s, whereas the older, European industrializing countries experienced an increase in unemployment (see table 4.5).[15] This largely reflects the very rapid expansion of industrial employment in the 'developing' world. Whereas total industrial employment in the 'developed' market economies declined, in the 1970s, total industrial employment in the 'developing' market economies grew very rapidly in the same period (see figure 4.3).[16]

Table 4.5   *Unemployment rates (as a percentage of total labour force)*

	1968	1970	1971	1972	1973	1974	1975	1976	1977
Ireland	5.3	5.8	5.8	6.3	5.9	5.7	7.9	9.5	9.4
Spain	1.9	1.5	1.9	2.9	2.7	3.1	4.5	5.1	6.1
Portugal		not available				2.1	5.5	6.3	7.4
Greece	2.2	1.5	0.9	0.7	0.7	0.8	1.1	0.9	0.9
Turkey	n/a	4.6	not available			6.3	6.3	7.4	8.6
Singapore	7.3	6.0	4.8	4.7	4.5	4.0	4.5	4.5	4.0
South Korea	5.1	4.5	4.5	4.5	4.5	4.1	4.1	3.9	3.8
Philippines	7.8	n/a	5.2	6.3	4.8	4.0	3.9	5.0	n/a

The most striking contrasts can be made between manufacturing employment in the EEC (particularly Britain) and in certain of the industrializing countries (see table 4.6).[17] The growth in industrial output and employment in the industrializing countries, and its effect on levels of unemployment, was more or less on a par with the rate and pattern of growth of industrial output in the advanced industrialized countries in the 1950s. Far from experiencing a recession, these countries experienced healthy rates of growth, with expanded employment opportunities, and in many of them unemployment declined.

I have suggested that the concept of a 'world recession'

after 1974 is of limited value in explaining the changes that have been taking place in the capitalist world economy since the mid-1960s. It does not show why some countries – particularly the older industrialized countries – were so much more vulnerable to recession than others. To a large extent this concept is used by politicians in these unsuccessful countries – originally mainly social democratic leaders, but increasingly also conservatives with monetarist leanings – to try to explain away the failures of their domestic economic policies, including high unemployment rates.

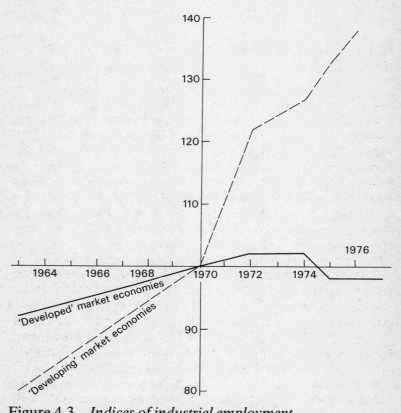

Figure 4.3   *Indices of industrial employment (mining, manufacturing, electricity, gas and water) (1970 = 100)*

Table 4.6   *Indices of employment in manufacturing (1970 = 100)*

	1968	1970	1971	1972	1973	1974	1975	1976	1977
EEC	96	100	99	98	99	99	95	93	93
UK	99	100	97	93	94	94	90	87	88
Ireland	94	100	98	99	102	103	94	96	99
Spain	94	100	101	105	111	115	115	116	n/a
Portugal	n/a	100	135	154	160	167	166	172	n/a
Greece	92	100	106	110	117	118	119	126	132
Turkey	94	100	108	120	131	125	136	154	162
Singapore		(1974 = 100)				100	91	100	110
Korea	93	100	96	116	145	173	194	234	248
Philippines		(1972 = 100)		100	110	118	122	126	132
Hong Kong	96	100	104	105	107	101	102	121	123

However, the oil price crisis was important in at least one respect. The considerable relative increase in the price of oil represents a formidable barrier to the type of continuous rapid expansion of the advanced industrialized economies that took place after the war. This partly reflects the determination of the OPEC countries to ensure that a finite and rapidly dwindling resource – their oil – should not be squandered by the rich nations of the capitalist world to satisfy their expansionist drive. But it also reinforces the pre-1974 tendency of international capital to diversify its production between the advanced and the industrializing countries, rather than concentrating it all in the former.

It is part of my argument, therefore, that the rise in oil prices makes a rapid boom in industrial production in the advanced industrialized countries of the capitalist world unlikely for at least the next decade. This is of crucial importance when we consider policies on unemployment.

Furthermore, this real obstacle to rapid growth has not been adequately acknowledged by economists or politicians. Both Keynesians and monetarists persistently suggest that the barriers to growth are institutional rather than in real resources. The monetarists argue that these institutional barriers take the form of restraints on free trade and on the operation of free market competitive forces. The Keynesians argue that they take the form of a long-term imbalance of trade, which has gradually been institutionalized, allowing the Japanese and Germans in particular to take too large a share of the market.

The difference between the two lies in which institutions they want to change. Thatcher and Reagan would leave capitalist world trading agreements largely intact, but want to change the internal domestic institutions of Britain and the United States to allow market forces freer rein. The British Keynesians would like to change the institutions of international trade.

The British Keynesians now offer an alternative explanation of the 'world recession' since 1974. The Cambridge group link together the problems of unemployment, slow growth and inflation, and suggest that to understand them the world economy must be analysed as a system.

> The existing framework of international economic relations, the rules by which it operates and the theories on which those rules are based, now serve to entrench unemployment and inflation in many countries, including the USA and the UK. The rules are not easy to change, particularly at the international level. Yet unless they are changed or broken, national policies are so tightly constrained by international interdependence that many governments are no longer able to resolve major economic problems in their own countries. The central problem is that the system of world trade no longer induces adequate economic growth . . . . the disturbance from which the world economy now suffers is not primarily due to high oil prices, but rather to a persistent and growing tendency to surplus on the part of Japan and a few European countries, notably Germany.[18]

Since 1979, the Cambridge group, with increasing support from the Labour Party, has therefore been advancing a new variation on the 'world recession' theme. These persistent imbalances in trade (particularly in manufactures) have become a serious obstacle to growth of world trade and GNP. What is needed is a 'growth-inducing system of trade' for the capitalist world. They suggest that three changes could benefit some or all countries without harm to others. These are: a sharp reduction in Japanese exports; reductions in the import propensities of the USA and certain other countries, such as Britain; and discrimination in favour of exports of manufactures from the developing nations by countries with strongly favourable balances of trade. Thus, defying Keynes, they advance a protectionist programme for restoring rapid growth and full employment to the advanced industrialized countries of the capitalist world.

One of several things that this analysis does not do is explain how the long-term shifts in the world balance of trade reflect long-term shifts in the location of capitalist production. It implies that the present system of international economic relations damages the interests of the largest and strongest capitalist nation, the United States, and benefits only two other major advanced countries. At first sight it seems unlikely that the United States would willingly have presided over the evolution of such a system, which inflicted long-term damage upon it, if there had been an alternative which was more in its own interests. On the face of it, it seems more likely that the development of international economic relations since 1965 has followed the logic of profit and the interests of capital in the major industrialized countries, including the United States.

The Cambridge group deal with this apparent contradiction by making the distinction – dear to Tony Benn – between international and national capital. In the 'quest for international profits' capital has ceased to heed national interests.[19] This distinction is given no analytic basis or accurate definition. The quest for international profits is seen as 'anarchy' – a kind of insane and random chase. National profits are seen as patriotic and acceptable.

In the next three chapters I shall argue that the development of international capitalism can only be understood as a system of commodity production, and not simply as a system of international trade. The intellectual tradition associated with this type of analysis is Marxism. In chapter 5, therefore, I shall turn to the Marxist explanation of mass unemployment.

REFERENCES

1   Harold Wilson, *Final Term: The Labour Government, 1974–76*, Weidenfeld and Nicolson and Michael Joseph, 1979, p. 110.
2   United Nations, *Statistical Yearbook, 1978*, Department of International Economic and Social Affairs, 1979, table 4. Index numbers of GDP, excluding services. Centrally planned economies include USSR, Albania, Bulgaria, Czechoslovakia, German Democratic Republic, Hungary, Poland, Romania and Yugoslavia.
3   United Nations, *Yearbook of National Accounts Statistics, 1979*, vol. 2, International Tables, United Nations, 1980, table 8B.
4   John G. Gurley, 'Economic development: a Marxist view', in K. P. Jameson and C. K. Wilber (eds), *Directions in Economic Development*, Notre Dame Press, 1979, pp. 187–8, tables 1 and 2.
5   Ibid.
6   United Nations, *Yearbook of the National Accounts Statistics, 1979*, vol. 2, table 8B. EEC figures include GDP of countries which joined in mid-1970s.
7   Ibid.
8   United Nations, *Statistical Yearbook, 1978*, table 4.8, and *Yearbook of National Accounts Statistics, 1979*.
9   Gurley, 'Economic development', p. 197, table 7.
10   Ibid., p. 188, table 2.
11   OECD, *Main Economic Indicators*, 1981, and United Nations, *Statistical Yearbook, 1978*.
12   E. Mandel, *Late Capitalism* (1972), New Left Books, 1975, p. 373.
13   Gurley, 'Economic development', p. 200, table 10.
14   OECD, *Main Economic Indicators*, 1970–81, and United Nations, *Yearbook of National Accounts Statistics, 1979*.
15   OECD, *Main Economic Indicators*, 1970–81, and United Nations, *Statistical Yearbook, 1978*.
16   *United Nations, Statistical Yearbook, 1978*, table 10.
17   Ibid., tables 10 and 21.

18   Cambridge Department of Applied Economics, *Cambridge Economic Policy Review*, April 1979, no. 5, Gower Press, p. 1.
19   F. Cripps, J. Griffith, F. Morrell, J. Reid, P. Townsend and S. Weir, *Manifesto: A Radical Strategy for Britain's Future*, Pan, 1981.

5
Unemployment as a Consequence of Class Conflict

The distinctive feature of the Marxist explanation of unemployment is that its analysis is framed in terms of conflict between labour and capital. In Marxist theory, it is a necessary feature of capitalism that labour should be exploited to produce profit. Unemployment is one part of the dynamic of this exploitation.

However, unemployment is also highly relevant to the struggle of labour to resist exploitation, and eventually to overthrow capitalism. The re-emergence of mass unemployment is therefore of considerable significance in the politics as well as the economics of class conflict. Marxists have never underestimated the revolutionary potential of mass unemployment.

Yet mass unemployment in the 1930s did not produce revolution on the scale that might have been predicted. Marxist theory has therefore to explain not only the tendency of capitalism towards recurring mass unemployment, but also its powers of recovery from this phenomenon. It has to offer an account of the post-war boom that followed the Depression, and of capitalism's subsequent difficulties.

The Marxist account of the capitalist world economy aims to do both these things. It shows how the boom conditions of the post-war period came about, and how they in turn gave rise to slower growth in the advanced industrialized countries in the 1970s. It also suggests the likely course of changes in the next decade.

In this chapter and chapter 7 I shall examine Marxist explanations in some detail. This difficult exercise seems worth while because the Marxist analysis sets itself to produce a model of capitalism as an international system in a way which other economic theories are beginning to acknowledge as necessary, but have not yet provided. It also seems important because Marxism offers by far the most coherent challenge to the capitalist system, and a source of ideas and ideals for critics of capitalism's structure in every part of the world.

In this chapter, I shall concentrate mainly on one account (Mandel's) of the development of the capitalist world economy, and in particular of the relationship between the advanced industrialized countries and the underdeveloped ones. I have chosen Mandel's account for three reasons: firstly because it is fairly well known; secondly because it is a comprehensive and coherent theory of the capitalist world system as a whole; and thirdly because Mandel was one of the Marxist economists who predicted the economic problems of the advanced industrialized countries and the re-emergence of mass unemployment.

Marxist economics has fundamentally different bases from 'bourgeois' economic theories, and I therefore need to start with a brief account of the theoretical underpinnings of explanations of the capitalist world economy.

VALUE, SURPLUS-VALUE AND THE RATE OF PROFIT

Marx was concerned to explain economic phenomena in terms of the relations between people in society, and particularly in terms of their productive relations. He pointed out that economic concepts such as 'money', 'wages' and 'capital' are treated as *things*, when in fact they are consequences of processes of production, which in turn crystallize relations among people.

'Value' was treated by many economists as if it was a property of things. But Marx argued that what was meant by value in commodities was always the labour-time that went into producing them. In considering the relations between people established through the production and exchange of commodities, the value of these commodities was demonstrably measured in this way. This value was not the same thing as the *price* of the commodities, nor was the value of the labour-time in them measured by the *wages* paid to the worker – actual levels of prices and wages were determined by quite other mechanisms. Labour-time was an abstract construct, a universal measure of value, according to which commodities could be exchanged. When two commodities were exchanged (for example, in an economy based on bartering), each had to be assessed according to some external measure. According to Marx, this was always labour-time, which could be compared in all commodities.

In capitalist production, although the methods used are immensely complex, the only value that is actually produced during the process is that added by each new amount of labour. At each stage of the process, there are two elements in this value. Firstly, there is the amount of labour necessary to produce what workers need for their day-to-day living. This is the equivalent labour-time of their wages, and is called 'necessary labour' – the amount of labour necessary for the 'reproduction of labour-power'. Secondly, there is *surplus labour*, which is the part of the day or week which the worker spends in creating *surplus-value*. This is the labour-time which is spent in reproducing capital. The worker has to work beyond the time needed to produce his wages, in order to sustain capital. 'What appears as surplus-value on capital's side appears identically on the worker's side as surplus labour in excess of his requirements as a worker, hence in excess of his immediate requirements for keeping himself alive.'[1]

Without surplus-value produced in this way by extra, unpaid labour-time there can be no profit. However, the rate of profit is not directly related to the rate of surplus-value. It depends on a number of other factors, including the *total value* of capital and the amount of raw materials. Because capital is never fully utilized, and there are always raw materials involved in production, the rate of profit is always lower than the rate of surplus-value. Within this general law, there is scope for changes in the rates of profit and of surplus-value which are divergent.

The development of capitalism is marked by the introduction of more and better machinery, whereby the *productivity* of labour is increased. As this occurs, the differences between forms of labour, such as those of the smith, the carpenter or the shoemaker, tend to be eroded through the adoption of methods of production based on machines. Thus labour becomes in fact close to being homogeneous. Marx writes of 'abstract' rather than homogeneous labour, and value analysis is based on units of such labour. 'Socially necessary labour' is the amount of such labour required to produce a given commodity with the aid of average skill and intensity, and of the best available techniques.

Thus value is determined by the quantity of labour needed to produce a commodity; but this quantity of labour depends on the productivity of labour. Every increase in the productivity of labour reduces the amount of labour needed to produce the commodity and simultaneously *lowers* the value of that commodity. For example, the introduction of a machine enables a jacket to be produced in seven hours instead of the ten hours that were needed before. Thus its value is reduced from £10 to £7 (assuming that an hour of the worker's labour creates a value of £1, and that this is 'average' rather than particularly skilled or unskilled labour). Cheaper jackets then enter the market and displace more expensive ones. Demand for jackets rises, and jacket production increases. More productive resources are transferred to jacket-making. The dynamic of the whole national economic system can thus be traced to a change in the technical process of production, worked out through the law of value.

One important law in Marx's account of the development of capitalism is that the more productive processes are developed, and the productivity of labour rises through the introduction of more machinery, the harder it is to go on increasing the rate of surplus-value. This is because, each time the productivity of labour is increased, surplus-value does not increase by the same amount, because some part of the working day must always be given over to the production of the worker's wages. With every increase in productivity, the relative growth in surplus-value becomes smaller. For instance, if the original introduction of a machine doubled the productivity of a worker, it would halve the proportion of his labour-time spent in producing his subsistence, assuming he was previously a self-employed hand-craftsman. But if the capitalist later introduced a new machine that again doubled his productivity, the same halving of his labour-time spent on producing his subsistence would only diminish this to a quarter of the working day. Thus the gain in surplus-value by the first doubling of productivity was half a day, while the second was only a quarter of a day. Marx pointed out that this meant that 'the more developed capital already is, . . . the more terribly it must develop the productive force in order to . . . add to surplus-value – because its barrier always remains the relation between the fractional part of the day which expresses necessary labour, and the entire working day.'[2]

This is the reason why Marx argued that there was a law of the falling rate of profit. As the amount of the working day given over to the creation of surplus-value increased with the introduction of new processes (i.e. as *relative surplus-value* increased), so it became harder to convert this increase into profit. 'Thus, in the same proportion as capital takes up a larger place as capital in the production process relative to immediate labour, i.e. the more relative surplus-value grows – the value-creating power of capital – *the more does the rate of profit fall*.'[3] There are various 'countervailing influences' which Marx mentions as checking this tendency for the rate of profit to fall. One important one is 'the creation of new branches of production in which more direct labour in relation to capital is needed, or where the productive power of labour is not yet developed.'[4]

Nonetheless, this long-run tendency which Marx identified has been the object of a great deal of controversy between Marxist economists seeking to explain the long period of expansion in the capitalist world economy, and particularly in the advanced industrialized nations, after the Second World War. Some economists have criticized or abandoned this part of Marx's theory. Others have suggested that it is still relevant and necessary to explain events of the 1970s. I shall follow the arguments of one of the latter, Ernest Mandel, whose systematic analysis of the capitalist world economy in *Late Capitalism* relies heavily on the notion of the falling rate of profit.

SURPLUS-PROFITS AND GROWTH

Mandel points out that one way in which the tendency for the rate of profit to fall can be checked derives from the uneven development of the capitalist world economy. Marx followed the classical economists in assuming that, because of competition between capitals, there was a tendency for the rate of profit to equalize between firms and branches of production in any country over time, with capital moving into industries in which it could earn surplus-profits, i.e. profits which exceed the rate of profit ruling in the economy as a whole. This movement caused profits in the industries in question to fall, except in so far as they were protected by a monopoly, which could postpone this equalization, but not avert it in the long run. However, at no time did Marx suggest that profits would equalize on a worldwide basis. In fact, Mandel suggests that rates of profit which differ as between different countries are characteristic of all eras of capitalism.

Mandel uses this as the basis of his explanation of the phenomenon of 'underdevelopment'. As capitalism gradually created a world commodity market, it did not create a uniform system of production. Indeed, the far higher productivity of labour in the more advanced industrialized countries co-existed with much less intensive methods of production in the less developed nations. Thus commodity values (the labour-time involved in producing commodities) were very different between those produced in the industrialized and the underdeveloped countries.

In the final analysis, this internationally hierarchized and differentiated system of varying commodity values is explained by an internationally hierarchized and differentiated system of varying degrees of labour productivity. Imperialism, far from equalizing the organic composition of capital on an international level – or leading to an international equalization of rates of profit, arrested and intensified international differences in the organic composition of capital and the level of the rates of profit.[5]

As 'the original capitalist countries' (the metropolitan countries) started with the highest concentration of capital, they are constantly struggling with the problems of the decline in the rate of profit, as relative surplus-value rises. In the short term they can overcome the problem by making surplus-profits. These are monopoly profits at above the average rate of profit that obtains, and they can be achieved in three main ways. The first is by technological innovation, leading to new and cheaper methods of production by a substantial improvement in labour productivity. During the period before these techniques can be adopted by competitors, the innovators are able to earn a monopoly surplus-profit, or 'technological rent'. The second is by the discovery of new cheap raw materials, which lower production costs; and the third is by the discovery of new sources of cheap labour-power.

Technological improvements in labour productivity are particularly important in late capitalism because they give rise to surplus-profits in two ways. Firstly they create a monopoly during the time lag between the innovator's and his competitors' adoption of the new method. But they also give rise to a process of 'unequal exchange' during this period. Through the introduction of new technology, labour productivity increases in the way described at the beginning of this chapter. Thus commodities produced in this branch of industry have a lower value (labour-time content) than the products of other industries in which technological innovation has not occurred, or has occurred more slowly. When these commodities are exchanged for each other, this difference in value results in 'unequal exchange'. Hence the technologically advanced industry drains off part of the surplus-value produced in other spheres – which adds to the surplus-profit.

Mandel argues that this 'unequal exchange' is always present in trade between advanced industrial nations, with their high labour productvity, and underdeveloped nations, and that it helps to explain why capital has continued to accumulate more rapidly in the metropolitan countries that in the colonial ones, in spite of the latter's abundant supplies of cheap labour.

However, since the vast bulk of commodities produced in any of the metropolitan (advanced industrialized) countries are sold in their home markets, this source of surplus-profits, through unequal exchange with the underdeveloped world, cannot be the main one. Mandel recognizes that there has until recently been another major source of unequal exchange within the metropolitan countries themselves. Each advanced economy had within it backward traditional areas, using less capitalized methods, with lower labour productivity, which functioned as 'internal colonies' for the creation of surplus-profits through unequal exchanges. Historically Ireland, the southern states of the USA, and the traditional sectors of the Japanese economy have played this role. In the nineteenth century, for example, Ireland (whose initial attempts at industrialization had been crushed by Britain in the eighteenth century) was kept in an underdeveloped state, and remained backward and extremely poor. But for many of the other metropolitan countries, this situation of having an 'internal colony' persisted until much more recently. 'The difference in the level of productivity between agriculture and industry . . . creates unequal exchange, or a steady transfer of value, from the underdeveloped to the industrialized regions of the same capitalist state.'[6]

Although Mandel does not emphasize this point, I consider it to be of the utmost importance in trying to understand different historical rates of growth between the advanced industrialized countries in this century. If we are trying to understand why Britain had such a relatively low rate of growth from the end of the First World War, this seems to offer a major contributory explanation. The mass migration of labour from the land had begun to slow down from the 1870s onwards, coinciding with the start of Britain's relative economic decline. British agriculture was very largely capitalized by the 1920s. In this way, Britain (which had also just released Ireland from its political dependence) had already lost a source of surplus profits in this previously backward internal sector. Mandel makes it clear that 'the exchange of agricultural products against industrial goods is an unequal exchange (always with the reservation that we are speaking of agricultural production by small peasants. . . . As soon as agriculture becomes fully capitalized, such unequal exchange disappears).'[7]

In the other metropolitan countries, this source of additional surplus-profits existed until well after the Second World War. Mandel himself points out that the capitalization of agricultural production was a major source of growth in the advanced industrial nations in the post-war period.

> The age of late capitalism . . . has been characterized by an even greater increase of labour productivity in agriculture than in industry. In West Germany in the period 1950–1970 there was a four-fold increase in the gross productivity of labour in agriculture. . . . This rate of growth was far higher than that of industry. In the U.S.A. there was an annual growth of 3.8% in production per unit of labour in agriculture in the period 1937–1948 (as against 1.9% outside agriculture), a growth of 5.7% (as against 2.6% outside agriculture) in the period 1949–1957, and of 6% in the period 1955–1970. Under capitalist relations of production, the escalation of the productivity of labour in agriculture takes the form of an increasing conversion of agriculture into purely capitalist enterprises – in other words, a radical diminution of the areas of simple commodity production or of individual small peasant farmers producing use-values.[8]

This can be seen from table 5.1, which shows strikingly how those advanced countries with the highest proportions of their populations employed in agriculture also had the most rapid

Table 5.1   *Percentage of total labour force employed in agriculture*

	1960	1970	1973
Japan	30.2	17.4	13.4
Italy	32.8	19.6	17.4
France	22.4	14.0	12.2
W. Germany	14.0	8.6	7.5
USA	8.3	4.4	4.1
UK	4.1	2.8	2.9

reductions in the proportional workforce employed in this sector.[9] Above all, small peasant farmers left the land, and were absorbed into the urban workforce, thus moving from very low-productivity subsistence production to relatively higher-productivity employment. In chapter 2 of this book I suggested that this accounted in large measure for the different rates of growth of the major industrialized countries during the post-war period. There is a correlation between the rank order of rates of growth and the proportion of the workforce employed in agriculture at the start of the period.

Mandel adds a further factor contributing to this correlation. In Europe, and particularly West Germany, the existence of a large pool of post-war refugees, and the subsequent immigration of workers from southern Europe, helped keep wages down while relative surplus-value was rising. Together with the influx of displaced peasant farmers, these constituted a source of cheap labour, another of the factors listed by Marx as giving rise to surplus-profits. Mandel writes:

> The absorption of over 10 million refugees and millions of foreign workers in post-war West Germany had its equivalent in Italy in the incorporation of millions of peasants and rural inhabitants from Southern Italy into North Italian industry, in Japan in the absorption of yet more millions of peasants and labourers occupied in traditional sectors of the economy by modern Japanese industry with similar effects, and in the USA by the absorption into the urban labour force of over 10 million married women, together with more than 4 million farmers, share-croppers and agricultural labourers. . . . These movements were the necessary and sufficient precondition for the long-term persistence of an above-average rate of surplus-value – in other words, for a long-term blockage of the fall of the average rate of profit, and hence for an above-average growth in the accumulation of capital. Thus, between 1950 and 1965, approximately 7 million labourers emigrated from the agricultural sector in Japan. In the same period the number of wage-earners in manufacturing industry

doubled (rising from 4.5 to 9 millions). . . . The secret of this imposing growth is easy to see: between 1960 and 1965 real wages per wage-earner in manufacturing industry rose by only 20%, while the physical productivity of labour per employee increased by 48%: hence a vast increase in the production of relative surplus-value.[10]

Mandel argues that, given the enormous increase in labour productivity that was made possible by the 'third technological revolution' during the Second World War, these conditions were ideal for a period of expansion in the capitalist world economy. In the USA, the 'industrialization' of agriculture and new automatic processes in industry meant that the annual growth rate of labour productivity exceeded the annual growth rate of production, with resulting relatively high rates of unemployment and modest rates of wage increases. In West Germany the share of wage and salary earners in national income in 1959 remained below its level of 1929, and the relative share of wages actually fell throughout the 1950s, to a level below that of 1938 (when it had been held down by five years of Nazi dictatorship which made trade unions illegal). Only after 1960 did the relative share of wages start to rise, with the advent of full employment. The years up to 1965 in the USA and Japan, and up to 1960 in Europe,

form genuine halcyon periods for late capitalism, in which all the factors appeared to promote expansion: a high rate of investment; rapid growth of labour productivity; a rising rate of surplus-value facilitated by the industrial reserve army, hence a slower growth of real wages as compared to the productivity of labour, with a simultaneous dampening of social tensions.[11]

Britain was the exception to this general rule, as Mandel recognizes. However, he attributes the low rate of growth in Britain entirely to the capacity of the British working class to resist capitalist exploitation.

Britain became the only imperialist power which proved

unable to increase the rate of exploitation of its working class significantly during or after the Second World War: the rate in the UK was now stabilized at the lower pre-war levels in the new epoch. From a capitalist point of view the result was evident: an erosion of the rate of profit, and a much slower rate of economic growth and accumulation than in the other imperialist countries (and the stimulating influence of international expansion on the British economy was responsible for a significant part even of this growth).[12]

This explanation of Britain's relatively poor post-war economic performance shows how heavily Mandel relies on the notion that the rate of profit is very closely related to movements in the rate of surplus-value and the organic composition of capital. In fact, there is little evidence from the 1960s to suggest that British workers were militant in their resistance to exploitation, or that they enjoyed more than modest improvements in their standards of living. It was the weakness of British capital rather than the strength of British labour that accounted for slow economic growth, and it is unclear from Mandel whether the low rate of profit in Britain was an expression or a cause of this weakness.

From Mandel's own account, however, it seems clear that the other major difference between Britain and the other metropolitan countries lay in the structure of its labour force, since Britain's agricultural sector had already been 'industrialized', and apart from the relatively small influx of workers from the Caribbean and the Indian sub-continent, there was little immigration. Thus an important element in the dynamic of growth among Britain's competitors was not available for British capital.

'LONG WAVES' AND UNEMPLOYMENT

Mandel's explanation of the slowing down of economic growth in the advanced industrialized countries is based on the re-appearance of a widespread fall in the rate of profit in the mid-1960s. All the conditions for expansion mentioned above began to disappear from that time, and with the disappearance of surplus-profits on the previous scale came a slower rate of growth.

Marxist economists had for many years drawn attention to a phenomenon described as 'long waves' in the development of capitalism. In addition to the seven to ten years of the industrial cycle – consisting of an upswing during which capital accumulates and the rate of profit rises, and a downswing when both the mass and rate of profit falls – there is an analogous cycle of about 50 years. During the 25 years of expansion, the constant undertone of each of the shorter cycles is of accelerated growth of capital, and the rate of profit is generally high. During the subsequent 25 years of stagnation, the undertone is of decelerated accumulation of capital, and a low rate of profit.

Although it was Marxists like Kondratieff and Trotsky who first drew attention to this phenomenon, economic historians are now broadly agreed that it is borne out to a great extent in rates of economic growth and rates of profit. According to the scheme used by Mandel, the period from 1894 to 1913 was one with a tendency towards accelerated growth, from 1914 to 1939 of decelerated growth, and from 1940 to 1966 of accelerated growth. The figures he quotes in support of his general argument are shown in tables 5.2[13] and 5.3[14].

Mandel's explanation for each of the periods of accelerated growth of capital accumulation is a technological revolution, giving rise to significant potential increases in labour productivity. But this potential can only be realized through a rise in

Table 5.2　*Annual cumulative rates of growth of industrial output (per cent)*

	1894–1913	1914–38	1939–67
UK	2.2	2.0	3.0
Germany (after 1945, West Germany)	4.3	2.2	3.9
USA	5.9	2.0	5.2

Table 5.3   *Average rate of post-tax profit
(commercial and industrial companies) (per cent)*

	1950–64	1965–70	1970–73
UK	6.9	5.1	4.5
USA	7.0	7.7	5.5

the rate of profit. Mandel implies that a 'reserve fund' of unused capital – ready for massive investment in new technology or products – builds up during the period of decelerated growth. Although this can be challenged (by pointing out that expansions are largely self-financing, and use the bank overdraft system to create new money), it seems that he is right to suggest that there have been points in time at which investment suddenly increased, based on new methods and new commodities.

The advent of consumer durables production in the USA, rearmament, and the success of fascism in forcing down real wages all contributed to a gradual rise in the rate of profit in the late 1930s. With the new technology invented during the Second World War, automatic methods of production were introduced in a far broader range of products. In addition, machines themselves were produced by new advanced processes, and the production of raw materials and foodstuffs were mechanized.

However, in spite of the exceptionally favourable conditions that prevailed for capital in the post-war period, a problem began to emerge at the end of the 25-year expansion. In essence it represented a special case of the general difficulty mentioned in the first section of this chapter. Although new technological processes could increase productivity greatly, they eventually run up against the same difficulty as all other productive processes – that of the diminishing rate of growth of relative surplus-value. The particular version of this problem associated with automation will be discussed in the next chapter.

As a result of this difficulty, Mandel argues, the rate of

profit began to fall from the mid-1960s onwards in the advanced industrialized countries. This has given rise to a period of decelerated capital accumulation. One of the functional features of this long wave of stagnation, from the standpoint of capital, is that unemployment increases, and with it the pressure for increases in real wages. According to the Marxist theory of wages, their level is controlled by capital, through the creation of an 'industrial reserve army' of unemployed workers, which can be exploited during periods of expansion, and discarded during periods of stagnation or crisis – both in the industrial cycle and in the long waves. This surplus population places at capital's disposal 'a mass of human material which can be exploited . . . for capital's changing requirements'. Thus

> The general movements of wages are exclusively regulated by the expansion and contraction of the in-dustrial reserve army . . . by the varying proportions in which the working class is divided into an active army and a reserve army, by the increase or diminution in the relative amount of surplus population, by the extent to which it is alternately absorbed and set free.[15]

Mandel points out that full employment did not begin to occur in the advanced industrialized countries in the long wave of post-war expansion until the 1960s, because of the availability of refugee, immigrant and displaced agricultural labour to reconstitute the industrial reserve army. However, from 1960 onwards, 'the high level of employment contri-buted to a significant increase in the strength of wage-earners, to whom extra-economic pressures were now applied in order to prevent them from diminishing the rate of surplus value'.[16] Among his evidence for this new struggle over the rate of surplus-value, Mandel includes economic planning, incomes policy and wage freezes. He describes Keynesian methods of 'economic management' as attempts to provide a state guarantee of profits for capital, and suggests that permanent inflation was part of the price of this system.

Mandel suggests that the transition from the long wave of expansion to the long wave of stagnation was closely related to this struggle over the rate of surplus-value, and that renewed class conflict will continue to be a feature of the period right up to the next technological revolution in methods of production, which could be expected at the end of the present decade. Thus high rates of unemployment and attempts to reduce the standards of living of the working class will, by this analysis, be features of the 1980s in the advanced industrialized nations, as will slow rates of growth of national income.

The only two other ways of combating the low rate of profit in the advanced industrialized countries are automation and the export of capital to countries with lower wages and higher rates of profit. Automation will be discussed in the next chapter. Mandel devotes relatively little attention to the export of capital. He suggests that the industrialization of certain previously underdeveloped countries is limited by a number of factors. In the first place 'it is the accumulation of industrial capital moving from the sphere of raw materials into that of manufacturing industry, but on average remaining one or two stages behind the technology or type of industrialization predominating in the metropolitan countries'.[17] Using obsolete machinery, or advanced machinery at very low capacity levels, the industrial sector of these countries also has a limited home market because of low earnings in other sectors, and cannot seriously compete with commodities produced in the metropolitan countries. Mandel does concede that in one sector the industrializing countries can compete with the industrialized ones – labour intensive industries producing finished goods which can operate with relatively cheap machine equipment. Here the advantage of cheap labour-power is considerable, and the only limits of growth are the costs of transport. While acknowledging the rapid expansion of manufacture of electronics equipment in South Korea, Taiwan and Hong Kong, of Asian textiles and African tinned foods, Mandel sees this as of limited significance because 'labour-intensive branches of industry are today declining in overall economic significance as compared with capital-intensive, semi-automated or automated branches which monopoly capital has no incentive to transfer to the semi-colonies'.[18]

CRITICISMS OF MANDEL'S ANALYSIS

Mandel's account of late capitalism was written in the late 1960s and early 1970s. He is concerned to show late capitalism as a new era of capitalism in which previous features of the development of capitalism are worked out. In the introduction he states:

> The era of Late Capitalism is not a new epoch of capitalist development. It is merely a further development of the imperialist monopoly—capitalist epoch. By implication the characteristics of the imperialist epoch enumerated by Lenin thus remain valid for late capitalism.[19]

Because he emphasizes the continuity with imperialism, Mandel's account of the interrelationship between development and underdevelopment, between the 'imperialist' and the 'semi-colonial' countries, is couched in dualistic terms. He does not differentiate between the 'metropolitan' or imperialist countries, or between the underdeveloped ones, and therefore gives no clear account either of the relative decline of Britain and the United States, or of the rapid emergence of the industrializing countries. Because he sees the advanced industrialized countries as dominating and controlling the expansion of the capitalist world economy, he does not conceive of any of them losing their positions of superiority.

Yet in his own account of economic growth through surplus-profits in late capitalism, Mandel recognizes the importance of unequal exchange between higher and lower productivity sectors of the same economy, and thus by implication of the same group of economies. This leads him to state that:

> limits to the process of capitalist growth are – from a purely economic point of view – in this sense always merely temporary, because while they proceed out of the very conditions of a difference in the level of productivity, they can reverse these conditions. Industrial zones flourish at the expense of agricultural regions, but their

expansion is limited by the very fact that their most important 'internal colony' is condemned to relative stagnation and sooner or later they therefore seek to overcome this limit by resorting to an 'external' colony. At the same time, however, the relationship 'industrial zone—agricultural region' does not remain eternally frozen under capitalism. It provides a new stimulus to the process of growth . . . and there is no reason why a zone which was industrialized early on should not be transformed into a relatively backward area, or a former agricultural district be transformed into an area of industrial concentration. Marx had already seen this possibility in his own time. . . .[20]

There are two very important implications of this statement. The first is that a zone (or nation) 'which industrialized early on' may come to have a lower level of productivity than a zone (or nation) which industrialized later. This is exactly what has occurred in the post-war era. Newly industrialized zones in Britain and the United States (the Midlands, the South and South-Western States) came to have higher rates of productivity than the old industrial centres (the North of England, the North-Eastern States). But in addition the rate of increase of productivity in industrializing Japan, France and West Germany outstripped that in both Britain and the United States. The enormous lead in productivity established first by Britain and then by the United States has been whittled away. In the case of Britain, its level of productivity is now lower than in any other major industrialized country, so that 'unequal exchange' occurs in trade between Britain and any of these countries. Britain is at risk of becoming a de-industrializing 'internal colony' of the metropolitan world.

The second implication is that the growth rates of industrialized zones and countries are no more limited by the processes that Mandel describes than those of industrializing zones or countries, so that advanced metropolitan countries are able to make as positive use of differentials in productivity as rapidly industrializing ones. Yet Mandel's own analysis gives strong reasons why this is not so. Partly this stems from the problems inherent in automation and the declining rate of growth of relative surplus-value. But principally it stems from the fact that historically the highest rates of relative economic growth, and of increases in labour productivity, have been associated with the process of industrialization and the capitalization of agriculture. The experience of the first zones to industrialize in Britain and the United States, and the experience of Britain itself in international competition, suggest that once this process has been completed, the opportunities for growth are much more limited, and other industrializing zones and nations grow more quickly.

Two possibilities arise from this which Mandel does not consider. The first is that the metropolitan imperialist countries may find it more difficult to reassert their international predominance and economic success in the next long wave of expansion, and that industrial production may continue to shift towards the newly industrializing countries. The second is that Britain in particular may come to serve the function of a source of unequal exchange, rather than as part of the prosperous metropolitan imperialist bloc.

If the first possibility came about, then rates of unemployment would continue to be high, and possibly growing, in the advanced industrialized countries, even after a renewed expansion of the capitalist world economy after 1990. If the second possibility arose, Britain would experience unprecedented mass unemployment for the foreseeable future.

REFERENCES

1. Karl Marx, *Grundrisse* (1857), Penguin, 1973, pp. 324–5. For a far more comprehensive explication of Marx's theory of value, see I. I. Rubin, *Essays on Marx's Theory of Value* (1928), Black and Red, 1972, and R. Rosdolsky, *The Making of Marx's 'Capital'* (1968), Pluto Press, 1977.
2   Ibid., p. 341.
3   Ibid., p. 747.
4   Ibid., p. 751.
5   E. Mandel, *Late Capitalism* (1972), New Left Books, 1975, p. 83. For a detailed critique of Mandel's analysis, see Bob Rowthorn, *Capitalism, Conflict and Inflation*, Lawrence and Wishart, 1980.
6   Ibid., pp. 89–90.

7   Ibid., p. 90.
8   Ibid., pp. 378–9.
9   OECD, *Labour Force Statistics.*
10   Mandel, *Late Capitalism*, pp. 171–2.
11   Ibid., p. 178.
12   Ibid., p. 179.
13   Ibid., pp. 141–2.
14   Ibid., pp. 212–13.
15   Karl Marx, *Capital*, vol. 1 (1867), Penguin, 1976, p. 790.
16   Mandel, *Late Capitalism*, p. 180.
17   Ibid., p. 368.
18   Ibid., p. 374.
19   Ibid., p. 10.
20   Ibid., p. 104.

6
Automation and Unemployment

We come now to the nub of the problem of rising unemployment in the advanced industrialized countries of the capitalist world – the relationship between 'automation' and unemployment.

It is now widely recognized that there is a crucial link between the degree and nature of automation of industrial production and the expansion or contraction of industrial employment, but neither orthodox economic theory nor political analysis provide a systematic or comprehensive account of this link. The result is a contradictory and ambivalent attitude towards new technology.

Much of the confusion stems from attempts to determine whether modern sophisticated technology 'causes' unemployment by making human labour redundant, or whether it 'provides' more employment by increasing productive potential. These attempts are futile so long as they fail to take account of the key factors which determine the relationship between productivity and output. In this chapter I shall try to show why precisely the same new technological processes have had such different effects on particular industries and areas according to these factors. I shall look at the reasons why new technology has assisted in the rapid expansion of industrial output and employment in the newly industrialized countries, while at the same time has contributed to falling industrial employment in the advanced industrialized countries.

First, however, it is necessary to clarify some issues over the definition of 'automation'.

TYPES OF AUTOMATION

In order to develop an adequate theory of the relationship between new technology and unemployment, we need to take account of the following historical facts:

(a) The increased use of machinery in production has been characteristic of every stage in the development of modern industry since the Industrial Revolution.

(b) New technology has constantly been introduced to increase the productivity of labour (output per worker). The development of industrial production thus depends on these two processes, the raising of labour productivity through the introduction of a proportionately greater mechanical element into productive methods.

(c) As well as increasing the productivity of labour, the introduction of new machinery may also have direct effects on the output and level of employment in the industry affected. New machinery does not always result in higher output, either in the firm that introduces it, or in the industry as a whole. It may be introduced with the primary intention of saving labour costs. If the effect of the machine is to increase the productivity of labour, but the output of the industry remains the same, or falls, then employment in that industry will decrease.

Productivity is measured by output per worker over a period of time (for instance, output per man-hour, or annual output per number of workers employed). Whichever way we measure productivity, it is possible to calculate the rate at which output per worker is rising or falling, and to compare this percentage rate of increase or decrease in productivity with the percentage rise or fall in output. If output is rising faster than productivity (or falling more slowly) then the number of workers in that industry (or the number of man-hours worked) must increase. If output is rising more slowly than productivity (or falling more quickly) then employment must decline.

(d) Historically there may have been many examples of industries and areas in which labour productivity has risen more rapidly than output, with the result that machines *replaced* workers. For example, in Britain there were fewer workers in manufacturing industry in 1938 than there had been in 1920. This was because, although manufacturing output increased by 58 per cent in this period, output per worker increased by an even larger amount (60 per cent) through new methods of production.[1]

Both Ricardo and Marx in the nineteenth century recognized the possibility of such a process, but Ricardo saw it as mainly a short-term feature in certain industries and geographical areas and thought that in the long term displaced workers would be absorbed elsewhere in the economy. He suggested that the circumstances in which machinery was introduced without increasing output proportionately were usually associated with very rapid technological innovation in a particular industry. Even so, he acknowledged, 'I am convinced that the substitution of machinery for human labour is often very injurious to the interests of the class of labourers. . . . The same cause which may increase the net revenue (profits) of the country may at the same time render the population redundant, and deteriorate the conditions of the labourer.'[2]

Marx, however, foresaw that in the long run the development of capitalism and the mechanization of production would lead to a stage at which 'living labour' would be replaced by 'dead labour' (machines produced from the surplus labour of past generations of workers). He referred to 'automata' in a way which foreshadowed industrial developments today. Unlike Ricardo, he saw this as the logical final stage of capital's development, and the stage towards which the whole history of capital's growth was progressing. But it would not necessarily and of itself free the working class from its life of toil; all it would achieve in the first instance would be to expose the latent contradictions in capitalism's development, and make the transition to socialism far easier. This was because the elimination of living labour from the process of production would bring capitalism face to face with the consequence of the law of value – the creation of surplus-value through surplus labour would cease to occur. Marx wrote: 'As soon as labour in the direct form has ceased to be the great well-spring of wealth, labour-time ceases and must cease to be

its measure. . . . With that, production based on exchange value breaks down. . . .'³
This was the unavoidable consequence of capital's tendency to mechanize production.

> The exchange of living labour for objectified labour . . . is the ultimate development of the value relation and of production resting on value. . . . to the degree that large industry develops, the creation of real wealth comes to depend less on labour-time and on the amount of labour employed than on the power of the agencies set in motion during labour-time, whose powerful effectiveness is . . . out of proportion to the direct labour-time spent on their production, but depends rather on the general state of science and on the progress of technology, or the application of science to production. . . . Labour no longer appears so much to be included within the production process; rather, the human being comes more to relate as nightwatchman and regulator to the production process itself. . . .⁴

If this passage is taken out of its context, Marx appears to be describing a process which will occur simultaneously in all the most advanced industrialized countries, and will bring about the end of capitalism as a world economic system. He also seems to be suggesting that the process itself depends on the 'powerful effectiveness' of the new technology itself – the intrinsic qualities of the new automatic processes, which can dispense with human labour. Yet clearly this cannot be the case, since living labour is not displaced simultaneously in all industries or in all geographical areas. Even a *fully* automatic method of production introduced into one industry will not necessarily reduce, still less eliminate, human labour in the whole productive process of the economy, so long as there continue to be new opportunities for employment in other non-automated industries elsewhere. Indeed, it has been one of the ironic consequences of the introduction of micro-electronic technology into industrial and commercial processes in the industrial countries that it has increased employment in the industrializing countries, which have been used as the main centres for manufacturing micro-electronic equipment.

Thus the only meaningful way in which the concept of automation can be discussed is in terms of the *relation* between the rise or fall in output in a given industry or area, and the rise or fall in employment in that industry or area. To discuss it in terms of a particular technological process is bound to be misleading, since the same new technology may have entirely different effects on output and employment levels. We need the following concepts to describe the various possibilities in this relation:

(a) *Mechanization*: I shall use this term to describe a situation in which the introduction of new technology is used to increase output more rapidly than it increases labour productivity.

(b) *Automation*: This term describes any situation in which new technology is used to increase productivity more rapidly than it increases output. Only in these circumstances is human labour substituted by machinery.

It should be clear that both these processes may be occurring simultaneously in different branches of the same industry, in different geographical areas, or in different parts of the world. The effects on employment and unemployment of the combination of these processes in different industries and areas can only be calculated by examining how the balance between them is maintained.

Within the category of automation, we may distinguish between four relationships between output and productivity, all of which can lead to reduced employment in an industry or area:

(i) Output increasing rapidly, employment falling. This may be the result of entirely new technology being introduced into an industry which is expanding production, thus increasing productivity even more rapidly than it increases output.

(ii) Output increasing slowly, employment falling. This is normally associated with less rapid technological change in an industry which is not expanding its output so fast.

(iii) Output stagnant, employment falling. This usually occurs in an idustry in which there is some technological change occurring in methods of production, but no growth of output.

(iv) Output falling, employment falling more rapidly. Under these circumstances, automation is occurring even though no new processes of production are being introduced. Thus during a period of reduced output, even without technological change of any kind, there may be a more rapid reduction of the workforce than there is of production (e.g. a drive to reduce 'overmanning').

This suggests several paradoxical results. For instance, it is quite possible that an expanding capital-intensive industry with a very small workforce and massive capital investment may be described as in the process of 'mechanization' (because even very large increases in labour productivity are being outstripped by even larger increases in output) while an old and declining industry may be said to be experiencing automation, because its fall in output is not matched by a corresponding fall in the productivity of labour.

Indeed, this is precisely what has occurred in several British industries recently. For example, the enormous increase in production of North Sea oil cannot be described as involving a process of automation because employment has risen, albeit very marginally, in this industry. On the other hand, a declining industry like iron and steel can be said to have experienced automation, since its workforce has fallen more rapidly than its output. Thus if automation is seen as a relation between output and employment rather than as a description of a particular productive process, there is no reason why a capital-intensive industry should be more likely to experience automation than a labour-intensive industry.

Another potential paradox is that automation in this sense is most likely to occur when an industry or area has relatively stagnant or falling output. While output is rising rapidly, productivity is unlikely to outstrip production, and thus rapid growth industries and areas seldom experience automation. On the other hand, areas with far slower growth in productivity may well experience automation as a result of even slower growth of output, if employers decide to use new investment to save labour costs. The reasons for such decisions will be discussed in chapter 8.

A third paradox is that the 'stage of automation' which Marx anticipated does not necessarily occur first in the most scientifically advanced industries, for the reasons given above. Indeed, I shall suggest in the next section that agriculture provides the best example of automation in the post-war advanced industrialized world. Thus the most backward and lowest-productivity sector of productive industry was the first to experience automation.

Nonetheless, Marx's prediction of a 'stage of automation' in the advanced industrialized nations, following after the 'stage of mechanization', and associated with rapid advances in science and technology, is highly relevant to the present situation in the industrialized countries of the capitalist world.

AUTOMATION IN THE POST-WAR YEARS

If we consider automation in this light, it becomes clear that none of the major advanced industrialized countries experienced automation in their industrial sectors between 1945 and 1966. In every one of them industrial employment rose, as output increased more rapidly than productivity. Thus all the considerable technological innovation of this era produced more employment in the industrial sphere.

Yet during this same period, every one of these countries experienced the automation of agriculture. Because agricultural output grew slowly, but new methods based on tractors, combine harvesters and so on, were introduced, the agricultural workforce declined rapidly in all the industrialized countries. In particular, peasant farmers were displaced as large units using more machinery were formed.

Tables 6.1, 6.2 and 6.3 indicate the relative increases in industrial and agricultural output, employment and productivity in the early 1960s. In each of these countries, the productivity of labour in agriculture was less than half that of industry at the start of the period. Thus the process that occurred in the post-war period was of the automation of the

Table 6.1   *Indices of industrial and agricultural production at 1960 prices (1960 = 100)*

	Industrial Production[5]		Agricultural Production[6]	
	1960	1968	1960	1968
Japan	100	270	100	190
Italy	100	180	100	127
France	100	147	100	126
W. Germany	100	147	100	118
USA	100	152	100	113
UK	100	113	100	121

lowest-productivity sector of the economy – displacing its least productive workers – and a simultaneous expansion of the higher-productivity sectors. This was the recipe for rapid and prolonged growth of national income, particularly in those countries with the largest surviving agricultural workforces.

As can be seen from the tables, productivity growth was not the only factor responsible for growth of output, or growth of national income. Germany and France had virtually identical rates of growth of output in both industry and agriculture, and also of national income (percentage increases of 57 and 58 per cent during this period). Yet labour productivity grew significantly faster in the industrial sector in Germany than it did in France. The explanation for the difference lies in the con-

Table 6.2   *Indices of industrial and agricultural employment (1960 = 100)*

	Industrial Employment[7]		Agricultural Employment[8]	
	1960	1968	1960	1968
Japan	100	137	100	74
Italy	100	105	100	65
France	100	109	100	75
W. Germany	100	100	100	73
USA	100	116	100	70
UK	100	98	100	74

Table 6.3   *Percentage increases in output per worker*

	Industry[9] 1960–68	Agriculture[10] 1960–68
Japan	97	157
Italy	71	95
France	35	68
W. Germany	47	62
USA	31	61
UK	15	63

tinued growth of industrial employment in France. This is explained partly by the larger proportion of agricultural workers in the French economy during the early 1960s (22.5 per cent in France, compared with only 14 per cent in Germany) and partly by the steady growth of the French civilian workforce (by 6 per cent from 1960 to 1968, compared with a *fall* of 0.5 per cent in civilian employment in Germany during the same period).

The beginnings of automation in the industrial sectors of the economies of the advanced industrialized countries occurred in Britain and Germany from 1966 onwards. If we compare the figures for industrial output, employment and productivity in the two countries during the period 1966–72, we can see that the automation that took place was of a diferent nature (see table 6.4). In Germany, industrial pro-

Table 6.4   *Indices of industrial production, employment and productivity in West Germany and the UK 1966–72*

	Industrial production[11]		Industrial employment[12]		Industrial productivity of labour	
	1966	1972	1966	1972	1966	1972
W. Germany	100	140	100	99	100	141
UK	100	117	100	84	100	139

duction continued to grow at a rate of approximately 5.8 per cent a year, but productivity grew even faster. In Britain, the rate of growth of industrial production was far slower, and the decline in employment was more rapid.

These countries provided the blueprints for what was about to occur in all the major advanced industrialized countries of Europe in the mid-1970s. Britain and Germany were the first European nations to industrialize, and had the highest proportions of industrial workers in the mid-1960s. It is therefore reasonable to argue that the long-term automation of industry in these countries indicated the pattern of advanced industrialization in the capitalist world. We can see this pattern repeated on a European scale if we consider figures for industrial production, employment and productivity in the EEC for the mid-1970s (see table 6.5). For purposes of comparison, I also include the equivalent figures for the 'developing' market economies in this period. From these figures it is clear that industrial labour productivity rose much more rapidly in the EEC countries in the 1970s than it did in the 'developing' countries, but that industrial employment expanded in the latter, while contracting in the former.

The automation of the industrial sector of the advanced industrialized countries had very different consequences from the automation of agriculture in the period up to 1966. Instead of displacing the lowest-productivity workers in the economy, and allowing them to be absorbed into higher-productivity

Table 6.5   *Indices of industrial production employment and productivity in the EEC and 'developing' countries 1970–77*

	Industrial production[13]			Industrial employment[14]			Industrial productivity of labour[15]		
	1970	1973	1977	1970	1973	1977	1970	1973	1977
EEC	100	115	118	100	98	92	100	115	125
'Developing' market economies	100	128	155	100	122	138 (1976)	100	102	109 (1976)

work, it displaced workers from the highest-productivity sector, at a time when the only expanding sectors of the economies of the industrialized countries were services, and particularly public services, in which increases in productivity were (at least at that time) more difficult to achieve. As government policy switched from deliberate expansion of these services in the early 1970s to deliberate control over this process, unemployment rose rapidly.

TYPES OF INDUSTRIAL AUTOMATION

To understand industrial automation in the advanced industrialized countries we need to disentangle the several kinds of automation that were occurring simultaneously in various industries and countries.

Firstly, there are certain clear examples of *industries* where rapid increases in production were accompanied by substantial decreases in employment. These are the industries where the most rapid technological innovations were occurring. The best example is the production of crude petroleum and natural gas. The figures for the EEC countries given in table 6.6 show that, from the early 1960s, the automation of this industry was very marked.[16] However, after 1970 this process was to a limited extent reversed, and productivity actually fell for a while.

In contrast with this industry, the production of metals (mainly iron and steel) in the EEC declined from 1968 onwards (see table 6.7).[17] However, as production fell, the workforce in this industry declined even more rapidly, so that there was an even greater fall in employment than in output. Hence although labour productivity remained relatively constant throughout the 1970s (reflecting little technological change in methods of production), automation was taking place in this industry from the early 1960s onwards. This contrast represents the extremes between a growth industry (petroleum and natural gas) and a declining industry (metals). It shows that the overall process of automation contained instances of rapid technological change and rapid decline in output.

Table 6.6   *Indices of production of crude petroleum and natural gas in the EEC (1970 = 100)*

	1960	1963	1968	1970	1973	1974	1975	1976	1977
Production	27	33	65	100	152	165	166	186	209
Employment	187	181	112	100	111	114	119	134	128
Productivity	17	22	58	100	137	145	139	139	163

Similarly, the contrast already made between West Germany and Britain indicates that the composite figures for the EEC disguise two contrasting patterns – automation of relatively successful economies (and regions), with continued growth of industrial production; and automation of stagnant or declining economies, with declining industrial production. The series quoted above continues as shown in table 6.8.[18] The picture is particularly gloomy for Britain if North Sea oil and gas are excluded. Hence in both industries and areas, the process of automation represents a combination of declining output and employment in some sectors and technological innovation in certain growth sectors. But the common factor to both is that labour is perceived as costly, and is eliminated from the process of production.

In the previous chapter we considered the Marxist explanation for this phenomenon. Mandel suggests that full employment in the industrialized countries was not reached until about 1960, and from that time onwards rising real wages created problems for capital in increasing relative surplus-value. The rate of profit on domestic investments began to fall in the industrialized countries from the mid-1960s onwards,

Table 6.7   *Indices of production of metals in the EEC (1970 = 100)*

	1960	1963	1968	1970	1973	1974	1975	1976	1977
Production	51	58	101	100	92	89	84	78	71
Employment	188	158	110	100	87	79	78	70	63
Productivity	28	37	92	100	106	113	108	112	114

Table 6.8   *Indices of industrial production, employment and productivity in West Germany and the UK 1973–80 (1975 = 100)*

	1973	1974	1975	1976	1977	1978	1979	1980
W. Germany								
Industrial production	107.8	106.6	100	110.3	111.1	112.9	117.4	117.4
Industrial employment	109.1	106.6	100	98.1	97.3	97.4	98.5	99.2
Industrial productivity	98.8	100.0	100	112.4	114.2	115.9	119.2	118.3
UK								
Industrial production	109.8	105.7	100	102.4	106.5	110.2	112.8	99.2 (Q4)
Industrial employment	104.5	104.1	100	97.5	97.3	96.9	96.1	88.0
Industrial productivity	105.0	101.6	100	105.1	109.6	113.7	117.4	112.7
UK if North Sea oil and natural gas are excluded								
Industrial production	109.6	105.8	100	101.1	102.6	104.4	104.5	90.3
Industrial employment	104.5	104.1	100	97.5	97.2	96.8	96.0	87.9
Industrial productivity	104.9	101.6	100	103.7	105.5	107.9	108.9	102.7

and the oil price crisis merely gave the final twist to a process that was already well established in Britain, Germany and the United States.

The reason why automation occurred in the industrial sectors of the advanced industrialized countries was therefore that new technology provided the *means* of saving labour costs, while rising real wages provided the *motive* for doing so. Mandel acknowledges that automation substantially increases relative surplus-value. However, he does not clearly demonstrate how it solves one of the barriers to capital's development mentioned by Marx. The problem for capital of a falling rate of increase of relative surplus-value rests of the irreducibility of necessary labour – that part of labour-time which is needed for workers to reproduce their own subsistence in the form of wages. So long as the *number* of workers in any industry or area is the same, this irreducible fraction cannot be changed, and any increase in productivity encounters Marx's arithmetical problem mentioned in the last chapter. However, as soon as the *number* of workers is reduced, this fraction is reduced also, since a smaller number of workers requires a smaller volume of subsistence. Hence relative surplus-value can be increased much more quickly by reducing the workforce, and capital has the strongest possible motive for doing this when the rate of profit is falling, and labour costs are rising.

The way in which automation is capable of saving labour costs and restoring the falling rate of profit can be gauged from the following examples from Britain during the inter-war years. The tables below illustrate the patterns of production, employment, wages and profits of mining and agriculture between the wars, both of which experienced automation in this period.[20]

In the case of mining and quarrying, it can be seen that between 1921 and 1925 the volume of wages rose (despite a small reduction in the workforce) while the volume of profits fell (table 6.9). Between 1925 and 1929, the workforce was greatly reduced, and profits (which fell to virtually nothing in 1927–28) rose again in 1929, while the volume of wages fell. In 1932, the deepest trough of the Depression, profits were again very low, and wages had continued to decline in volume. But by 1938 the volume of profits was 77 per cent higher than it had been in 1921, whereas the volume of wages was the same.

In the case of farming and fishing, profits declined more rapidly than wages from 1921 (when they were very high) to 1932, but from 1932 to 1938, the volume of profits rose while the volume of wages fell (table 6.10).[20]

Thus reductions in the workforce (automation) can be shown to save labour costs and to increase profits, and this is why they were made in the industrial sector of the advanced capitalist countries from the mid-1960s onwards. However, this created two problems – higher unemployment, and lower incomes for the working class. These problems in turn have limited the scope for industrial expansion in the advanced

Table 6.9   *Mining and quarrying at constant 1913 prices*
(1921 = 100)

	1921	1925	1929	1932	1938
Total production	100	149.5	168.8	130.7	147.2
Total employment	100	99.5	87.2	74.5	74.7
Total volume of wages	100	110.5	93.3	84.4	100.4
Total volume of gross profits and other trading income	100	87.1	105.7	65.0	177.3

industrialized countries. The cost of taxation to raise revenue
for maintaining the unemployed has further reduced the incomes of those still in work so that both employed and unemployed have had to spend a higher proportion of their incomes
on subsistence commodities. Thus demand for the more expensive range of industrial products has been diminished.

I have suggested that no political or economic theory gives a
clear account of the causes or consequences of automation.
However, Mandel attempts to do so, within a Marxist
framework, and in the next chapter I shall consider some of
the shortcomings of his account of the process. This is necessary in order to disentangle the likely consequences of the

Table 6.10   *Agriculture, forestry and fishing*
(1921 = 100)

	1921	1925	1929	1932	1938
Total production	100	107.4	117.6	115.0	117.7
Total employment	100	94.4	90.0	84.7	76.2
Total volume of wages	100	87.4	92.6	96.9	88.3
Total volume of income from self-employment, rent and other trading income	100	74.5	67.3	67.3	78.4

automation of industry for unemployment and for the future of the working class in the advanced capitalist countries. Mandel's theory posits a limit to capitalism's potential for automation, and we need to consider whether there is in fact such a limit, or whether capital's potential for self-perpetuation through automation is infinite.

REFERENCES

1   C. H. Feinstein, *Statistical Tables of National Income, Expenditure and Output of the United Kingdom, 1855–1965*, Cambridge University Press, 1972, tables 51 and 59.
2   David Ricardo, *Principles of Political Economy and Taxation* (1817), Everyman Edition, Dent, 1912, p. 264.
3   Karl Marx, *Grundrisse* (1857), Penguin, 1973, pp. 705–6.
4   Ibid.
5   OECD, *Industrial Production: Historical Statistics (1955–1964)* and *Main Economic Indicators*, 1967–70.
6   United Nations, *Statistical Yearbook, 1969*, United Nations, 1970, table 24.
7   OECD, *Labour Force Statistics*, 1958–69.
8   Ibid.
9   OECD, *Industrial Production: Historical Statistics* and *Labour Force Statistics*.
10 United Nations, *Statistical Yearbook*, 1969, and OECD, *Labour Force Statistics*, 1958–69.
11 OECD, *Main Economic Indicators*, 1967–70.
12 OECD, *Labour Force Statistics*, 1958–69.
13 United Nations, *Yearbook of National Accounts Statistics, 1979*, index numbers of industrial production, table 8B.
14 Ibid., index numbers of industrial employment.
15 Ibid., index numbers of labour productivity in industry.
16 Ibid., industrial production.
17 Ibid.
18 OECD, *Main Economic Indicators*, OECD, *Labour Force Statistics*, and Department of Employment, *Employment Gazette*, vol. 89, no. 4, April 1981.
19 Feinstein, *Statistical Tables*, tables 8, 9, 22, 51 and 59, using price inflators for retail prices and capital goods, tables 61 and 65.
20 Ibid.

7
Limits to Automation

In the 1970s, the advanced industrialized countries of the capitalist world dispensed with large numbers of their industrial workers. In this chapter I shall consider whether the consequent phenomenon of mass unemployment represented a temporary phase in the regeneration of capital, corresponding with a 'long wave' of slow accumulation, or whether it betokened an important new era in the development of world capitalism.

Marxist theorists seem strangely ambivalent about this issue. Since it is precisely the longest-established industrialized countries that are experiencing the most noticeable versions of this phenomenon, one might have supposed that they would have drawn attention to the way in which this finally justified Marx's own predictions. Particularly in the less successful advanced nations – Britain and the United States – mass unemployment could be seen as emerging as a long-term structural phenomenon, leading to an increase in inequality and a progressively more visible maldistribution of resources. Thus the process of automation could be directly linked with a visible arrival of the 'progressive immiseration of the working class'.

Indeed, Marx himself drew attention to the revolutionary potential of precisely this situation.

A development in the productive forces that would reduce the absolute number of workers, and actually enable the whole nation to accomplish its entire production in a shorter period of time, would produce a revolution, since it would put the majority of the population out of action.'[1]

Yet this aspect of the recent development of capitalism has not yet been fully analysed, nor has its potential for class struggle been sufficiently emphasized, in Marxist literature. In this chapter I shall suggest that this is because of certain theoretical problems in the Marxist analysis, which I shall try to identify.

In particular, I shall pay some attention to disputes among Marxist theorists about how to apply Marx's theory of value to the situation of automation; and to much more fierce disputes about how to interpret the emergence of the newly industrializing countries and the decline of some of the advanced industrialized ones. These disputes indicate the sources of their ambivalence on the connections between automation and class struggle. First, however, I shall follow Mandel's account of automation, since this links directly with his analysis of world capitalist developments that I have already described.

MANDEL'S ACCOUNT OF AUTOMATION

We saw in chapter 5 that Mandel's account of 'late capitalism' suggested that automation in the industrial sector of the metropolitan capitalist countries was a response to the falling rate of profit in the late 1960s and early 1970s. However, Mandel argues that there are limits to the scope of automation, and that it exposes the contradictions of late capitalism.

> For if fully automated enterprises and branches, and semi-automated concerns, grow so numerous that they become decisive for the structure of the whole of industry, reducing 'classical' industrial enterprises to only a relatively small share of total production, then the contradictions of late capitalism assume an explosive character. . . . All the historical contradictions of capitalism are concentrated in the . . . character of automation.[2]

I shall argue that Mandel's account of the potential limits to automation rests on a very serious confusion about the nature of this process, and that the true limits are much more complex and ambiguous than he suggests.

Mandel never defines automation satisfactorily. On the one hand, he quotes Marx's definition in terms of displacement of 'living labour' by 'objectified' labour (machinery). But soon after this he reverts to an implicitly 'technological' definition. Mandel thus describes automation as if it were a property of machinery, rather than a change in productive relations.

> The technical possibility of automation springs from the arms economy, or from the technical necessities corresponding to the particular degree of development reached by the arms economy. This applies to the general principle of automatic, continuous processes of production, completely emancipated from direct control by human hands (which becomes a physiological necessity with the age of nuclear energy). It also applies to the compulsion to construct automatic calculators, produced by direct derivation from cybernetic principles, which can collect data at lightning speed, and draw conclusions from them for the determination of decisions – for example, the precise guidance of automatic air defence missiles to knock out bomber planes.[3]

In fact, of course, while this new technology provided the means for automation, it did not result in automation throughout the period 1945–66. Such automation as did occur in this period was mainly in agriculture, and was accomplished by means of unsophisticated machines like tractors and combine harvesters. It was only in this sphere (as Mandel himself acknowledges elsewhere) that 'living labour' was displaced in the post-war era.

Next, Mandel goes on to compound this confusion. He describes the 'automation' of American industry in technological terms. He mentions the number of 'automatic control and measurement devices' used by US manufacturing establishments in the 1960s, but says nothing about the effect these had on employment. He suggests that new technology casts workers in a more supervisory role, but again does not show that this resulted in 'living labour' being displaced. Indeed, employment in manufacturing industry rose throughout the 1960s in the United States.

At this point, Mandel reveals the source of his muddle over automation. In explaining how semi-automatic processes of production give rise to 'substantial increases in the production of relative surplus-value', he quotes another author's account of the fact that 'the industries producing food and drink and the textile industry in West Germany registered a decline in the number of working hours needed to produce commodities to the value DM 1,000 from 77 to 37 and 210 to 89 hours respectively between 1950 and 1964'.[4]

This, of course, says nothing about automation. It has been on the essence of every technological innovation since the Industrial Revolution that it enabled the same quantity of commodities to be produced with less labour-time (i.e that it increased the productivity of labour). If Mandel is to use Marx's definition of automation, he would need to show that the number of man-hours worked in these industries was actually reduced, not that more could be produced in the same number of man-hours. Mandel says nothing about this, and the figures available are rather sketchy. They suggest that the numbers of workers employed in these industries in Germany were increasing throughout the 1950s, though they started to decline slightly in 1962.[5]

Next, Mandel makes a distinction between 'semi-automation' and 'full automation' which is far from helpful. These terms are never properly defined, but 'full automation' is mentioned as occurring when 'the displacement of living by dead labour . . . is virtually total'.[6] From the footnote attached to this passage Mandel appears to mean by this that the proportion of production costs representing wages and salaries is extremely small (a petrochemical works with 0.02 per cent labour costs is mentioned). Here again, Mandel fails to distinguish between increases in productivity achieved through higher organic composition of capital, and actual displacement of labour. He gives no example of displacement of workers in the petrochemical industry. Mandel goes on to say that

if semi-automatic processes of production are introduced into certain branches of production on a massive
scale, this merely reproduces at a higher level the inherent tendency for capital to increase its organic composition and does not raise any important theoretical
issues. . . . If, however, fully automated production
processes are introduced on a mass scale into certain
realms of production, the whole picture alters. In these
realms, the production of absolute or relative surplus-
value ceases to rise and the entire underlying tendency of
capitalism turns to its own negation: *in these realms
surplus-value hardly continues to be produced at all.*[7]
[Mandel's italics]

Here we come to the nub of the problem. It stems from the
fact that every reduction in the workforce, by reducing
labour-time, necessarily also reduces the *value* of the commodities produced. We saw in chapter 5 that according to
Marx (and incidentally also according to Ricardo), the only
measure of value in commodities produced was the labour-
time spent producing them. Thus increases in productivity
necessarily lowered the value of commodities by reducing the
labour-time spent in their production. However, as long as
the workforce goes on increasing, the total value of production goes on rising, even though the value of *each commodity
produced* continues to fall.

Once the process of automation begins in any industry or
area, then the value of the total output of commodities in that
industry or area must decline. This is as true of the process
that Mandel calls 'semi-automation (a fall in the number of
workers employed, presumably) as it is of 'full automation'
(the elimination of virtually the whole workforce). In either
case, if workers are displaced, total value falls.

Hence, this leads to a remarkable paradox. One of the
problems for capital in Marxist theory is the 'irreducibility' of
necessary labour – that part of the working day spent by the
worker in earning the means of his subsistence, his wage.
Because this fraction always remains, capital cannot maintain
its rate of increase of surplus-value simply by increasing
productivity. Hence, automation: the reduction of the work-

force reduces the total volume of wages, and allows relative surplus-value to grow more rapidly. What Mandel calls 'full automation' is a radical solution to this problem. It increases *relative* surplus-value to almost 100 per cent.

We might imagine Mandel's notion of 'full automation' coming about from two possible directions. On the other hand, there might be *new* industries which, from the start, had such a high organic composition of capital that they employed almost no workers. Thus, even though no *process* of automation occurred, only a tiny proportion of labour-time is consumed by the production of wages. In Mandel's example of the petrochemical plant, each of the very few workers employed would spend 99.98 per cent of his day in surplus labour, producing surplus-value.

In the case of *old* industries, by reducing the workforce, capital would achieve a similar result. Since the proportion of necessary labour in a given workforce could not be cut without reducing real wages, redundancy is the only way to go on increasing relative surplus-value. There is no logical reason why the displacement of workers by machines should not continue until the whole workforce is redundant, and relative surplus-value is as high a proportion as in the new industry.

However, at the same time as this process was developing, the total value of production would be falling. The more that labour-time was reduced, the less would be the value of total output. Hence, we have the paradox that capital could maximize relative surplus-value through automation, but at precisely the moment when relative surplus-value reached 100 per cent, total value would be nil. In its drive to maximize profits, in order to sustain itself, capital would have entirely destroyed the value of its production.

Mandel never makes this paradox clear, but he does assert that full automation would destroy surplus-value.

> . . . we have here arrived at the absolute inner limit of the capitalist mode of production. This absolute limit lies . . . in the fact that the *mass of surplus-value itself necessarily diminishes as a result of the elimination of living labour from the production process in the course of the final stage of mechanisation – automation.* Capitalism is incom-

patible with fully automated production in the whole of industry and agriculture, because this no longer allows the creation of surplus-value or the valorisation of capital. It is hence impossible for automation to spread to the entire realm of production in the age of late capitalism.[8]

In support of this assertion, Mandel goes on to quote the passage in Marx already recorded in chapter 6 (see page 97), in which Marx suggests that when labour-time ceases to be the universal measure of value, then production based on exchange value will break down.

This paradox focuses attention on a theoretical problem about which there has been great and anxious debate among Marxist economists in recent years. The central issue in this debate is whether or not the whole labour theory of value is indispensable to Marxist theory. For instance, in a recent article Hodgson explicitly rejected the theory of value, and argued that the crucial feature of the capitalist mode of production is capital's ability to *compel* the worker to sell his labour-power. In this article, Hodgson used the possibility of a full automated society, in which production took place without labour, as conclusive evidence *against* the notion that all value was derived from labour.[9] Mandel, of course, uses it as crucial confirmation of the theory.

This whole area is of key importance in Marx's theory, yet it has been the subject of the most fundamental disagreements between his followers. For instance, Rowthorn has written of Marx's definitions of 'constant' and 'variable' capital (dead labour and labour-power):

These definitions are so simple and so clearly given by Marx, that it would seem impossible for anyone who has read even the First Volume of *Capital* to misunderstand them or fail to see their importance. Yet generations of economists, both Left and Right, have done just this. Such is the power of tradition over men's minds, a tradition that insists on reading Marx as though he were an English classical economist.[10]

It is particularly unfortunate that Mandel, who adheres strongly to both the labour theory of value and the law of the declining rate of profit, and who develops such a powerful and comprehensive model of how these two elements in Marx's theory can be seen at work in the post-war development of international capitalism, should have provided such a confused account of automation. By describing it as a technological phenomenon, rather than showing how it reflected changes in productive relations between people under these two laws, Mandel provides still futher scope for the disputes which have characterized the recent history of Marxist economics. Much time and energy has been spent on necessary clarification of these theoretical fundamentals, and relatively little has been available for the analysis of phenomena which are of enormous significance to the future of the working class in every country.

In his description of the eventual breakdown of production based on exchange values, Marx does indeed raise the possibility of both production and wealth-creation without labour.[11] Since all machinery used in production up to that point would consist of the past surplus labour of workers in previous industrial cycles, it would represent in itself the objectification of the *historical* mass of surplus-value. It would be this mass of objectified surplus-value (made up from the man-hours of surplus labour worked by past generations of workers) that would then become the relevant factor in methods of production. With full automation, the entire production process would be accomplished by 'dead labour', and the costs of reproducing labour-power would be nil. What is not clear is whether capital (in theory at least) could then be presumed to be able to use this 'stock' of surplus-value to reproduce itself and accumulate.

It is hardly surprising that Marx, anticipating the process of automation over a hundred years ago, should not have predicted the exact course that the process would take. In the relevant passage of the *Grundrisse*, he was mainly concerned to argue that science and machinery had the *potential* to eliminate living labour from production, and that in this potential lay both one of the contradictions in capitalism, and a great future hope for a socialist society. But Marxist economists have not yet developed the theory or clarified how this process might be worked out in the capitalist world economy during the period of transition.

Although this period of transition seems already to have started, what has occurred so far is not enough to require any modification of the law of value. For such automation as occurred in the advanced industrialized countries after 1966 was only marginal. Even in Germany and Britain the reduction in the number of working hours spent on industrial production between 1966 and 1980 cannot have been greater than 25 per cent while in many other industrialized countries (such as the USA and Japan) the total labour-time increased. The overall decline in working hours in the advanced industrialized world was more than matched by the enormous growth in industrial employment in those countries which were industrializing in this period. Because of this growth in employment, the total number of man-hours expended on industrial production in the capitalist world must have increased considerably.

Furthermore, even a fully automated industrialized economy would continue to appropriate part of the surplus-value of non-automated industry in other countries through the process of unequal exchange in trade. Thus, capital in the advanced industrialized countries which were experiencing automation could continue to drain off surplus-value from the underdeveloped and industrializing countries, even if the mass of their 'own' surplus-value was declining. This could be achieved both through unequal exchange and through the profits of multinational corporations. (This will be discussed more fully later in this chapter.) Hence, there is no reason to assume that the mass of surplus-value appropriated by capital in the advanced industrialized countries necessarily declines through automation of their own industrial sectors.

Does this imply that there is no limit to the potential process of automation in the capitalist world economy? I shall argue that there are limits, but that they have to be understood rather differently from the way in which Mandel (in this section of his book) presents them.

AUTOMATION AND WORKING-CLASS INCOMES

The real limits to automation lie in the problem of the falling total volume of working-class incomes. If the only way in which firms and individual capitalists can combat a falling rate of profit is to eliminate living labour from its production costs, then they will decrease their workforces and increase relative surplus-value. However, they must still sell their products. Someone must buy the commodities produced, and since the whole point of displacing labour is to avoid having to pay the costs of the reproduction of labour-power (wages), clearly those workers who are displaced are going to have to derive their incomes from elsewhere. Thus what is a solution to a problem for particular capitalists becomes a problem for the capitalist system as a whole.

We saw in the first part of chapter 6 that this process presents no problems where a backward, low-productivity sector or region of an economy is experiencing automation, and an advanced, high-productivity sector or region is expanding production and employment. It was precisely this that occurred in all the major advanced industrialized countries of the capitalist world between 1945 and 1966. Agriculture was automated, and the displaced workers were able to find industrial work at higher wages. Such a bald statement belies the toll of human disruption and misery caused by the break-up of rural communities, the displacement of peasant farmers who had tilled their land for many generations and the drift of workers into urban ghettos and slums. Yet despite all this suffering the average real standards of living of the working class in all the advanced industrialized capitalist world undoubtedly rose during this period.

The same is not true when automation occurs in a high-productivity sector or region. Under these circumstances, the total volume of the real incomes of the whole working class is likely to fall. Whether or not this occurs must depend on the type of automation that takes place. If it is automation associated with increased output and rapid technological change, then a rise in the real incomes of those workers who remain in employment may well compensate for the loss of income of those made redundant. However, if automation is associated with stagnant output in a high-productivity sector or region, then the volume of wages in that sector or region will fall and the income of the working class will decline. As we have already seen, historically automation is much more likely to occur in a whole sector or area under the latter circumstances than the former. If working-class incomes fall, this in turn limits the potential profitability of industry, because the volume of sales must fall. Obviously this is not true of any one industry, but where whole sectors or regions experience automation, this entails a limit upon the demand for all the commodities consumed by the workforce on that sector or region.

The best example of this occurring in the whole economy is to be found in Britain in the 1970s. If we exclude the North Sea oil and natural gas industries where growth in output has been enormous and outstrips growth in productivity, British industry has been characterized since the mid-1970s by stagnant production and falling incomes for its workers. During periods of slow growth of production (1971 to 1973 and 1976 to 1979) productivity has risen more rapidly and the downward trend in the size of the workforce has only been very briefly checked. When government economic and monetary policies have cut back demand in the economy (1974–76 and 1979 onwards) output has fallen back so sharply that, even though productivity has itself declined, working-class employment and incomes have fallen. The whole cycle of Britain's industrial problems therefore rests on the failure of automation to induce industrial growth. British capital's attempt to combat the falling rate of profit from 1966 onwards by automation has had only a limited success, because domestic demand for its own products has been limited by the falling levels of the income it distributed to its own workers, with the result that production has tended to decline.

Table 7.1 demonstrates these developments in the 1970s, and shows that the total incomes from employment of industrial workers (before tax) were lower in 1980 than they had been in 1973.[12] (It should be noted here that Mandel recognizes the possibility of this occurring, though he gives no examples in *Late Capitalism* of its having occurred. He records in passing that one of the possible problems to be encountered in automation is the reduction of incomes, and asks, 'who is supposed to buy a doubled volume of consumer durable goods if, with a constant selling price, the nominal income of the population is reduced by half?')[13]

Table 7.1 *Indices of output, employment, productivity and total wages and salaries in British industry (excluding North Sea oil and natural gas) at 1975 prices (1975 = 100)*

	1970	1971	1972	1973	1974	1975	1976	1977	1978	1979	1980
Output	99.9	99.6	101.5	109.6	105.8	100	101.1	102.6	104.4	104.5	90.3
Employed labour force	108.7	105.5	103.1	104.5	104.1	100	97.5	97.2	96.8	96.0	87.9
Output per person employed	91.9	94.5	98.5	104.9	101.6	100	103.7	105.5	107.9	108.9	102.7
Total wages and salaries in production industries (before tax)	90.4	90.7	92.9	98.3	101.8	100	97.0	92.4	96.4	99.1	96.0

In fact, capital has been much more successful in overcoming this potential limit to its development through automation in other countries than it has been in Britain. In most European countries and Japan, a considerable degree of automation has taken place in a number of industries in the 1970s, but the effects on the industrial sector as a whole, and on working-class incomes, have not been so damaging. This is because industry in these countries, unlike British industry, has been able to go on increasing output at a steady, if reduced, rate, since automation occurred. Table 7.2 illustrates the increase in industrial production in Germany and Japan, despite the decline (in Germany) or very slow growth (since 1973 in Japan) of industrial employment.[14]

The most striking example here is Germany. We have seen that, as in Britain, there has been automation of the *whole*

Table 7.2 *Indices of industrial production and employment in West Germany and Japan (1970 = 100)*

	1970	1971	1972	1973	1974	1975	1976	1977	1978	1979	1980
W. Germany											
Industrial production	100	101.8	105.7	113.2	111.9	105.0	115.8	116.7	118.5	123.3	123.3
Industrial employment	100	99.6	98.2	97.1	94.9	89.2	86.8	86.0	84.2	85.1	85.8
Japan											
Industrial production	100	102.7	110.2	127.4	122.5	109.6	121.7	126.7	134.5	145.5	155.4
Industrial employment	100	101.3	101.9	107.5	106.5	103.0	103.8	103.8	104.1	105.2	107.5

industrial sector in Germany since 1966. Yet despite this, German industry has gone on increasing its output and, when British industry was experiencing its most drastic setback (1980) actually increasing its workforce. Given the potential limit to automation in falling domestic demand, how has this been achieved?

The answer, as far as Germany is concerned, lies in its industry's continued success in capturing a larger and larger share of world trade. While Britain's share of exports of industrial products has been falling, Germany's share of such exports has been rising (as of course has Japan's). Indeed, German and Japanese penetration of the British market has been a contributory factor to the limits on demand for British industrial products.

This exporting success has enabled Germany to counter the potential limits on automation. By keeping production high and growing, working-class incomes have been sustained, despite the fact that productivity has risen more rapidly than output. This has also ensured that unemployment, though it has risen in Germany as in all the other advanced industrialized countries, has not reached anything like the levels in Britain or the United States. This in turn has meant that employed workers have not had to suffer such a considerable futher loss of income through higher taxes and social security contributions as their counterparts have in Britain. Increasing industrial exports are thus very necessary to countries like Germany and Japan.

In the case of Japan, what is particularly striking is that industrial employment as a proportion of all civilian employment has fallen from 37.2 per cent in 1973 to 35.6 per cent in 1980, despite an increase of 22 per cent in industrial production during that period. At the same time, employment in non-industrial (mainly service) jobs has increased from 49.4 to 54.6 per cent of the civilian workforce.[15] Japan's proportion of industrial workers is still slightly lower than Britain's while its proportion of non-industrial workers is rising more rapidly. This shows that automation of industry can allow an expansion of the service sector without undue harm to the total economy, so long as industrial exports go on rising (Japan's visible trade surplus stood at some 3.26 billion dollars a month in September 1981). In other words, the notion that Britain's economic problem consists in having 'too few producers' is clearly refuted by Japan's success. The real problem of automation in unsuccessful economies is falling working-class incomes. But although this partly explains how the potential limits of automation have been avoided in the more successful advanced industrialized economies, the picture of how this has been achieved would not be complete without a wider look at the capitalist world economy.

MULTINATIONAL CORPORATIONS AND
THE CAPITALIST WORLD MARKET

In my analysis so far, I have tended to write as if capital in each country was a separate entity, and as if the firms in any one country, as well as competing with each other, competed also with those of other countries. In fact, of course, this is by no means a realistic description of the present situation in the capitalist world economy. As long ago as 1967, the ten leading capitalist industrialized nations had subsidiaries and branches abroad which produced 240 billion dollars worth of production. This was almost double the total value of all exports from these ten countries. By 1971, multinational corporations are estimated as having produced more commodities outside their home countries than the total value of world trade.[16]

The motive behind the rapid growth of multinational corporations in the post-war era was that they provided capital with opportunities for the development of world markets, the diversification of products and of methods of production. They were associated both with the concentration and centralization of capital, and with the exploitation of new sources of cheap labour.

The form which the subsidiaries and production centres of multinational corporations take is varied, but generally they comprise a mixture of capital from one or more of the major advanced industrialized countries and capital from the country in which production actually takes place. Control, planning and decision-making rests with the major company, which is located in one of the advanced industrialized countries in the enormous majority of cases (94 per cent in 1976).[17]

Between 1945 and 1966 the vast bulk of the investment abroad by such corporations was between one advanced industrialized country and another. In particular, American-controlled corporations invested heavily in European subsidiaries. From 1966 onwards two trends were evident. Firstly the proportion of all foreign investment stemming from the United States and Britain fell as Germany and Japan rapidly increased their share in international investment abroad. Secondly, while investment in the advanced industrialized countries remained high, investment in several newly industrializing countries grew much more rapidly.

The extent of the growth in overseas investment by Germany and Japan can be gauged from the fact that the value of the stock of German foreign investments increased from 3 billion dollars in 1967 to 19.9 billion dollars in 1976, while Japanese foreign investments were valued at 7.5 billion dollars in 1967 and 19.4 billion dollars in 1976.[18] While the average number of new manufacturing subsidiaries formed by American parent companies reached its highest peak in 1968–69 (508 per year) when roughly half these subsidiaries were being located in Europe, Japanese and German parent companies continued to increase their new manufacturing subsidiaries in the 1970s. In the case of Japan, some 70 per cent of these new subsidiaries were located in the newly industrializing countries of Asia and the Pacific.[19]

An indication of the increase in investment by multi-national corporations based in the advanced industrialized states in the newly industrializing countries can be seen in table 7.3, which gives figures of direct investment stocks in 1967 and 1975.[20] In 1974, foreign controlled companies owned 41 per cent of all assets in manufacturing industry in Turkey, and 29 per cent in Brazil. Multinational corporations had a 70 per cent share of the manufactured exports of Singapore in 1972 and 43 per cent of those of Brazil.[21]

Table 7.3   *Direct investment stock (million dollars)*[20]

Host country	1967	1975
Spain	1,777	4,605
Greece	598	946
Turkey	398	495
Brazil	3,560	10,466
Mexico	3,082	4,634
Singapore	1,340	1,742
Hong Kong	746	1,379
Philippines	805	1,372
Korea	439	1,033

The industrialization of these countries, accomplished mainly through multinational corporations based in the advanced industrialized nations, achieved a number of aims for capital in the latter countries.

(a) We have seen that from the early 1960s onwards real wages started to rise more rapidly in the advanced industrialized countries, because full employment had been reached. In particular, in Britain, Germany and the United States, the source of new, cheap labour from the agricultural sector of the economy began to dry up. By 1966 the agricultural workforces of these countries had been reduced to 3.2 per cent, 10.8 per cent and 5.5 per cent of the civilian workforce respectively, and by 1980 the proportion employed in agriculture in Britain had actually started to rise. The obvious alternative source of new cheap labour was the 'developing' world. However, to avoid sucking this labour into a domestic market in which wages were rising, investment abroad allowed far lower wages to be paid. The continued drift from the land in the industrializing countries provided a continuous supply of cheap labour.

(b) On the other hand, the very low levels of *per capita* incomes in the most backward underdeveloped countries represented a formidable barrier to sales of industrially produced commodities in those territories. By developing certain less backward countries, whose *per capita* income was rather higher, the advanced industrialized countries were able to create an industrial proletariat which would be able to afford to buy a proportion of the surplus of industrially produced goods from the industrialized world. By selling these products abroad, capital was able to increase the otherwise limited demand in the home markets because of automation. Advanced industrialized countries created substantial trade surpluses with the industrializing states, selling more of their industrial production to them than they bought from them.

(c) Multinational corporations were able to diversify their production between the advanced industrialized countries and the industrializing ones. Products that could most profitably be produced by advanced technology continued to be developed in the industrialized countries. These were not confined to manufactured goods; they included the production of raw materials, such as offshore oil, which had a very low labour content in its production factors. On the other hand, products with a high labour content were increasingly produced in the industrializing countries, taking advantage of lower wages. In some industries a more 'old-fashioned' type of technology was used for production undertaken in the industrializing countries, using more labour, than the methods used for producing the same commodities in the industrialized states. Harberger suggests that in modern industrial activities the typical developing country uses an average of four times the amount of labour used in similar activities in the United States per dollar of return to capital.[22] By diversifying both products and locations of production, multinational corporations were able to maximize the benefits of automation and 'technological rents' and take advantage of the higher rate of profit in the industrializing countries.

(d) In Marxist terms, the combined effect of these developments was to allow relative surplus-value to rise through automation in the industrialized countries, while in the industrialized countries the mass of surplus-value was rising through increased production and high productivity. Thus capital was able to neutralize the effect of automation through investment in the industrializing countries.

(e) Finally, labour productivity in industry in the industrialized countries remained far higher than in the industrializing countries, because of the greater concentration of capital and the selection of high technology production there. The process of automation maintained this differential – in fact, labour productivity grew much more rapidly in the industrialized countries in the 1970s than it did in the industrializing ones. This enabled unequal exchange to take place, as commodities with a lower labour-time content from the industrialized countries could be traded for commodities with a higher labour-time content from the newly industrializing countries.

Some Marxist economists have noted these developments and seen them as highly significant. In an article published in 1973, which provoked much dispute, Bill Warren argued that during the post-war period the balance of economic power had shifted away from the dominance of a few major imperialist countries towards a more even distribution. He suggested that there was a major upsurge of national capitalisms throughout the underdeveloped world in that period, giving evidence that 'imperialism declines as capitalism grows'.[23] He argued that formal political independence had given underdeveloped countries a degree of freedom for manoeuvre and initiative which they could, in the long term, use to their economic advantage. He concluded that:

. . . empirical observation suggests that the prospects for successful capitalist economic development (implying industrialization) of a significant number of major underdeveloped countries are quite good; that substantial progress in capitalist industrialization has already been achieved; . . . and that the imperialist countries' policies and their overall impact on the Third World actually favour its industrialization. . . .[24]

Even more significantly, and more recently, André Gunder Frank, one of the major protagonists of the 'dependency theories' of underdevelopment, has published a book which revises his earlier views. In discussing the major crisis in the capitalist world economy – which like Mandel he attributes to a long wave of decelerated capital accumulation, associated with a falling rate of profit – he describes important changes in the international division of labour which have occurred during this crisis.

A rapid qualitative differentiation is taking place in the underdeveloped world. For example, the Third World countries, which underwent a certain kind of industrial development based on what has been called import substitution, . . . have become, to a certain extent, economies that could be classified as intermediate, or semiperipheral. After the Brazilian experience, these began to be called sub-imperialist. These countries already participate in the international division of labour in a different way, exporting not so much raw materials or simple manufactured goods but industrial goods coming from heavy industry, engineering, and – significantly – from the armaments industry. . . . Up to a point, this also applies to Mexico. There are other more or less industrialized intermediate economies which have tried to become part of the international division of labour by following the Brazilian model. . . . Another group of underdeveloped economies, which has been growing rapidly since the beginning of the 1970s, has won its place in the international division of labour by specializing in the production of manufactured goods for the world market based on cheap labour. This process began in the early 1960s in South Korea and later in

Taiwan. . . . Later on, this form of specialization was developed in Hong Kong and Singapore and is now expanding to Malaysia and the Philippines.[25]

Unlike Warren, Frank explicitly relates these developments to a crisis in capital accumulation in the advanced industrialized countries, and draws attention to (though he does not analyse) a similar differentiation of production *within* the imperialist group. Thus Marxist theorists are increasingly recognizing the relevance of these changes in the overall balance of production between the industrialized and the industrializing world, but they have been slow to work out their implications. In the next chapter, I shall examine these developments and their impact on unemployment in the advanced industrialized countries. I shall particularly consider the role of Britain in relation to these changes in the capitalist world economy.

REFERENCES

1   Karl Marx, *Capital*, vol. 3, Penguin, 1981, p. 372.
2   E. Mandel, *Late Capitalism* (1972), New Left Books, 1975, pp. 204, 216.
3   Ibid., p. 193.
4   Ibid., p. 198.
5   OECD, *Manpower Statistics*, 1950–60 and *Labour Force Statistics*, 1958–69.
6   Mandel, *Late Capitalism*, p. 195.
7   Ibid., p. 198.
8   Ibid., p. 207.
9   Geoff Hodgson, 'A theory of exploitation without the labour theory of value', *Science and Society*, Fall 1980, vol. 44, no. 3, pp. 257–73. See also David Laibman, 'Exploitation, commodity relations and capitalism: a defense of the labor-value formulation', ibid., pp. 274–88.
10 Bob Rowthorn, 'Neo-classicism, neo-Ricardianism and Marxism', *New Left Review*, no. 86, 1974, p. 87.
11 For the origins of the debate about the labour theory of value and surplus-value, see I. I. Rubin, *A History of Economic Thought* (1929), Ink Links, 1979, especially pp. 248–60 and 307–12. See also R. Rosdolsky, *The Making of Marx's 'Capital'*

(1968), Pluto Press, 1977, pp. 413–36, and Rowthorn, 'Neo-classicism, neo-Ricardianism and Marxism'.

12   Department of Employment, *Employment Gazette*, April 1981, table 1.8, and Central Statistical Office, *National Income and Expenditure, 1981*, HMSO, 1981, tables 3.1 and 2.6 (using implied deflator for consumers' expenditure).

13   Mandel, *Late Capitalism*, p. 205. See also, E. Mandel, *An Introduction to Marxist Economic Theory* (1969), Pathfinder, 1973, pp. 27–8.

14   OECD, *Main Economic Indicators*, 1970–1981, and OECD, *Labour Force Statistics*, 1967–78, and quarterly summary, February 1981.

15   OECD, *Labour Force Statistics*.

16   C. Tugendhat, *The Multinationals*, Eyre and Spottiswoode, 1973, p. 21.

17   N. Hood and S. Young, *The Economics of Multinational Enterpise*, Longman, 1979, p. 18, table 1.4.

18   Ibid., p. 18.

19   Ibid., p. 22, table 1.5.

20   Isaiah Frank, *Foreign Enterprise in Developing Countries*, Johns Hopkins University Press, 1980, pp. 18–19, table 5.

21   Mandel, *Late Capitalism*, p. 373.

22   A. C. Harberger, 'Perspectives in capital and technology in less developed countries', in K. P. Jameson and C. K. Wilber (eds), *Directions in Economic Development*, Notre Dame Press, 1979, p. 71.

23   Bill Warren, 'Imperialism and capitalist industrialisation', *New Left Review*, no. 81, September–October 1973, p. 41.

24   Ibid., pp. 3–4.

25   A. G. Frank, *Reflections on the World Economic Crisis*, Hutchinson, 1981, pp. 55–7.

8
Why Unemployment in Britain will go on Rising

In the first part of this book I have considered the explanations of mass unemployment offered by the major economic theories that inform the political process in the capitalist world, and drawn attention to some shortcomings of these explanations, in theory and in practice. I have also tried to develop my own analysis of the recent changes in the capitalist world economy, showing the relationship between increasing automation in the advanced industrialized countries and increasing production and employment in the 'developing' countries. By understanding the emergence of the newly industrializing countries we can also grasp the significance of the relative decline of some of the advanced countries, and particularly of Britain.

In this chapter I shall argue that the relative decline of the British economy is now so evident and long-standing that it requires its own explanation within any account of the development of the capitalist world system. The Marxist analysis is the only one that provides a coherent model of international capitalism as a system, but because of its dualistic nature (imperialist and colonial nations) such an explanation of Britain's role has been slow to emerge from that school of thought.

On the other hand, the Keynesians and monetarists have both tried to explain Britain's relative decline in terms of its institutional structure, and their political adherents have adopted economic strategies in line with these explanations. Because they did not take into account the changes in the capitalist world economy, these policies have failed.

All this may help us to understand the emergence in Britain of an analysis associated with the Cambridge group of Keynesian economists, and with Tony Benn and his followers in the Labour Party. This suggests that Britain's decline must indeed be seen in terms of the post-war development of international capitalism, and that a future Labour government should pursue policies which counteract the weaknesses in Britain's trading position.

In many ways, Benn and his supporters give important indications of recognizing the true nature of Britain's position in the capitalist world system. Unfortunately, these are often expressed in 'throwaway lines', which sound rather glib or exaggerated when they are not linked with hard economic analysis. Furthermore, the more rigorous application of economic theory to the features of Britain's situation that they identify would suggest that their remedies are unlikely to succeed.

One example of such a 'throwaway line' occurred in the newspaper interview with Tony Benn mentioned in the first chapter. Referring to the loss of democratic control over national decision-making, Benn said:

Britain is now the last colony left in the British Empire. Britain alone it seems is left with a colonial-type administration led by an establishment which itself is defeatist and is actually frightened of the potentiality and strength of the British labour movement working through parliamentary democracy. They have handed over the keys of power to others outside this country to govern us, so that they can be protected from the British working class.[1]

This notion of Britain as a 'colony' seems to be mainly in terms of its administrative structure, and lack of autonomy in political decision-making. But there is a more fundamental sense in which Britain's position resembles a colony, as I shall suggest in this chapter. The newly industrializing countries are emerging in a form which meets certain of the needs of capital in the advanced industrialized states. These countries are ceasing to serve the traditional purposes of 'semi-colonies' in the post-

war capitalist world; they are no longer in the same sense
'underdeveloped'. But at the same time Britain's role is also
changing. I shall argue that it is becoming the 'internal colony
of the advanced capitalist world – a kind of post-industrial
equivalent of the backward, rural internal colonies that each
advanced nation had during its development. In this context
Benn's other phrase, 'the Northern Ireland of the EEC' is
particularly apt.

The other 'throwaway line' that captures an important truth
about Britain's emerging role occurs in *Manifesto*: *A Radical
Strategy for Britain's Future*. This recently published work is
co-authored by leading respected Labour Party figures from
several fields, including one member of the Cambridge
economic group and Tony Benn's former political adviser. In
discussing the neglect of Britain's industries by multinational
corporations, *Manifesto* states: 'Overseas investment by
British multinational companies has been increasing two and
a half times faster than their investment in Britain. They tend
to regard Britain as a valuable market rather than as a production base.'[2]

I would argue that there is a deeper sense in which this is
true, not merely for British multinational companies, but
increasingly of the structural role of Britain in the capitalist
world economy. Britain's historically low rates of growth and
profit have provided few opportunities (outside North Sea oil
and natural gas) for the surplus profits and technological rents
upon which advanced capitalism depends for its development. Hence the type of automation that has occurred in
Britain (other than in the fields mentioned above) has mainly
been associated with stagnant industrial output.

Although productivity has risen far more rapidly than output in British industry, it has lagged well behind the increases
of industrial productivity in most of the other advanced
industrialized countries. Hence Britain is more attractive as a
market for foreign exports than it is as a location for multinational investment. Average levels of income, though they
have dropped well behind those of the other European
countries and the United States, are still well above those of
the industrializing countries (though the gap is closing fast).
Britain has a large population, and therefore a large market

for the sale of consumer durables, electronic equipment and other manufactures from the advanced capitalist countries.

Because of its lower level of labour productivity it is also a potential source of unequal exchange, as the products of higher-productivity countries can be traded for those with a higher labour content. In other words Britain has come to occupy a position much more akin to that of the old colonies in relation to the capital of the other advanced industrialized nations. Just as capital from the imperialist countries did not develop industry in colonial countries for as long as it could exchange its manufactures for cheaply produced raw materials, so modern international capital will not want to develop British industry while it can more profitably sell its own, more efficiently produced industrial goods on the British market, and import raw materials from Britain.

To this argument it might be objected that once the British unemployment rate reaches a certain level, Britain will be ripe for re-development by international capital. This may well be so eventually, but I shall argue that this process will take a very long time. To understand why, we need to consider in more detail the emergence of the newly industrializing countries and the parallel decline in the British economy.

THE ROLE OF THE INDUSTRIALIZING
COUNTRIES

The roles of Britain and the industrializing countries are essentially complementary, and between them they meet the needs of international capital in an age of automation in the advanced industrialized countries.

In the 1970s, the industrial production of the 'developing' countries increased rapidly, but productivity remained fairly constant, increasing gradually after the middle of the decade. Table 8.1 includes figures for the group of industrializing countries which are members of the OECD and therefore not classified as 'developing countries' in the United Nations figures.[3] From these it is clear that industrial employment grew far more slowly in the older industrializing countries of Europe than in the newer ones of Asia and Latin America,

Table 8.1   *Indices of industrial production, employment and productivity in industrializing countries (1970 = 100)*

	1970	1971	1972	1973	1974	1975	1976	1977	1978
'Developing'									
market economies									
Industrial production	100	106	116	128	135	137	148	155	n/a
Industrial employment	100	105	112	122	127	134	138	n/a	n/a
Labour productivity in industry	100	101	104	100	100	102	109	n/a	n/a
Ireland									
Industrial production	100	104	109	121	125	117	126	137	147
Industrial employment	100	104	102	104	106	101	97	99	102
Labour productivity	100	100	107	116	118	116	130	138	144
Spain									
Industrial production	100	104	122	140	153	143	152	170	164
Industrial employment	100	101	102	106	108	109	105	105	101
Labour productivity	100	103	120	132	142	131	145	162	162
Portugal									
Industrial production	100	108	122	136	149	132	138	155	166
Industrial employment	100	101	102	103	104	101	101	100	105
Labour productivity	100	107	120	132	143	131	137	155	158
Greece									
Industrial production	100	111	127	147	144	151	166	170	191
Industrial employment (manufacturing)	100	106	112	121	134	135	not available		
Labour productivity	100	105	113	121	107	112	not available		
Turkey									
Industrial production	100	109	120	135	144	158	172	n/a	n/a
Industrial employment	100	not available			116	119	124	130	133
Labour productivity	100	not available			124	133	139	n/a	n/a

while the productivity of labour in the former grew far more quickly than in the latter.

As I have suggested earlier, this increase in industrial output and employment was accompanied by a massive reduction in the agricultural workforce in the industrializing countries, which released workers from the rural areas to come to urban centres of industrial production. The decline in agricultural employment in some of the industrializing countries is shown in table 8.2.[4]

That this was accomplished through the introduction of machinery into agriculture is indicated by table 8.3, which shows the numbers of tractors in use in these countries in 1969 and in 1977.[5] By way of comparison, figures for a group of industrialized countries are included, from which it can be seen that the number of tractors in use was actually *falling* in the United States and rising only very slowly in Germany, Britain and France. There was a very similar pattern in the growth of numbers of combine harvesters in use in the industrializing countries during the same period.

Thus the pattern of automation of agriculture and expansion of industrial production in these countries was precisely the same as had prevailed in the advanced countries during the 1950s. The only difference was that industrial productivity rose far more slowly in the newer industrializing countries during the 1970s than it had in the advanced nations during the 1950s and 1960s, and more slowly than it continued to rise in the advanced countries during the 1970s. In other words, the process of industrialization in these newly developed countries concentrated on the exploitation of cheap labour power, released from the farming sector of these economies, and not on raising the productivity of this labour. Increases in productivity based on the newest technology were still concentrated in the advanced industrialized world, where the objective of capital was to save the costs of labour-power.

The role of the newly industrializing countries during this period was to provide production sites for capital's expansion of the output of commodities which contained a relatively high proportion of labour-time. Contrary to popular opinion, these included the manufacture of micro-electronic equipment, in which labour forms a rather high percentage of

Table 8.2 *Numbers employed in agriculture (thousands)*

	Agricultural workforce 1962	Percentage of civilian workforce 1962	Agricultural workforce 1973	Percentage of civilian workforce 1973	Agricultural workforce 1980	Percentage of civilian workforce 1980
Ireland	370	35.2	261	25.0	not available	not available
Spain	4,507	38.9	3,406	26.5	2,128	18.7
Portugal	1,358	41.2	895	28.8	750(1978)	23.0
Greece	1,959(1961)	53.8(1961)	1,222(1971)	38.9(1974)	not available	not available
Turkey	9,742	76.8	9,426(1974)	65.2(1974)	9,085(1978)	60.9

Table 8.3   *Tractors in use on farms*

	1969	1977	Percentage increase 1969–77
Industrializing countries			
Ireland	77,700	125,000	60.9
Spain	239,544	421,393	75.9
Portugal	25,314	57,238	126.1
Greece	57,000	110,000	93.0
Turkey	95,709	324,669	239.2
Brazil	155,400	280,000	80.2
Mexico	87,600	150,000	71.2
Philippines	7,000	13,800	97.1
S. Korea	100	1,121	1021.0
Industrialized countries			
West Germany	1,339,781	1,452,661	8.4
France	1,209,013	1,382,000	14.3
United Kingdom	462,376	496,900	7.5
United States	4,619,000	4,370,000	−5.4

production costs. The expansion of output of these goods was largely developed in countries like Brazil, Hong Kong, Taiwan and Korea.

BRITAIN'S ROLE IN THE INTERNATIONAL
CAPITALIST SYSTEM

Britain's relative decline as an industrial producer can be traced back as far as 1870. In the early nineteenth century, Britain had industrialized earlier and more completely than any other country. From 1846, when protection of British agriculture was abandoned, it committed itself to a radical free trade policy never adopted by any other nation before or since. Britain specialized in the industrial production of commodities for the world market, building upon the productivity lead it had established over its rivals to produce such goods more cheaply, and exchange them for essential food and raw materials. Up to 1870, Britain not only maintained its lead in industrial labour productivity, but also went on expanding its share of world trade.

However, from 1870 onwards its rivals began to close the gap, and Britain's share in world manufacturing exports gradually declined. By the First World War the United States had achieved higher rates of labour productivity in industry, and after the war Britain ceased to dominate the world's industrial trade. There were many contributory factors to Britain's relative decline, but once this dominant position was lost, its commitment to industrial specialization and free trade made it increasingly vulnerable to competition from countries that industrialized later, and which were more adaptable in response to economic challenges and opportunities.

No single factor in Britain's recent institutional or economic development can account for its failures, since the rate of growth of national income has been higher in this century than it was for the final quarter of the last. What has happened since the Second World War has been that Britain did not exploit the very favourable conditions for economic growth as successfully as others did – that Britain did not adapt and change fast enough, rather than that it changed for the worse.

Increasingly in the post-war period, the unequal exchange process on which Britain's nineteenth-century success was based has been reversed. Britain originally specialized in industrial production because of its lead in productivity. Thus it could produce such commodities more cheaply than its rivals, and exchange these goods for others – mainly food and materials – with a higher labour content. But since the war, many industrialized countries have achieved higher rates of industrial productivity than Britain. As a result, the process of unequal exchange now works against Britain, so that manufactured goods are increasingly imported from these more efficient rival producers, and British goods with a higher labour-time content are exchanged for them.

Britain's role as an industrial producer in the 1970s declined markedly outside the field of certain raw materials (notably North Sea oil and natural gas) (see chapter 6, p. 107). Industrial labour productivity increased more quickly in Britain than in the newly industrializing countries, but this was mainly because cutbacks in the workforce exceeded cuts in production. In few industries was the workforce actually expanding. Outside North Sea oil and natural gas, the phenomenon of rapidly increasing production matched by even more rapidly increasing productivity did not occur in Britain, as it did in the more successful industrialized countries.

Indeed, in this respect Britain's economic performance in the 1970s should be contrasted very unfavourably with British industry in the 1930s. During and after the Great Depression, a number of new industries in Britain were rapidly expanding both their output and their workforce (see table 8.4).[6] It was

Table 8.4   *Indices of real product and employment in Britain (1930 = 100)*

	1930	1932	1934	1936	1938
Electrical engineering					
Real product	100	103.7	128.2	166.9	177.3
Employment	100	104.2	114.9	118.8	126.6
Food, drink and tobacco					
Real product	100	97.1	106.3	118.7	125.7
Employment	100	101.4	106.7	111.2	117.5
Chemicals and allied industries					
Real product	100	102.3	116.0	131.0	132.3
Employment	100	96.1	102.2	103.5	120.2
Vehicles					
Real product	100	83.2	109.4	156.0	175.8
Employment	100	100.2	103.3	102.2	99.7
Gas, electricity and water					
Real product	100	107.3	119.7	144.3	162.1
Employment	100	105.2	109.1	118.3	126.5

precisely these industries in which production and employment continued to expand after the Second World War. In other words, the 1930s gave an indication of which British industries would provide the basis for the post-war boom and which would not. By the same token, industries whose output remained stagnant or fell in the 1930s (mining, textiles, leather and clothing, for example) were precisely those in which production remained stagnant after the war and employment continued to decline. In general, the 1930s were a period of expanding output and employment in manufacturing industry (except for the years 1931–32); between 1930 and 1938 output increased by 35 per cent in manufacturing, and employment by 15 per cent.

The 1970s thus form a dismal contrast with the 1930s in British industry, in so far as output remained stagnant or declined in industry as a whole, and particularly in manufacturing industry, and employment diminished throughout the decade, and indeed during the previous four years. This is a clear indication that, using the same indicators which revealed the potential expansion of British industry after the 1930s, there are no grounds for optimism about a similar expansion after the 1980s.

As far as international capital is concerned, Britain is not an attractive prospect for major investment. Historically, the rate of growth of the economy has been low by international standards since 1920, and so has the rate of profit. More recently, these problems have been compounded by high and growing rates of unemployment, which have further restricted the potential for expansion of domestic demand.

Because Britain has pursued free trade policies, multinational corporations have been aware that they could sell their products readily in Britain, whether they were produced in other advanced industrialized countries, or in the newly industrializing countries. Thus they had no incentives from protection to locate production sites in Britain.

British capital invested a higher proportion of national income abroad than any other country except the United States. The rate of profit on British investments abroad was considerably higher than on home investments, and this in turn further restricted the growth of British industrial output.

Many British companies preferred to invest in production sites in European countries, with faster growth rates and better prospects of increasing demand.

On the other hand, Britain provided an excellent potential market for the sale of the industrial products of international capital, both from advanced and industrializing countries. Capital in the advanced countries had stronger and stronger needs to export its products made in those countries in the 1970s, because productivity had been growing so much more rapidly in those countries than in Britain, and hence the same commodities could be more efficiently produced there.

British industry is often criticized for being so much less efficient than German or Japanese industry, and British workers for being less hard-working. But the efficiency and high productivity of German and Japanese firms can be understood only in terms of the dynamic of their post-war developments. For 20 years after the war they had conditions ideal for capitalist expansion. Not only did they have the structural potential for further industrialization that Britain lacked; they also had enormous pools of displaced persons who could be absorbed into industry at low wage rates. Quite apart from the disruption of war, they inherited from their pre-war political regimes situations in which labour had been exploited to an extent that would have been impossible under democratic governments.

These conditions enabled a rate of expansion that produced its own virtuous circle. Rapid growth of output and of productivity, unaccompanied initially by proportionate rises in real wages, produced high rates of profit, which allowed the whole process to continue. Thus the considerable lead in labour productivity which Britain still possessed was rapidly overhauled, as German and Japanese firms were able to adopt new techniques and processes in a climate of optimism, of expanding industrial employment and – by the 1960s – of rising real wages. The same virtuous circle applied in most European countries.

By contrast, Britain's industry was beset by a vicious circle arising directly from its earlier industrialization and its role in the international capitalist system. I have shown in chapter 2 that the rate of growth of national income in Britain had been the slowest of the advanced industrialized countries as long ago as 1920. But in addition to this historically low rate of growth, Britain had a historically low rate of profit. For the whole of the post-war period, the rate of profit in Britain was among the very lowest in the capitalist world. This stemmed directly from the same structural factors that determined the low rate of growth, and the two were inextricably linked. As the first country to industrialize, Britain could benefit from none of the features of the post-war situation as fully as those countries which were still in the process of industrialization.

It has recently been suggested that differences in the rates of profit between the advanced industrialized countries, and between these and the developing countries, have been exaggerated. Harberger has produced figures of real rates of return to capital in the period 1969–71, which suggest that private, after-tax rates of return in Britain were not so much lower than those in Greece and Portugal, for instance (see table 8.5).[7] The weakness of this argument is that it looks at a single snapshot of the situation, rather than considering the rates over a period of time. The significant fact about Britain is that its rate of profit (both before and after tax) has always been low in relation to those of other countries. This long-term feature of the British economy in comparison with others has contributed to Britain's emerging special role in the capitalist world system.

During the post-war boom, British industry was constantly

Table 8.5 *Private after-tax rate of return to capital (per cent)*

	1969–71		1969–71
United States	7.6	Portugal	5.7
Canada	6.4	Greece	5.9
Germany	5.6	Jamaica	9.4
Belgium	5.8	Argentina	10.6
Finland	4.8	South Korea	15.2
UK	4.4		
Sweden	3.1		

under pressure to increase its labour productivity, but to do this defensively, in order to combat competition from foreign imports. Since the mid-1960s, such improvements in efficiency and productivity as have taken place (and these have been more substantial than in the United States) have been achieved against a background of stagnant or even falling output, of reduced employment and rising unemployment. It is no wonder that British workers cannot be easily persuaded of the advantages of higher productivity, when they see that the gains that are made in efficiency do not lead to higher working-class living standards or better job prospects. Hence once overtaken, Britain has fallen further and further behind its competitors in productivity, reinforcing the vicious circle.

The consequence has been increasing import penetration of manufactured goods from these more successful economies. Table 8.6 shows the way in which foreign manufactured imports invaded the British market in the early 1970s, and how this occurred only marginally in Japan, and was successfully resisted in Germany.[8]

This trend continued throughout the 1970s. But the problem of increased manufactured imports was not confined to Britain. Several other EEC countries – notably Italy – and the USA also had considerable increases in the volume of their manufactured imports from Germany, Japan and the new industrialized countries. Furthermore, Britain's own *volume* of manufactured exports increased slightly in this period, as all the advanced industrialized countries strove to increase their exports, in order to offset the effects of automation.

Table 8.6 *Manufactured imports as a percentage of the domestic market*

	1969	1974	Percentage change 1969–74
UK	10.2	16.7	+63.7
Japan	3.1	3.7	+19.4
West Germany	13.4	11.8	−11.9

However, in spite of this, as world trade expanded, Britain's share of trade in manufactures declined, and the ratio of its manufactured imports to GNP grew more rapidly than in either the rest of the EEC or the USA (see table 8.7).[9]

Table 8.7   *Trade in manufactures*

	Shares of world trade in manufactures (per cent)			Ratio of volume of manufactured imports to GNP		
	1961	1969	1978	1961	1969	1978
UK	12.7	8.6	7.0	4.6	8.0	14.2
Rest of EEC	33.9	35.0	37.1	6.1	10.1	15.8
USA	17.9	15.5	11.5	1.5	3.4	4.5
Japan	5.0	8.3	11.5	1.8	2.2	2.4

From tables 8.6 and 8.7 it is clear that between 1961 and 1978, Britain's role in the international capitalist system changed as dramatically as did the roles of the previously semi-colonial industrializing countries in the same period. In 1961 Britain still had a large share as a producer in world trade in manufactured commodities. By 1978 its share as a producer was reduced to little over half what it had been in 1961. But whereas Britain imported very few manufactured goods in 1961 (4.6 per cent of national income), by 1978 it had become a major importer of overseas-produced manufactures. Thus Britain's role was transformed from that of an important producer to an important market in less than 20 years.

This transformation was more dramatic than anything that took place in any other advanced industrialized country. Both the United States and Italy suffered some of these consequences during the same period. In the case of the United States, its declining share of world trade was balanced by an exceptionally low propensity to import manufactured goods, so that even by 1978 its proportion of imports of manufactures to GNP was lower than Britain's had been in 1961.[10] In the case of Italy, although its tendency to import manufactured commodities increased alarmingly from an already high proportion (from 15.2 per cent to 20.1 per cent of the domestic market between 1969 to 1974), nonetheless its own success in exporting manufactures was considerable. Hence Italy's share of world trade was rising in this period, and between 1963 and 1974 its share in the exports of each of the six major industrialized countries to each other increased. In consequence, greater import penetration in manufactured goods from Germany, Japan and the newly industrialized countries did not affect industrial production in the USA and Italy anything like as adversely as in Britain, as can be seen from figure 8.1. [11]

Even so, *per capita* incomes grew more rapidly in Japan, Germany and France in the 1970s than they did in the USA, Italy or Britain. In the USA in particular, growth in industrial production did not result in the same fairly rapid increase in national income per head as had occurred during the post-war boom. Britain's position, near the bottom of the table of living

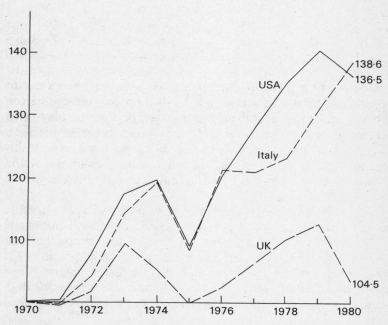

Figure 8.1   *Indices of industrial production (1970 = 100)*

standards, is even worse than it appears, because Italy's income per head has been increasing more quickly (see table 8.8).[12] Even so, average British incomes are still a good deal higher than average incomes in the newly industrializing countries, and the size of the British market continues to make it an attractive target for manufactured goods from abroad.

Table 8.8   *GNP per head of population at 1975 prices and exchange rates (US dollars)*

	1970	1980	Percentage growth 1970–80
Japan	3,845.5	5,464.8	42
West Germany	6,256.3	8,144.8	30
France	5,485.9	7,423.6	35
USA	6,643.6	8,125.0	22
Italy	3,176.4	4,078.1	28
UK	3,750.0	4,464.7	19

It might be thought that I have exaggerated the extent to which capital is able and willing to shift production away from an advanced industrialized country, and change its role from a major producing nation to a much less important one. In fact, this change in Britain's role has been unfolding for most of this century. A far more dramatic and sudden example of the same kind of change is to be found in a smaller country, Switzerland.

Up to 1973, the Swiss economy was still growing at a healthy rate (about 6 per cent per year since 1960), and industrial production was expanding at the same rate. Investment had increased by nearly 8 per cent a year between 1960 and 1973. But from 1973 to 1975 national income fell by nearly 8 per cent, and in 1979 still stood over 4 per cent below its 1973 figure, while investment remained 20 per cent below its 1973 level.[13]

The main explanation for this was the sudden decline in the

traditional Swiss watchmaking industry, and the rapid growth of manufacture of electronically operated watches in the newly industrializing countries and Japan. But Swiss capital itself was quick to transfer its investments out of Switzerland. Between 1971 and 1976 the stock of Swiss investments abroad rose from 9.5 to 18.6 billion dollars, and Switzerland's proportion of world overseas investments rose from 4.8 to 6.5 per cent.[14] By the end of 1977, Switzerland's stock of investments in the developing countries stood at 1,870 million dollars, almost half of which had been invested in the period 1973–77.[15]

The main difference between the British and the Swiss experience lies in the very long-term nature of Britain's relative industrial decline, and the problems of adapting a large, complex and antiquated industrial structure, such as Britain possessed, to the rapid pace of change.

CONCLUSIONS

In the first part of this book, I have tried to show that it is necessary to have a model of international capitalism as a system in order to understand the re-emergence of mass unemployment in the advanced industrialized countries. In this chapter I have argued that Britain's recent role in this system suggests that unemployment here – already at the highest rate among the OECD countries – will go on rising under present trading conditions.

This explains the increasing demands within the Labour movement in Britain for protective tariffs and import quotas on manufactured products, to slow the rise in import of these commodities. The aim would be not merely to stop the rapid erosion of the British market by overseas competition, but also to give multinational corporations stronger motives for locating their production sites here, thus attracting more investment from abroad, and allowing our industry to modernize and expand. In the second part of the book I shall evaluate this strategy, and suggest that it makes over-optimistic estimates of the potential gains of protectionism, and underestimates the difficulties of achieving planned economic growth.

My own analysis points strongly to structural features of Britain's economy and to trends in the international capitalist system which indicate that low growth or stagnation are likely in Britain for at least a decade, and probably for longer. Since we already have a high standard of living compared with the vast majority of the population of the rest of the world, this is not meant to be a gloomy or defeatist conclusion, but simply a realistic one, on which we should base our economic and social planning.

However, I am extremely pessimistic about the chances of achieving any measure of social justice under the present political and economic order in Britain. Within our current institutional framework, stagnation inevitably entails higher unemployment. For the past 15 years we have seen that this produces gross distortions in the distribution of our national resources. Therefore a far more radical approach to the issues of redistribution of work, income and leisure needs to be adopted. Yet (as will become clear in the second part of the book) our present institutional framework is certain to be vigorously defended. To change it will require a challenge to the capitalist mode of production, and to all the assumptions behind our 'mixed economy'.

The radical issue raised by my analysis of Britain's role in the world capitalist system is whether Britain stands to gain from continuing to be part of that system. For if its role is to be primarily as a market for goods produced abroad, the downward spiral of falling industrial production and employment, rising unemployment and falling working-class living standards must tend to continue, whatever policies are pursued by British governments. The question – relevant for every country which is a 'colony' – must be whether we want to play this role in the capitalist empire.

Meanwhile, the immediate political issue in Britain raised by mass unemployment is whether the present political system can contain the polarization of class interest that it creates. Already a new alignment has emerged in British politics, and the pace of change is accelerating. At the same time, the trade union movement is having to redefine its objectives and methods, in industrial as well as political affairs.

Finally, the unemployed themselves, and especially the

young who form such a disproportionate section of the un-employed, are taking action which, if not overtly political, has potentially profound political consequences. All these matters will be the subjects of the second part of this book.

REFERENCES

1   Tony Benn, *Guardian* interview, 29 September 1980.
2   Francis Cripps, John Griffith, Frances Morrell, Jimmy Reid, Peter Townsend and Stuart Weir, *Manifesto: A Radical Strategy for Britain's Future*, Pan, 1981, p. 38.
3   United Nations, *Statistical Yearbook, 1978*, tables 9 and 10, and OECD, *Main Economic Indicators*, and *Labour Force Statistics*, 1967–78.
4   OECD, *Labour Force Statistics*, 1967–78.
5   United Nations, *Statistical Yearbook, 1978*.
6   C.H. Feinstein, *Statistical Tables of National Income, Expenditure and Output of the U.K., 1855–1965*, Cambridge University Press, 1972, tables 51, 52 and 59.
7   Arnold C. Harberger, 'Perspectives on capital and technology in less developed countries', in K.P. Jameson and C.K. Wilber (eds), *Directions in Economic Development*, Notre Dame Press, 1979, p. 55, table 1.
8   B. Moore and J. Rhodes, 'The relative decline of the U.K. manufacturing sector', in *Cambridge Economic Policy Group Economic Review*, 1976, no. 2, p. 37, table 4.3.
9   Cambridge Department of Applied Economics, *Cambridge Economic Policy Review*, Gower Press, 1979, no. 5, p. 2, table 1.
10 Moore and Rhodes, 'Relative decline of the UK manufacturing sector', p. 37.
11 OECD, *Main Economic Indicators* and Department of Employment, *Employment Gazette*, 1981.
12 OECD, *Main Economic Indicators*, 1981.
13 Ibid.
14 Neil Hood and Stephen Young, *The Economics of Multinational Enterprise*, Longman, 1979, p. 18, table 1.4.
15 Isaiah Frank, *Foreign Enterprise in Developing Countries*, Johns Hopkins University Press, 1980, p. 13, table 3.

9

The Conservative Party

Between the wars, the Conservatives earned the reputation of being the party of unemployment. In the 1950s they become known as the party of prosperity. The Macmillan era – 'you've never had it so good' – did much to dispel the memories of the 1930s.

Unlike right-wing parties in many countries, the Conservatives have never been chiefly the party of business, still less of big business. They are as much the party of the countryman, the churchman, the royalist and the patriot as the party of the businessman. Nonetheless, since the 1950s, the Conservatives have carefully fostered the impression that the post-war boom owed much to their knowledgeable management of the economy. They have often repeated that they enjoy the confidence of the business world at home, and of international high finance, and that this trust is a vital element in creating the conditions for prosperity which they claim to be the hallmark of periods of Conservative government.

Yet in the 1970s it became increasingly difficult for the Conservatives to sustain this image of themselves. Whereas in the 1950s and early 1960s, Conservative governments were able to claim that they could equally achieve 'expansion' and 'sound finance', in the 1970s these became alternatives. Throughout the decade, the party was divided (often less discreetly than is usual among Conservatives) between those who gave priority to one aim, and those who emphasized the other. In the Heath era the expansionists dominated the government; under Margaret Thatcher the monetarists prevailed. In each case the ruling principle for a time totally displaced the other, so that the Heath government was as notorious for its rate of inflation as the Thatcher government has been for its rates of recession and unemployment. What was even more evident in Conservative circles was that although banks and other financial institutions did very well under both these administrations, industry fared well under neither. Despite the hectic expansion of the Heath period, the profits of British industry continued to decline. Under Thatcher, industrialists have at times openly criticized government policies and dissented from the direction of economic management.

In this chapter I shall suggest that the division of opinion in the Conservative Party over economic policy reflects the increasing impotence of national governments in the face of the power of international capital, and that in Britain's case neither of the two wings of the Conservative Party can restore British industry's profitability in the face of powerful adverse trends in the world economy.

This leaves the Conservatives with a very serious political problem. Although the monetarist critique has shown itself to be an effective weapon in discrediting Keynesian policies and social democratic governments, it has been far less impressive as an instrument for running the economy. Above all, high rates of unemployment give monthly evidence that a large proportion of the population have been excluded from economic activity, while riots and protests increasingly suggest that those excluded will not accept their situation submissively.

As a result, the Conservative government is on the defensive. Because of its poor record, it is forced to try to discredit attacks from the left and the centre, and even from within its own party, over its handling of the economy. But it is also forced to deal with the problems created by its failures – with unemployment itself, and with the revolt of inner-city youth. Many of the policies called forth by these problems require action that is inconsistent with the government's other aims. Whereas the strength of the monetarist critique was the monolithic logical consistency between its economic and social policies, in office the Conservatives have been inconsistent in much of what they have been forced to do – both in attempting to forestall unemployment through intervention in industry, and in having to increase public spending in order to provide subsistence for the unemployed.

THE OVERTHROW OF EDWARD HEATH

As I have shown in chapter 2 (p. 30), the Heath government of 1970–74 was elected on a programme of reduced government intervention, cuts in public spending and taxation, and the restoration of competition. At the start of the 1970s the Conservatives seemed united in an attempt to dismantle many of Labour's institutions of economic planning and management, which had been introduced during the Wilson government. In its manifesto the Conservative Party declared itself confidently against government intervention in industry, against prices and incomes policy, and in favour of expansion based on market forces.

Yet in the period from the autumn of 1972 to February 1974 the Heath government's actions went directly against every one of these declared aims. The rescue of ailing industrial firms (Rolls-Royce, Upper Clyde Shipbuilders) had occurred even earlier. In November 1972 the government adopted a compulsory wage freeze. Above all, public spending increased far more rapidly than it had done under Labour – in 1973 by as much as 11 per cent in real terms.

The rebellion against these 'U-turns' by Conservative MPs was confined to backbenchers. A group of 'economic radicals' consistently criticized government decisions from the standpoint of orthodox monetarist theory, drawing attention to the inflationary consequences of all of them, and insisting that control of the money supply and of public spending was the only way to fight inflation. On the other hand, Enoch Powell was probably expressing the feelings of a large section of Conservative opinion when he accused the Heath government of being socialists in disguise, and attacked them as much for their lack of commitment to Tory principles as for the Keynesian flavour of their economic policies.

Following the defeat of the Conservatives in the two general elections of 1974, the leadership contest was therefore as much about Heath's reliability as a champion of Toryism as about the specifics of his government's economic policies. His two chief critics, Sir Keith Joseph and Margaret Thatcher, had both served in his cabinet and neither had resigned. But Joseph had made his public repentance for the government's record (and his part in it) in his speech at Preston in June 1974, in which he rejected Keynes and all his works, and embraced monetarism, and at the cost of higher rates of unemployment. Thatcher's campaign for the leadership owed everything to Joseph's outspoken recognition of Conservative priorities. It was he who had spelt out the need to repudiate the 'semi-socialism' of the Heath era and to return to sound money, thrift, the market economy, responsibility, patriotism and middle-class moral standards.

Much of Joseph's rhetoric was indistinguishable in content from the criticisms that Enoch Powell (who left the Conservative Party in 1974) had been making of the Heath administration. Since Powell had long since been seen as an extremist, it appeared that the overthrow of Heath represented a victory for the radical right wing of the party. But several changes in the political and economic climate combined to make the change in Conservative policies appear much less fundamental over the next two years. Above all, the Labour government had abandoned its ambitious programme of 1974, and reverted to a modified form of monetarism. The control of the money supply, cuts in public spending, reductions in social services, the transfer of resources to private industry, an emphasis on restoring profits and investment, had all become official government policy under the Callaghan-Healey regime. The new Conservative leadership were able to take advantage of this process to legitimize their own views.

Secondly, the fear that undoubtedly influenced the Heath government – that unemployment of over a million would be politically disastrous – was finally dissipated under Labour. The Heath government attempted rapid expansion, induced rapid inflation, and fell over incomes policy. The Labour government allowed unemployment to double and survived – only to fall over its attempt to limit public sector wage settlements. The message was plain: unemployment was not the political threat it had once been, incomes policy was the new danger area. Thus the main charge against the monetarists –

that they took little account of the consequences of their policies in unemployment – lost much of its force.

The new Conservative leadership on economic affairs published a pamphlet in 1977, *The Right Approach to Economy*, which set out its objectives. Written by Howe, Joseph, Prior and Howell, and representing a compromise between Thatcherites and former Heath supporters, its tone was a good deal less strident than that adopted by Heath's critics during the leadership struggle. Introducing its proposals as the logical steps to follow from Labour's new and more 'realistic' policies, it went on to introduce the familiar monetarist package:

> We must now work towards sensible economic objectives. Some of these the Labour government began by ignoring and is now belatedly trying to pursue, some it has continued to ignore, some it has rejected in favour of goals which lie in the opposite direction. Our prime and overriding objective is to unwind the inflationary coils which have gripped our economy and which threaten to throttle the free enterprise system.[1]

In two years the new Conservative leadership had made rapid progress in gaining legitimation for policies that during Heath's government were heretical. In particular, their own diagnosis of the root of Britain's economic problems was remarkably similar to that of the Labour leadership. James Callaghan said in the House of Commons on 27 April 1976:

> It is important that productive jobs should be created and that we should rely on investments on which a successful return can be expected. That is the way to achieve more employment rather than by transferring more and more jobs to the public sector.[2]

Under the heading 'The Real Problem', the Conservative leadership set out a very similar, if rather more detailed, account of national economic decline:

> What has been happening in the last four years has gone far towards destroying Britain's capacity for the creation

of wealth – on which all else depends. Industry expands, develops, changes and adapts, creates jobs, more or less successfully in accordance with its ability to earn the profits from which these activities must be financed. Those who fondly imagine that 'the State' can finance them instead forget that 'the State' neither has nor can create any wealth of its own, but can only tax and redistribute the wealth that is created by others. Business firms will not and often cannot invest, unless they see the prospect of a profitable return on the investment at the end of the day. . . . And the plain fact is – whatever impression some people may derive from the apparently large cash profits occasionally announced by some companies – that over whole sectors of industry the trend of *real* profits (taking account of inflation) has been steadily falling, sometimes actually representing a negative rate of return on capital invested. Over a wide area, profitability is now so low as seriously to restrict investment – the investment that could make our industry more competitive and create new wealth and new jobs.[3]

THE THATCHER GOVERNMENT

The new Conservative government therefore came to power in 1979 with the avowed intention of restoring the rate of profit and boosting the level of investment in private industry. The party manifesto declared that the restoration of profits was a higher priority than the preservation of jobs:

Profits are the foundation of a free enterprise economy. In Britain profits are still dangerously low. Price controls can prevent them from reaching a level adequate for the investment we need. . . . Too much emphasis has been placed on attempts to preserve existing jobs. We need to concentrate more on the creation of conditions in which new, more modern, more secure, better paid jobs come into existence. This is the best way to help the unemployed and those threatened with the loss of their jobs in the future.[4]

Assuming that the Conservative leadership actually believed the logic of their own argument, the whole of their economic strategy thus rested on the notion that lower taxation and lower public spending could enable higher investment, leading to higher earnings and more jobs. But this logic presupposed

(a) that the rate of investment in British industry was low,
(b) that higher investment would lead to higher output, and
(c) that this in turn would lead to more employment opportunities in private industry.

In fact, there was no evidence to support any of these propositions.

(a) Investment as a proportion of GDP in Britain had fallen from over 20 per cent in 1972 to 17.8 per cent in 1979. But the vast bulk of this fall could be explained in terms of the decline in house-building and other construction during the late 1970s. Investment in plant, machinery and vehicles still stood at 9.9 per cent of GDP. This was one of the highest proportions in the advanced industrialized world, exceeded only by Japan.[5]

(b) High rates of investment had not given rise to increases in output in British industry since the mid-1960s. The overwhelming motive behind investment decisions since that period had been the saving of labour costs. Thus between 1972 and 1979 the numbers of workers employed in British industry as a whole fell by 7 per cent, and in manufacturing by 8 per cent, while output increased by only 10 per cent in all industries and by only 4 per cent in manufacturing.[6]

(c) As a consequence of this long-term feature of British industrial investment, there was no evidence for supposing that even if Conservative policy could increase the rate of investment in plant and machinery in the private sectors of industry, this would create more employment. On the contrary, there was some evidence that there might be a net loss of jobs.

Table 9.1 shows the proportion of GDP spent on plant and machinery and vehicles in Britain since 1972. They indicate that this proportion never fell below 9 per cent throughout this period, and that it was therefore never accurate to describe investment in British industry as low in the 1970s. Also included in the table are the figures for all investment (including new buildings and works) in two important sectors of industry – petroleum/natural gas and manufacturing. These show that although in the mid-1970s investment in North Sea oil and natural gas was growing very rapidly, and investment in manufacturing industry was falling slightly, by 1979 this trend had been reversed, and it was manufacturing investment that was increasing and investment in the oil and natural gas industries that was diminishing.[7]

Table 9.1   *Gross domestic fixed capital formation*

	1972	1973	1974	1975	1976	1977	1978	1979
Plant, machinery and vehicles as % of GDP	9.2	9.7	9.7	9.0	9.0	9.5	9.9	9.9
Petroleum and natural gas (£ million at 1975 prices)	211	327	698	1,369	1,843	1,699	1,577	1,292
Manufacturing (£ million at 1975 prices)	3,372	3,440	3,782	3,522	3,326	3,510	3,773	3,873

When we consider the relationship between these rates of investment and the output of British industry, the striking fact is how low the rate of growth of production was in the 1970s for this high rate of investment. Even including North Sea oil and natural gas, a rate of growth of only 1.5 per cent a year in British industry's output is a very poor return for this volume of investment. By contrast, West Germany and France, each of which invested a lower proportion of GDP in plant, machinery and vehicles in the late 1970s, were expanding industrial production at the rate of 2.3 per cent and 3.4 per cent a year respectively in the period 1970–79. If manufacturing industry alone is considered, the contrast is even more striking. British manufacturing output increased by only 0.6 per cent a year, while Germany's increased by 2.3 per cent and France's by 3.5 per cent a year.[8]

These facts indicate clearly that the nature and purpose of

British industrial investment (outside North Sea oil and natural gas) was quite different from that of our major competitors. The primary purpose of investment in Britain was to remain competitive with our overseas rivals by saving labour costs without increasing output. Thus there was every reason for supposing that the same trend would continue under the Conservatives, and that increased investment would not yield significantly higher output, still less a growth in industrial employment.

If the Conservative leadership had conducted a serious analysis of trends in the British economy for the previous 15 years, instead of relying on doctrinaire monetarist othodoxies, they could have anticipated all the difficulties that the Thatcher government encountered. High interest rates, cuts in the money supply and in public spending merely further reduced demand for industrial products, and reinforced the tendency for industrial output to remain stagnant or to fall, and for investment to be aimed at reducing the workforce. The industrial recession was therefore accompanied by a much more rapid rise in unemployment than the government had anticipated.

As a result, instead of creating a climate of incentive, modernization and ultimately expansion, the new government found itself trapped in a greatly exaggerated version of the vicious circle that had ensnared the Labour government. As unemployment rose, taxation and public borrowing had to increase to pay the costs of social security benefits, of job creation schemes, and of bailing out the ailing industrial giants. As the party of the wealthy and the middle classes, the Conservatives were committed to keep down taxes on the higher incomes; they were also committed to reducing taxes on companies. Hence an even greater burden of taxation fell on ordinary households, whose incomes were already declining. Promises of reducing taxation and of raising tax thresholds were abandoned.

The burden imposed by the failures of Conservative policy fell disproportionately on the working class, and particularly on industrial workers. Between 1979 and 1980, total household disposable income at constant prices rose by 2.4 per cent.[9] But this relatively small increase concealed very large differences between sectors of the economy. For instance, total incomes from employment in insurance, banking and finance (a growth sector) rose by 8.7 per cent in real terms in that year; in other professional and scientific services, total incomes from employment rose by 9.9 per cent.[10] But in the manufacturing industries, where employment was declining most rapidly, total wages and salaries fell by 4.6 per cent at constant prices; and in metal manufacture the decline in total wages and salaries was a spectacular 16.9 per cent in real terms.[11] At the same time, total receipts from taxes on incomes increased by 6.1 per cent and taxes on expenditure by 6.3 per cent at constant prices.[12]

Despite major cuts in a number of services, the Conservatives failed to reduce total public spending. Total current spending by central government increased by 4.9 per cent in real terms between 1979 and 1980.[13] The main explanation for this failure of Conservative policy was increased unemployment. The real value of all state benefits was considerably reduced during the year, yet total spending on National Insurance benefits increased by 4.5 per cent and on supplementary benefits by 6.9 per cent.[14] The whole of this increase was attributable to the rise in unemployment. Total payments of unemployment benefit increased by 48.5 per cent in real terms (despite heavy cuts in its value), during a year when total payments of retirement pensions rose by 3.1 per cent in real terms.[15]

CONTRADICTIONS IN CONSERVATIVE POLICIES

Because the Conservative government's strategies have not been successful in breaking out of the circle of falling industrial production, rising unemployment, falling incomes and rising public expenditure, the apparently cohesive logic of its policies has collapsed. The three areas where this is most visible are youth employment, income maintenance and the relations between central and local government.

Youth unemployment
Britain has one of the highest proportions of young people among its unemployed in the OECD. In 1980, 46.6 per cent of

unemployed people in Britain were under 24 years of age. Only Italy (62.3 per cent) and Australia (55.5 per cent) had higher proportions of youth unemployment.[16]

There is much evidence that this troubles the Conservatives more than the unemployment rate itself, and has done ever since the new government came to power in 1979. The obvious reason for political sensitivity on this issue is the dismal picture presented to millions of families for the future of their children, when half of all school-leavers are out of work. The government has had to counter the growing impression that there will never be enough jobs for the new generation of children who will leave school in the 1980s.

But the other major fear that was undoubtedly in the government's mind, even before 1981, was the threat to law and order posed by millions of young people out of work, particularly in inner-city areas. The Conservatives made law and order a high priority in their election manifesto, and were very critical of Labour over mounting figures for juvenile delinquency and adult crime. Indeed, social policy analysts have suggested that the Conservatives have tried to establish a 'law and order consensus' as the basis of their political support, to replace the loosely welfare-orientated social democratic consensus of the 1960s. Certainly spokesmen like Sir Keith Joseph and Margaret Thatcher have placed great emphasis on personal and moral responsibility, and the need for discipline and authority in families and in society.

Yet in terms of actual policy, the Conservatives were limited to a few retrogressive measures, designed to introduce 'short, sharp shocks' into the juvenile justice system. The more intelligent members of the Conservative government, or those with any criminological knowledge, must have been aware that these measures would be wholly ineffective and irrelevant in the face of the problems of disaffection and lawlessness among city youth. Although they could rely on a section of public opinion to rally to calls for harder penalties for hooligans and vandals, this kind of response was hopelessly shallow when public disorder became widespread and alarming.

In opposition, the Conservatives had been cynical and dismissive about Labour's attempts at providing employment for young people without jobs. But in power, their administration was punctuated by increasingly anxious attempts to allay public concern about youth unemployment and to enlarge the programmes for artificially created jobs and 'training' for this group.

The key figure in this continuing dialogue with the public was James Prior, then Secretary of State for Employment. On the one hand, he frequently spoke of unemployment as a long-term problem, requiring new ways of thinking and changes in lifestyle and expectations. On the other hand, he floated various schemes to alleviate the effects of youth unemployment – some highly speculative.

During the summer of 1980 he spoke on several occasions of schemes to get unemployed people, especially the young, doing 'voluntary work' or 'social work'. In September 1980 he expressed concern that the unemployed were not required to do any work as a condition of receiving benefit, and announced that he was looking into schemes to get a better return for the money handed out in unemployment benefit.[17] At the end of April 1981 the notion of voluntary military service for unemployed youth was floated, and he announced to the House of Commons that the government intended to pursue the idea, even though it was opposed by the Manpower Services Commission.[18] This last idea had obvious appeal for Conservatives, with its connotations of discipline and national service.

During this public speculation, however, Prior was clearly trying hard to persuade his cabinet colleagues to spend more on enlarging the existing schemes for temporary employment, work experience and training. One such extension was announced during the winter, but failed to keep pace with mounting numbers of young people out of work.

The riots in Brixton, Toxteth, Moss Side and other inner-city areas in June and July 1981 shook the Conservative government much more than anything the Labour opposition or the trade union movement had done in the previous two years. They provided a dramatic demonstration of the scale of alienation, anger and despair in such areas, and the destructive potential of the violence unleashed by these feelings. If the Conservatives feared a breakdown in law and order, they certainly did not anticipate anything on this scale, and the government's reaction showed that they were vividly aware of the connections between youth unemployment and the riots.

On 27 July the Prime Minister announced measures costing between £400 and £500 million in the following financial year designed to supplement existing programmes for reducing unemployment. These included extra finance to encourage young people to stay on at school or college, and a new scheme for paying £15 per week to firms willing to take on young employees at £40 or less in wages. She also announced that the government was reviewing the whole Youth Opportunities Programme, and looking at ways of introducing a more comprehensive traning scheme for all school-leavers so that they could receive either further education or vocational training if no jobs were available.[19]

If such a scheme, which seems to have been urged upon the cabinet by Prior, comes into existence it will represent a very radical departure from the Conservatives' intentions when they took office. Having insisted that only the free market could provide work opportunities which offer young people a secure future, they would have been driven to concede that the state should intervene to provide a vast new service for young people.

Income maintenance and taxation

In opposition, the Conservatives were highly critical of Labour's record in increasing the burden of taxation. They insisted that this burden was both excessive and unfair, and resulted from Labour's extravagant public spending and its socialist notions about the distribution of income. As part of their overall critique of personal taxes, they pointed out that the rate of income tax in Britain started very high, and fell increasingly heavily on lower wage earners. In *The Right Approach to the Economy* the Conservative leaders wrote:

(1) We shall reduce the basic rate of income tax, which hits the taxpayer with such force at a very modest level.
(2) We shall raise the thresholds. In 1952 income tax only struck when a family man's income stood at 103 per cent of average national earnings. By 1970 it was 56 per cent; after rising slightly, it has since fallen to an esti-

mated 47 per cent for the current year. . . . to restore the thresholds to the equivalent levels of 1973 would now cost about £2½ billion. That is the amount by which Mr Healey has stealthily increased the burden of taxation on the man in the street.[20]

In this same section of their statement on economic policy, the Conservative leaders noted that low tax thresholds, combined with non-taxable benefits, created a problem over work incentives:

. . . thousands of people have been caught in the Poverty Trap, where income tax falls to be paid by people living well below the officially defined poverty line. More and more people, who receive almost as much in tax-free social benefits when out of work as they can earn in post-tax income from employment, are asking themselves the question: why work?[21]

One Conservative MP, Ralph Howell, was already putting this argument much more strongly. From 1976 onwards he published a series of pamphlets entitled *Why Work? A Radical Solution*, setting out the problem in a far more detailed and cogent fashion. Insisting that a large proportion of people with low earnings cannot get as much in work as they receive when unemployed, and that many with slightly higher earning power receive virtually no extra reward for their efforts and skills, Howell pointed out that the problem is caused by two factors additional to the ones mentioned by the Conservative leadership. The first was that benefits for children are lower when parents are in work than when they are out of work, and the second was the excessive reliance of the British income maintenance system on a multiplicity of means-tested benefits. He estimated that 40 per cent of the working population is affected by this problem.

In government, the Conservatives addressed themselves to only one aspect of the problem. Their reduction in the basic rate of income tax was more than offset by their increase in VAT and other indirect taxes, which fell disproportionately on the worse off. Tax thresholds were not raised in line with inflation, in spite of election promises. The only area of change was the government's abolition of earnings-related supplements to sickness and unemployment benefits, their holding down of the rates of these benefits below the rate of inflation, and their announcement of their intention to make these benefits taxable in the future. In other words, the government's attempts to restore incentives to work were confined to reductions in the value of National Insurance benefits paid to people of working age.

Thus Howell's calculations suggest that in November 1980 a married man with two children aged 4 and 6 earning £55 a week had a net weekly spending power (given average housing costs) of £63.26, whereas the same man earning £105 per week had a net weekly spending power of £72.47 – a net gain of just over £9 for an extra £60 of earnings. On the other hand, the same man normally earning £55 a week would receive £72.02 per week (including tax refund) if out of work, and £69.49 if his normal earnings were £105 a week.[22]

Howell's radicalism and honesty forced him to draw attention to the failure of the Conservative government to tackle the main issues. On the one hand, the net earnings of the average worker did not keep pace with inflation. Using Howell's figures, the net weekly spending power of a family with two children in which the man received the average weekly earnings, increased by 25 per cent between November 1978 and November 1980, while the retail price index increased by 35 per cent in the same period. On the other hand, '. . . at variance with the 1979 Election Manifesto, the supplementary benefits scheme has today become Britain's main growth area.'[23] As a result of cuts in National Insurance benefits, and because the level of supplementary benefits was raised in line with inflation, it is only those unemployed who qualify for means-tested income maintenance support whose standards of living are being maintained under the Conservative government. All workers earning average or less than average wages, and the sick and unemployed who do not qualify for supplementary benefit, have suffered a decline in their incomes. Howell concludes that the poverty trap has enormously extended under the Conservatives, and that only very radical changes can break the vicious circle. His own recommendations include raising all tax thresholds well clear of the benefit ceilings, a much more progressive scale of tax rates, starting at only 15 per cent for lower incomes, a national minimum wage or minimum income for all citizens, in or out of work, uniform rates of child benefit, and minimal reliance on means-tested benefits.

While Howell's criticisms of the effects of Conservative policies are refreshing, he makes no attempt to examine the economic roots of the government's failures. Because unemployment has increased so rapidly, and earnings from employment have actually fallen, the government has been forced to raise more revenue to support the unemployed from those still at work. Even after cutting National Insurance benefits, and relying much more extensively on the cheapest method of paying a minimum subsistence level income to people out of work – supplementary benefits – the government was forced to choose between increasing taxes on the rich or increasing taxes on the poor. With its massive commitment to reductions in the higher rates of taxation at the top of the scale, the government has clearly decided to soak the poor. But even so, it has also been forced to depart from its declared intentions by increasing employers' National Insurance contributions. Thus the whole field of taxation and income maintenance has proved to be a source of constant tension and contradiction for the Conservative government.

Central and local government

The third contradiction in the Conservative government's policies concerns the relationship between central and local government. Traditionally, the Conservatives have championed local democracy and autonomy, and the right of local authorities to exert real control over their own services. Indeed, British local government follows a pattern largely laid down by Neville Chamberlain. But the Conservative government has been forced to adopt a strongly centralist line by the consequences of the failure of its economic policies.

The cities have been most affected by the recession. It is in the cities that unemployment and other forms of social deprivation are most concentrated. But the cities were penalized in the Conservatives' redistribution of central government block grants. Hence the metropolitan authorities are the ones that have most strongly resisted government spending limits.

On the other hand, it is also in the cities that industry is concentrated, and the Conservatives want to restore the rate of profit, or at least to protect industry from having to bear the burden of social deprivation. The aim of government policy has been to force local authorities to cut spending on housing, education and social services, and to ensure that commerce and industry are not hurt by any councils that get local support in their resistance to these cuts.

Accordingly, in the Bill announced by Michael Heseltine in September 1981, all businesses will get protection in the supplementary rate, which local authorities will still be allowed to levy each year. The higher the demand, the lower the share paid by commerce and industry will be, according to a statutory scale. Thus domestic ratepayers will have to bear the brunt of the supplement. If authorities require more than is allowed by the limits on this, they may go for a second supplementary rate in the autumn, but only after a mandatory referendum of their local electorate.

Heseltine presents these measures as a triumph for local democracy, but in fact it is highly centralist. The Secretary of the Association of Metropolitan Authorities described it as 'the most extreme direct control by central government over local government that we have ever seen'.[24] Heseltine is confident that a referendum in the form 'Do you want a second supplementary rate?' will – as in Coventry during the summer of 1981 – result in a defeat for the local authority. But the Coventry result showed that there was little democratic in the process; only a quarter of the electorate voted. The Association of Metropolitan Authorities felt sufficiently incensed by the Bill to take a full-page advertisment in the national press, claiming: 'The Government want you to believe that they are going to control your rates. But make no mistake. They're going behind your back. Soon you won't have any hand in your affairs. Don't be whitewashed by Whitehall, keep it local.'[25]

The *Guardian* leader comment expressed itself as 'baffled' by this legislation from a 'minister who has always declared his belief in local democracy'.[26] Yet the move follows logically from the failures of government economic policy. The Conservatives aim above all else at avoiding hurting better-off individuals and private industry. But someone has to pay to provide for the millions of unemployed and impoverished workers its policies have made dependent on the state. These measures contradict Conservative principles on local autonomy, but they are consistent with the class basis of government policy.

CONCLUSION

The Conservatives came to power with over-optimistic hopes that their 'enterprise package' would create a climate of confidence in industry. They wrongly diagnosed the problem of Britain's economy as low investment when in fact it was low output. Nothing the Conservative government did encouraged British or foreign capital to increase industrial production. On the contrary, high interest rates and restrictions on demand reinforced every tendency for industrial output to stagnate or contract.

Consequently every other characteristic problem of the British economy since the mid-1970s became exacerbated, and particularly unemployment. In opposition, the Conservatives had prepared themselves, and to some extent the electorate, for the political consequences of a rise in unemployment. But they had not prepared themselves for the massive and rapid rise in unemployment that their policies precipitated. Because of the high cost of maintaining the unemployed, the government could neither cut public spending nor cut taxes in the way it had planned.

Because of the change in the political climate after 1975, the Conservatives had achieved some degree of unity in their leadership. Labour policies had given the Conservatives' 'enterprise package' a certain legitimation, and former supporters of Edward Heath had rallied behind it. However, the failure of monetarist strategies provoked a reappearance of the basic division in the Conservative Party between those favouring 'sound money' above every other economic goal, and the more pragmatic advocates of expansion. Faced with a near breakdown of law and order in the cities, the Conservatives have been forced to make choices between conflicting alternatives.

There was clear evidence of the divisions in the party during the first two days of the 1981 party conference. The increasingly monolithic monetarist cabinet was openly criticized by a growing group of discarded ministers and young MPs. In economic policy, cautious advocacy of increasing public investment was heard – for instance from Sir Ian Gilmour. The law and order debate showed a division between the more moderate leaders (e.g. Whitelaw) and the majority of the party members, who called for the restoration of capital and corporal punishment.

The debates indicated that the cabinet still enjoys the support of the majority of the party in its hard line. But Thatcher's triumphant populism has clearly waned. Her 1979 success depended on massive support from lower-middle-class people and better-off workers, who would have voted Labour in the 1960s. Many of these will probably shift their votes to the SDP or Liberals in the next election.

The Conservative Party is highly unlikely to split; it is far too deeply traditional and cohesive in its loyalties. However, many MPs who have despaired of making progress in their ministerial ambitions under Thatcher are registering dissent and showing themselves to be available to serve another leader. Yet major changes in Conservative policies are unlikely. The government is pledged above all else to pursue the interests of capital, and British industry and commerce supports the monetarist line, despite high interest rates and falling sales. The notion that there is 'no alternative' to the government's strategy derives directly from the experience of the Heath government. Expansion via increased public spending damaged profits more than deflation and recession have so far. That is why the criticisms of the government made by the chairman of the CBI in 1980 were so quickly withdrawn. Capital has no alternative but to support Margaret Thatcher.

REFERENCES

1 Geoffrey Howe, James Prior, Keith Joseph and David Howell, *The Right Approach to the Economy: Outline of an Economic Strategy for the next Conservative Government*, Conservative Central Office, 1977, p. 8.

2 James Callaghan, speech in House of Commons, 27 April 1976.

3 Howe, Prior, Joseph and Howell, *The Right Approach to the Economy*, pp. 40–1.

4 *Conservative Party Manifesto 1979*, Keesing's Contemporary Archives, Longman, 1979, p. 29635.

5 Central Statistical Office, *National Income and Expenditure, 1981*, HMSO, 1981, tables 10.1 and 10.2.

6 Ibid., tables 1.12 and 2.3.

7 Ibid., table 10.6.

8 OECD, *Main Economic Indicators*, and United Nations, *Statistical Yearbook, 1979*.

9 Central Stastical Office, *National Income and Expenditure, 1981*, table 4.4.

10 Ibid., table 3.1, using implied index numbers of costs and prices for consumers' expenditure, table 2.6.

11 Ibid., table 3.3, using table 2.6.

12 Ibid., table 1.5.

13 Ibid., table 7.1.

14 Ibid., table 7.6 and 4.4.

15 Ibid., table 7.6.

16 OECD, *Labour Force Statistics*, quarterly summary, 1981.

17 *Guardian*, 10 September 1980.

18 Ibid., 29 April 1981.

19 Ibid., 28 July 1981.

20 Howe, Prior, Joseph and Howell, *The Right Approach to the Economy*, p. 26.

21 Ibid., pp. 25–6.

22 Ralph Howell, *Why Work? A Radical Solution*, Conservative Political Centre, 1981, p. 10.

23 Ibid., p. 25.

24 *Guardian*, 25 September 1981.

25 Ibid., 14 October 1981.

26 Ibid., 25 September 1981.

10

The Liberal–SDP Alliance

The emergence of the Social Democratic Party in 1981 and its alliance with the Liberals have been hailed as a new alignment in British politics. Roy Jenkins has frequently claimed that his new party has 'broken the mould' of the two-party system in Britain. In this chapter I shall examine the Liberal–SDP alliance, with particular reference to its claim to represent a moderate centre alternative to the extremism of the policies of the two major parties.

The claim to be a bastion against doctrinaire tendencies was made by David Steel of his party's role in the Lib-Lab pact of March 1977 to July 1978. He argued then that the Liberals, in return for propping up the Labour government in the House of Commons, gave the country a period of 'stability and consistency', in which the excesses of Labour's left wing were effectively curbed.[1]

In similar vein, when the Social Democratic Party held its first annual conference, Jenkins opened by defining it as an alternative to 'the dogmatism of two monopoly parties'. He contrasted it with the Conservatives, wedded to 'doctrinaire and incompetent monetarism' and Labour, offering 'a recipe not for prosperity and security but for a big move towards a Polish-type economy'.[2]

Since both parties reject 'the politics of detailed manifestos', it is difficult to discern how these sentiments might be translated into policies. There are important differences in style between the two parties. Never having experienced the burdens of office in the post-war period, the Liberals retain a kind of idealism and radicalism, linked with a surviving faith in the orthodoxies of the post-war era. They seem more Keynesian than the SDP, and to have a greater belief in the welfare state. Steel claims that they are the more radical of the two parties, with their stronger emphasis on community politics, on decentralization, political reform and popular consent, worker participation and disarmament. 'Certainly, our new alliance is a coalition. It contains a broad spread of opinion, from the moderate centre to the constructively radical.'[3]

The Social Democrat leaders are much more compromised, having served in several unsuccessful Labour governments. Jenkins emphasizes that the party represents neither big business nor organized labour.

> A Social Democrat–Liberal Alliance Government, drawing its electoral financial and moral support from all groups and classes, would start with an immeasurably greater fund of national goodwill than a Conservative or Labour Government identified with one or other side of industry. . . . We reject both the current desperate experiments from the Right and Left's bankrupt alternatives of nationalization and centralized state control.

It seems obvious that the new alliance is making a strong bid for the many lower-middle-class and upper-working-class votes which the Conservatives won at the 1979 election. The alliance is hoping that people who transferred their votes from Labour to the Conservatives in 1979, and have quickly been disillusioned by monetarism in practice, will now transfer to the SDP or Liberals. There is some encouragement from the opinion polls for this hope.

The real question, however, is whether a coalition between a left-of-centre radical party and a diverse collection of centre 'moderates' would in fact represent a successful bastion against extremism, either on the left or right, in a situation of mass unemployment and relative economic decline. In this chapter I shall argue that such a government, if it did come to power, would be the most likely precursor to the rapid rise of a fascist or neo-Nazi party in Britain.

THE GERMAN INTER-WAR EXPERIENCE

This assertion is based on careful analyses of what happened in German politics immediately before Hitler's seizure of power. Research indicates that the rise of the Nazis was based on support drawn away from the regional, radical and centre parties, and predominantly on lower-middle-class and self-employed people, including small farmers.

The Weimar Republic had been ruled by coalitions of radical and centre parties. In the elections of 1928, the Socialists won most seats (achieving 30 per cent of the total vote) and their leader became Chancellor. The Socialists, unlike the British SDP, were a workers' party with a long tradition. The several middle-class radical and centre parties got 27.5 per cent of the total vote between them; the two Catholic parties (the Conservatives and the Catholic Centre Party) got nearly 30 per cent; and the Communists 10.5 per cent. The Nazis received a mere 2.6 per cent of the total vote.[5]

By 1930 the Depression had begun to hit Germany very hard. Unemployment had risen from just over a million in 1928 to over 3 million that year, and the Socialist Chancellor had resigned, giving way to a new government, under the leader of the Catholic Centre Party. The Nazi vote in the election of 1930 increased to 18.3 per cent, at that time apparently mainly at the expense of the Socialists and the Conservatives.

But the decisive election in the rise of the Nazis was the one in 1932 – the last free election before Hitler took over as dictator. By 1932 unemployment in Germany had reached nearly 6 million, and the industrial system was collapsing. In the election, the Nazis increased their share of the vote to 33.1 per cent. Simultaneously, the Communist share rose to nearly 17 per cent. Of the other parties, only the Catholic Centre had a slightly higher percentage than it had achieved in 1928. The Conservatives' and Socialists' shares of the vote were down by 40 and 30 per cent respectively on their 1928 total. But by far the biggest decline was in the middle-class radical and centre parties, which sank to 5.8 per cent of the total vote. These parties therefore suffered an 80 per cent reduction in their support, and it seems clear that the vast majority of this was transferred to the Nazis.[6]

The combination of a weak centre government, based on the middle-class parties, and a very adverse economic situation, with rapidly rising unemployment, which it was quite powerless to influence, provided the ideal conditions in Germany for the rise of the Nazi party. As the government lost control of the economy and unemployment grew, support for the authoritarian parties of left and right increased dramatically during its term of office. In different parts of Germany, Nazism gained support from different groups, and for different reasons, but everywhere the Nazis benefited from middle-class disillusionment and insecurity.

The centre and regional middle-class parties had appealed mainly to voters who identified neither with big business nor organized labour. As the sociologist S. M. Lipset writes;

> In large measure they gave voice to the objections felt by the rural and urban middle classes of provincial areas to the increasing bureaucratization of modern industrial society and sought to turn the clock back by decentralizing government authority. At first glance, the decentralist aspirations of the regional autonomy parties and the glorification of the state inherent in fascism or Nazism seem to reflect totally dissimilar needs and sentiments. But in fact the 'states' rights' ideology of the regionalists and the Nazis' ideological antagonism to the 'big' forces of industrial society appealed to those who felt uprooted or challenged. In their economic ideology, the regional parties expressed sentiments similar to those voiced by the Nazis before the latter were strong. . . . The ideal-typical Nazi voter in 1932 was a middle class self-employed Protestant who lived either on a farm or in a small community, and who had previously voted for a centrist or regionalist political party strongly opposed to the power and influence of big business and big labour.[7]

Research also shows that the Nazis succeeded in winning support from previously Conservative voters only in areas where nationalist issues were of great importance, particularly in border districts. Heberle states that in 1932: '. . . the Conservatives were weakest where the Nazis were strongest and the Nazis were relatively weak where the Conservatives were strong.'[8]

There is also evidence that large-scale industry did not begin to offer financial support to Hitler until after the Nazis had achieved the status of a major political party.[9]

THATCHER, POPULISM AND THE CENTRE ALLIANCE

Margaret Thatcher's appeal to the electorate in 1979 was a populist rather than a traditional Conservative one. It was presented in political and economic terms as individualistic and middle class in its ideology. It appealed to small shop-keepers and people in small provincial towns – people whose background was similar to her own. It took up many of the moral and intellectual themes of nineteenth-century liberalism, and translated them into a popular twentieth-century form, aimed at the insecurities of these groups. It also appealed directly to the experiences of better-off workers, striving for higher status and income and with middle-class aspirations for their children. It encouraged resentment of the burdens imposed by taxation and by rising public expenditure on welfare beneficiaries.

Such voters were largely drawn from outside the Conservative Party, and had supported Labour in 1974. The SDP–Liberal alliance plans to take advantage of the disillusionment of this sector of the electorate, and to advance its prospects of power by the kind of populist campaign that Thatcher conducted in 1979. The alliance is well aware that it is unlikely to win much support from the traditional sources of Conservative or Labour votes. Neither large-scale industry nor organized labour will transfer its allegiance to the new grouping. Hence its hopes rest almost entirely on gaining massive support from the lower middle class, from aspiring workers and from those areas of the country where decentralization and regional autonomy are important issues.

There has already been strong evidence to encourage these hopes from the by-election in Croydon North West. The constituency, won by the Conservatives in 1979 by a small majority from Labour, was just the sort of area in which the lower middle-class and upper working-class vote could be won over to the new alliance. A newspaper report the week before the by-election suggested that:

> If there is a middle ground in British politics, it is concealed behind the curtains of these modest, well-kempt, undemonstrative Edwardian terraces. . . . to a striking extent this is an area of small owner-occupied terraced houses (average price: £25,000). . . . Unemployment is half the national average, but people have begun to hear the wind whistling outside. Salaries in this moderately ambitious group of craftsmen and lower managers are in the £6,000–£10,000 range. Some, like draughtsmen and engineers, have skills that would allow them to start up on their own if the economy were expanding. Many work in small firms, where staff tend to be more conscious of business costs than in bigger companies.[10]

The constituency therefore provided an opportunity for the alliance to show that this group of voters could be attracted away from the major parties, and particularly from the Conservatives. In the event, the Liberal candidate, who had lost his deposit in several previous elections, won handsomely, with Labour beaten into third place.

Yet it is precisely such voters, who elected the Liberal at Croydon, who form the only potential support for a British fascist party. Experience in many other countries besides Germany – particularly Austria, Italy and France – suggests that middle-class populism is a seedbed for fascism. As Saposs put it: 'Fascism . . . [is] the extreme expression of middle-classism or populism. . . . The basic ideology of the middle class is populism.'[11]

This is not to say that the present SDP or Liberal leaderships are crypto-fascists, any more than Margaret Thatcher was. However, there are important reasons why the centre parties might, as in Germany, collapse into a fascist party, while the Conservative Party is highly unlikely to do so. Organizationally, the centre parties are extremely loosely structured, and have no direct links with major hierarchies or networks in the community. Unlike the major parties, they are simply collections of individuals, coming together for a political purpose which is not tied down to a common economic activity or structure. They are also individualist rather than collectivist in their ideology. As a result they are far more politically volatile, and open to organizational irregularities. The Jeremy Thorpe trial provided several examples of the latter.

There is one clear and ominous precedent for a breakaway from the Labour Party that ended in fascism. In February 1931 Sir Oswald Mosley and four other MPs left the Labour Party and set up the New Party, on a radical programme of reform designed to attract middle-class support. In October 1932 the New Party became the British Union of Fascists. None of the Gang of Four shows signs of following Mosley's style, still less his policies, but the supporters that they are attracting could easily transfer their loyalty to fascist leaders.

The Conservative Party, for all its racist and authoritarian tendencies, has none of the hallmarks of a fascist organization. Its structural and financial links with large-scale industry, its upper-class traditions and its religious affiliations all mark it out as a party which, while it might not oppose fascism at all effectively, would be unlikely to embrace it in an active way. Thatcher's populism, while electorally effective in 1979, seems unlikely to be taken to its logical conclusion by the Conservatives, even though it provided an ideological legitimation for many fascist policies.

THE ALLIANCE AND UNEMPLOYMENT

I have suggested that the prospects of a rise in fascism in Britain would be increased if the Liberal–SDP alliance were to form a government. This prediction necessarily depends on a number of assumptions about immediate future developments in the British economy, and the likely consequences of SDP–Liberal policies. It also depends on a notion of how some sections of the electorate are likely to react to these events.

It seems unlikely that the British economy will immediately suffer a slump as intense as that experienced by Germany in the years 1929–32. Although unemployment doubled between 1979 and 1981, there will probably be a levelling-off somewhere between 3 and 4 million in 1982–83, and the Conservative government will take all possible steps to prevent further rises before the next general election.

The key factor for any SDP–Liberal government, therefore, will not be the seriousness of the situation it will inherit. Although Britain's long-term economic prospects as part of the capitalist system are poor, it seems improbable that the Conservatives will allow an election to take place during a crisis. Rather, the new government's main problem will be the unrealistic expectations that it would itself have created, not so much by its actual pronouncements or pledges, but by the bandwagon effect of its meteoric rise to power, through the extravagant support of the media, and through the investment of millions of dreams and fantasies in its largely shapeless and vacuous ectoplasm.

Since 1970, the lower middle-class and skilled working-class vote, which forms such an important section of the British electorate, has proved to be highly volatile. First it swung to Edward Heath in 1970. Then it briefly rallied to the Liberals in the by-elections of 1972 and 1973. Then it swung to the Labour Party just enough to allow Harold Wilson to win the election of 1974. There is some evidence that former Liberal voters contributed to the brief waxing of the National Front's fortunes in the mid-1970s. In 1978 (at the local elections) and 1979 it swung dramatically to the Conservatives. Finally in 1981 it has switched even more dramatically to the SDP–Liberal alliance.

The sudden nature of this final switch to a new and unknown political force, with few clear policies, suggests a desperate leap of faith. It indicates that lower middle-class and upper working-class voters are seeking new and untried sources of vision, leadership and hope, and that they are projecting on to the alliance many of their cherished illusions, including some that even the euphoric new leaders would disown. One voter in Croydon, interviewed shortly after being canvassed by the alliance candidate, and presumably still star-struck by the experience, declared that she would be voting for Mr Pitt because he was for reintroducing hanging.

If the election of an alliance government contained a great deal of this desperate and fantastic hope, born of frustration and insecurity, then such a government would be especially vulnerable to the process of disillusion that has progressively afflicted all British governments since 1966, but perhaps most dramatically the Thatcher government. In particular, it would be this section of the electorate, which as already shown itself to be mercurial, which might finally turn to a new political group which promised to do what Thacher, Tebbit and Joseph only hinted at – to cut wages, dismantle the welfare state, curb trade unions, reimpose law and order and repatriate immigrants.

My analysis also assumes that the SDP–Liberal government would be, as in Germany in the 1930s, a weak middle-class administration, without reliable links with or support from either large-scale industry or the labour movement. It is always possible, of course, that by the next election some such links will have been made, and that sections of industry or some trade unions may make tactical alliances with the new political group. However, any such support would be likely to be very conditional and temporary, and to be quickly withdrawn if things did not go well for the government. My own expectation would be that the alliance would quickly show itself to be impotent in the face of mass unemployment and its attendant political conflicts, and that precisely those voters who elected it would be most likely to transfer their allegiance to a new fascist party.

Much might also depend on whether the new government implemented its promises on proportional representation. If it were able to do so, this might well enable a fascist party to make a much greater impact than the National Front has ever done. Unlike the National Front, a new, smoother, more plausible and sophisticated party, emphasizing patriotism and national solidarity, might well fuse together a substantial middle-class vote with some support from the authoritarian sections of the right-wing working class, especially among urban youth.

In the absence of clear indications of what the alliance's

economic policies might be, it is difficult to prove that they will be ineffective. The Liberals are rather tentative Keynesians. In their 1979 manifesto, they argued that 'it is dangerous to pretend that the government can be taken out of economic and industrial planning.'[12] But the actual policies to be pursued by government were left extremely vague. The manifesto announced that Liberals believed in:

(1) Controlled and steady economic growth (in co-operation with our European partners), with greater attention to conservation of scarce resources, especially energy and land.
(2) Harnessing the potential of all at work to improve enterprise and productivity.
(3) Providing opportunities for useful work for all.
(4) Protecting the citizen from inflation by reconciling rises in incomes with the real rate of growth of the economy.
(5) Ensuring that the primary aim of government intervention in industry should be the promotion of viable market enterprises.[13]

It is all very well to believe in these things, but I have given reasons in this book why it has been so difficult to achieve any of them in Britain, still less all of them simultaneously. Because they are ideologically committed to free trade, yet lack the links with industry to inspire confidence in the business and financial worlds, the Liberals would be particularly at risk from an enormous emigration of British capital into overseas investment. They would also be likely to encounter much greater intransigence from the trade union movement.

Between 1945 and 1974 the basic aim of government economic policy under both the major parties was to manage the economy in such a way as to guarantee an adequate rate of profit to private industry, while at the same time allowing a share of national income to wage earners sufficient to ensure their electoral support. This became increasingly difficult from 1965 onwards, and since 1974 it has been impossible. The Labour government of 1974 tried briefly to redistribute national income in favour of the working class, but quickly changed to a policy of trying to raise the profits of industry, which the Conservatives have attempted even more vigorously to do. The Liberals yearn for the pre-1974 era, when the choice between these two alternatives seemed unnecessary. However, if they took office they would soon discover that their 'middle way' ended up by pleasing neither side of industry, or causing an even deeper recession through simultaneous export of capital and non-co-operation by the trade unions, stung to renewed fury by the imposition of wage controls.

The SDP leadership is much more clearly in line with the Callaghan-Healey tradition in declaring itself as determined to restore profits and limit wage increases. The SDP addresses itself directly to unemployment, but Jenkins makes it clear that he considers that the way towards a steady reduction ('aimed at removing one million people from the dole queue in two years') is 'to tell the electorate quite openly that any increase in real national income for the first two or three years of the government's term of office must be devoted to rebuilding profits in industry and commerce and creating new jobs in both the private and public sectors.'[14]

Although the Social Democrats speak of public investment programmes, they are also concerned with monetary stability. It could well be argued that Jenkins was Britain's first post-war monetarist Chancellor of the Exchequer; he was certainly the first to cut public spending (in 1968–69). Even the Conservative press recognizes his credentials in this. A *Daily Telegraph* editorial drew attention to:

. . . the essential Tory soundness of Mr Jenkins as a financial strategist. He may make speeches about watching more than one dial but that monetary dial would receive plenty of attention from either himself or Mr Rodgers, both notorious opponents in office of heavy public expenditure. . . . the [SDP] conference showed a broad spontaneous uncharity towards the trade unions which Mr Norman Tebbit himself will have to bid high to beat.[15]

Jenkins makes it clear that an incomes policy of some kind

would be an integral part of his economic strategy. It is not difficult to imagine the reaction to this from the labour movement, particularly in view of the SDP leaders' desertion of the Labour Party and the political damage this has caused. The SDP would thus in at least two respects – wage restraint and political treachery – start with a considerably worse relationship with the labour movement than the Conservatives have had.

The alliance therefore consists of a mixture of 1960s-style Keynesianism (the Liberals) and the monetarism of the Callaghan government (the SDP). Since policies of both kinds ended by drifting in the directions required by capital, the lack of detailed programmes by the alliance is probably realistic. History has shown that they would not be able to restore the rate of profit, achieve growth or reduce unemployment. Without the organized support of either industry or the trade unions, they would be helpless and ineffective. It is difficult to imagine such a government lasting for long, but it is easy to imagine the impetus given by the chaos that would attend its collapse to authoritarian parties, and particularly to fascism.

In fact, it seems to me far from certain that the alliance will be given an opportunity to fail. As the economic crisis deepens, the real polarization of class interests, whose political expression they denounce, may well force the middle classes to choose sides before the next general election. Even so, the alliance is likely to achieve a large enough share of the poll in the next election to ensure that there is no clear-cut victor.

REFERENCES

1 David Steel, Foreword to *Liberal Party Manifesto, 1979*, Keesing's Contemporary Archives, Longman, 1979, p. 29639.
2 Roy Jenkins, 'The SDP's plan for picking up the pieces', *Guardian*, 5 October 1981.
3 David Steel, 'Liberal answer to Benn's false radicalism', *Guardian*, 5 October 1981.
4 Jenkins, 'The SDP's plan'.
5 S. M. Lipset, *Political Man* (1960), Heinemann, 1969, p. 141.
6 Ibid.

7   Ibid., pp. 144–5, 149.
8   R. Heberle, *'From Democracy to Nazism'*, Louisiana State University Press, 1945, p. 113.
9   Lipset, *Political Man*, p. 148.
10   *Observer*, 7 October 1981.
11   D. J. Saposs, 'The role of the middle class in social development: Fascism, Populism, Communism, Socialism', in *Economic Essays in Honour of Wesley Clair Mitchell*, Columbia University Press, 1935, p. 395.
12   *Liberal Manifesto, 1979*, p. 29639.
13   Ibid.
14   Jenkins, 'The SDP's plan'.
15   *Daily Telegraph*, 10 October 1981.

11
The Labour Party

Since the mid-1960s, the Labour Party has been the party of government in Britain, holding power for 10 out of 15 years. Under Harold Wilson it seemed to have found a recipe for electoral success, appealing to a broad range of middle-income voters as well as its traditional working-class supporters.

Yet since 1966, Labour's vote in general elections has been steadily declining. In spite of an extra 6 million voters between 1945 and 1979, the highest total vote for Labour in the post-war era was in 1951. The crushing defeat of 1979 was in many ways a confirmation of a long-term trend. Perhaps the most worrying aspect of this defeat was the fact that only half of the trade union members who voted gave their votes to Labour candidates.[1] The much-publicized struggle for power in the Labour Party since then has been the sign of a fundamental reassessment of the direction of Labour policies.

Unemployment has been one of the symbols of the challenge to the leadership of the Labour Party by constituency members and rank-and-file trade unionists. The numbers of unemployed people doubled during each period of Labour government (1964–70 and 1974–79). At the time this seemed to have surprisingly little political significance. In each election defeat Labour governments' attempts to limit pay settlements seemed more influential than increasing unemployment.

Taking a broader and longer look at the problems of the Labour Party, however, it becomes clear that the emergence of structural unemployment was an important indication of the origins of Labour's declining vote. Quite simply 1966 was the peak year for industrial employment in Britain, and between then and 1980 the numbers of industrial jobs diminished by 30 per cent. Industrial workers were traditionally Labour's most reliable source of support. There were fewer of them in the 1970s, and their numbers kept falling all the time.

The Labour leadership seemed to take this into account in the way in which it presented its policies. Under the influence of people like Crosland and Jenkins, Labour ceased to be a party of the working class; they declared class to be an increasingly irrelevant issue. As the numbers of manual workers shrank, so there emerged a new group of technicians and white-collar workers, many of them in the public sector, who were middle class in much of their lifestyle, but unionized and potentially left-of-centre in their political affiliations. The leadership of the Wilson and Callaghan era made a direct appeal to this group, emphasizing its importance for Britain's economic success. To the traditional working class, Labour's leaders offered a vision of their sons and daughters escaping from manual toil through education, technical training, and the modernization of the whole industrial sector. It allowed them to look forward to a new generation of white-coated workers with clean hands, suburban, owner-occupying, continental-holiday-making, and increasingly classless in their culture.

The theoretical underpinnings of this prospect were set out as long ago as 1956 in Crosland's *The Future of Socialism.* He argued that Keynesian economic management had made the classless society possible because

. . . the government can exert any influence it likes on income distribution, and can also determine within broad limits the division of total output between consumption, investment, exports and social expenditure . . . traditional capitalism has been reformed and modified almost out of existence. . . . Instead of glaring and conspicuous evils, squalor and injustice and distressed areas, we have to fuss about the balance of payments, and incentives, and higher productivity.[2]

The Labour leadership's strategy depended heavily on the success of economic management. It required steady growth, not only of national income, but also of employment in the technical, scientific and administrative fields. It also required steadily rising wages and salaries, to support the promise of more affluent lifestyles. As the availability of rented properties and council houses became more restricted, it required rising wages and salaries simply to support the only lifestyles available, as young couples were forced into owner-occupation, with all its attendant expenses and expectations.

In fact, there was a substantial increase in employment in these fields – between 1970 and 1980 the number of jobs in insurance, banking, finance, business services, professional, scientific and miscellaneous services rose by 29 per cent. But these were by no means all reliable Labour voters, and could quickly be disillusioned when a Labour government failed to fulfil its promises on growth. For instance, in 1970 Heath promised much the same as Wilson had six years earlier – modernization of industry, efficient economic management, faster growth – and won a large proportion of their votes.

Meanwhile, the traditional working class, through the trade unions, was expressing its dissatisfaction with the Wilson government's performance. In the election of February 1974, the Labour leadership was forced by the terms of its 'social contract' with the TUC to adopt a programme for 'a fundamental and irreversible shift in the balance of power and wealth in favour of working people and their families'. Although the 1974 elections, with their much clearer class issues, did not greatly boost Labour's share of the vote, they did result in a record low vote for the Conservatives.

The subsequent Labour government's failure to implement most of its manifesto has been the subject of much bitter debate since 1979, and contributed very largely to the determination of party members to control the leadership in office. But the policies of Wilson and Callaghan from 1975 onwards were not merely a return to those of the 1960s. In the name of the national interest, they committed themselves to the restoration of the profits of private industry, control of the money supply, cuts in public spending and curbs on workers' pay. In other words, the promise to pursue class interests, even in the limited field of the 'social wage', was completely overturned in favour of a strong support for the needs of capital – under the guise of a 'classless' appeal to the national interest.

It was industrial workers' incomes that suffered most from these policies. Between 1974 and 1979 the total volume of wages and salaries in the whole economy, less the total volume of taxes on income and National Insurance contributions, increased by 8.2 per cent.[3] But the total wages and salaries of the manufacturing industries *before* tax fell by 2.2 per cent in this period.[4] In the metal manufacturing industries, total wages and salaries fell by 8.2 per cent, and in textiles by 14.1 per cent, before tax.[5] During the same period, total income tax and National Insurance contributions increased by 6.9 per cent.[6]

It is therefore not at all surprising that workers should have rejected the Labour government, and that since 1979 Tony Benn and his supporters should call for greater democratic control over policy-making and implementation. Since the election, even moderate voices among the Labour Party membership have called for a return to class politics, to counter the very clear identification of the Conservative government with capitalist – and particularly international capitalist – interests. Once this is understood, the whole new orientation of Labour policy – anti-Common Market, anti-nuclear, protectionist – becomes comprehensible. In order to fight for the interests of the British working class, the Labour Party membership wants to break free from ties to international capital.

Thus the very rapid shift to the left in Labour Party policy since 1979 cannot be seen as a minority takeover; rather it should be seen as a direct response to the failures of the Labour government and to the overtly class politics of the Conservatives. Since the Conservatives adopted such policies in 1975, the surprising thing is that Labour was so slow to answer them in kind. The rise of Tony Benn certainly does not represent the 'extreme' element in this bid to get the Labour Party to represent the working class; indeed he is in many ways part of the respectable centre of the Labour spectrum. Since the argument of this book is that appeals such as his to national interests – to democratic control over decision-making in political and economic affairs – are not likely to be sufficient to protect the interests of the working class, his leadership of the left of the party will probably be shortlived. The future is more likely to lie with groups whose views are far more thoroughgoing in their rejection of the capitalist system.

LABOUR SINCE 1979

Compared with its manifesto of 1974, the Labour Party's appeal to the electorate in 1979 was a pallid affair. It declared five priorities, of which the first two were the control of inflation and better industrial relations. Full employment came third, followed by greater freedom and strengthening world peace. The manifesto gave most prominent attention to 'the fight against rising prices'. On industrial policy: '. . . for the private sector, we declare our aim to be a high wage, high productivity, low unit-cost economy.' Providing few clues as to how this would be achieved, the manifesto announced: 'The Labour Government will pursue policies which give high priority to the return to full employment. This must go hand in hand with keeping down inflation. We therefore aim at a rate of growth of 3 per cent or more.'[7]

From this anodyne appeal to social democratic aspirations, the movement since 1979 towards a socialist programme has been quite dramatic. All the evidence suggests that the leadership, including Tony Benn, have devoted much of their energy to holding back this tide of radicalism. One of the best indications of this changing climate of opinion was provided in the debate on unemployment, industry and economic strategy on the first morning of the 1980 Labour Party conference. The speakers in the debate could be classified into three groups. The first group represented the traditional leadership of the party and the trade unions; the second group represented the alternative economic strategy; and the third group were those explicitly committed to overthrowing British capitalism. Tony Benn was clearly one of the second group.

Speaking for the first group, Michael Foot deplored the fact that the technological problems of the 1980s were being exacerbated by 'the international slump' and by 'a home-made British catastrophe directed from No. 10 Downing Street'. These thoughts were embedded in a speech largely devoted to defending the record of the previous Labour government.[8]

For the second group, David Basnett of the General and Municipal Workers' Union moved the composite resolution on economic strategy, which called on a future Labour government to restrict the export of capital, extend public ownership (with industrial democracy), reflate the public service sector, cut arms expenditure substantially, tax wealth, introduce import controls on a range of industrial products, and initiate a 35-hour week with no loss of pay. But Basnett's speech was highly pragmatic:

> Ideological arguments about the desirability of more nationalization, and arguments for or against the so-called mixed economy, are almost irrelevant. In the circumstance that will face us the hankering for a 1960s-type industrial policy of incentives and tax concessions, or a 1976-type industrial strategy, are in themselves as irrelevant as the demands for the nationalization of the top 200 companies. . . . We will need a whole range of pragmatic policies and a determined intervention by government to retrieve a crisis situation.[9]

The third group's views could be taken as represented by the composite resolution moved by Pauline Dunlop of Liverpool Edge Hill Constituency Labour Party. Her speech started from the facts of mass unemployment in Merseyside, and the ratio of 8.5 school-leavers per job vacancy. She pointed out that only the United States among the advanced capitalist countries was suffering a similar recession.

> It is partly as a result of a world crisis in the system and partly because of the unique crisis of British capitalism which has been telescoped into a far shorter space of time than any of the other capitalist countries. There has been a lot of talk about return to the 1930s, but the 1930s are already here and now, as then, half-hearted measures

are not enough. We cannot tinker with the system. We have to fundamentally change society or we are doomed to offer youth the kind of system that means a permanent pool of large unemployment, mass poverty and the appalling social conditions that happen today. For 30 years we were led to believe that the capitalist tiger had been tamed, that living standards would improve and now they throw their hands in the air and say that it is not the fault of the last Labour government that unemployment rose and productivity stagnated, it was all the world recession. In many ways that was true, but any attempt to preside over capitalism means accepting its laws and means no lasting improvements. [10]

The resolution called on

the next Labour Government to implement a programme of public ownership and control of industry as a socialist alternative to the problem of mass unemployment, high inflation and cuts in public expenditure.
(a) an end to redundancy: any firm refusing to pay a living wage or threatening redundancy, to be taken into public ownership;
(b) work or full pay: a minimum wage of £80 per week, tied to the cost of living: voluntary retirement at 60 on the average wage;
(c) work to be shared out: a legal maximum of 35-hour week with no loss of pay: at least 6 weeks' holiday for all workers;
(d) a programme of useful public works and a crash training programme under the control of the trade union movement. [11]

In his speech at the end of the general economic debate, Tony Benn referred to this resolution, and explained that the party's National Executive Committee was not recommending its adoption:

because, although based on a deep socialist conviction, which I share, [these proposals] are not yet fully worked out between the Party and the trade unions and they contain pledges which we cannot be sure that we would honour if we came to power with those resolutions in that form.[12]

These, therefore, are the three strands of Labour Party opinion on economic management and unemployment. Since the 1980 conference, the party has made known its 'alternative economic strategy', which has the support of the trade unions and of Benn and his followers. But is it adequate to the problems of an economy in the position Britain's will be in 1985?

THE ALTERNATIVE ECONOMIC STRATEGY

Throughout the first part of this book I have considered Labour's new approach to economic policy and unemployment, and suggested that it did no justice to the developments in the international capitalist system that it claimed to combat. While pointing policy in the right directions, it is over-optimistic about growth and about its potential effects on employment levels.

The strategy implies, quite correctly, that withdrawal from the Common Market is a necessary condition both for independent action and for socialist measures. It is right in concluding that Britain will do no better in future out of EEC membership (or membership of the other international capitalist organizations) than it has done in the past. It is also right in suggesting that a programme of large-scale public investment is urgently needed, not only in the railways and other public utilities, but also in house-building. But it is wrong in basing all its other policies on the assumption that, granted import controls or tariffs to protect British industry, a period of sustained growth could be achieved. This defies the historical evidence of 60 years of slow and halting growth, the evidence of the links between a highly industrialized structure and slow growth, but above all the evidence about Britain's position in world trade.

Because Britain is by no means self-sufficient in raw

materials and food, it must export manufactured goods in order to buy imports of these materials. This means selling British manufactures abroad, in competition with the manufactures of other industrial producers. The major industrialized countries – especially Germany, Japan and France – now have such a lead in productivity and efficiency that it is increasingly difficult for Britain to compete with their manufactures. The industrializing countries can take advantage of much lower labour costs, and can thus beat British prices in labour-intensive production.

The only ways in which Britain could become significantly more successful in international competition would be through very rapid increases in productivity or a very rapid fall in real wages. Assuming that the Labour Party is aiming at the former, its strategy requires massive investment in manufacturing industry, and the co-operation of trade unions in a programme of ruthless modernization.

Labour's hopes of the former lie in two policies. Firstly, after exchange controls were abolished altogether by the Conservatives, investment abroad trebled in one year. In 1980 net investment abroad stood at £3,206 million.[13] In the first six months of 1981 British investment in overseas stocks and shares rose again to nearly three times the amount in the same period of 1980. In the first quarter of 1981, the financial institutions – pension funds, insurance companies and investment trusts – invested nearly twice as much money in foreign company shares as in UK company shares.[14] By reimposing exchange controls, Labour argues, this drain of capital abroad could be checked.

Secondly, import controls would guarantee a large share of the domestic market to British industry, and thus give it the prospect of a rising rate of profit. Since the main obstacles to growth have been the failure of industrial output to expand, and the tendency of manufactured imports to increase, this policy would solve the two problems at a stroke, by providing an inducement for capital to produce more. Planning agreements and threats of nationalization could be used to bring capital into line with Labour's aims. Thus by a mixture of coercion and cajoling, British capital could be harnessed to Labour's new strategy.

This sounds very logical, but it ignores the effects of three enormous time-lags in the processes described. In the first place, if import controls or tariffs were imposed, British consumers would be forced either to buy more expensively produced British goods, or to pay more for imported commodities. Either of these would result in a real fall in the standards of living of British consumers, throughout the period until British industry was capable of producing the same commodities as efficiently. It would mean that British consumers had less to spend on other British products throughout that period.

Secondly, there would be a long time-lag between the introduction of these policies and the improvement in the rate of profit in manufacturing industry. Particularly in view of the first factor mentioned above, demand for British goods would not increase instantly or rapidly. British capital would therefore have few if any short-term inducements to invest in line with Labour's plans. It would be likely to devote a great deal of its energy and resources to evading restrictions, sabotaging plans and refusing co-operation. So long as any alternative outlets for investment (e.g. in land or property) were available within the British economy, it would be likely to seek them.

Thirdly, the longest time-lag of all would be between the implementation of the domestic strategy for improved efficiency and the actual achievement of better competitiveness abroad. During this lag (prolonged by the two factors above) Britain's trading position would be rather weak, and there would be a constant difficulty in maintaining the necessary volume of exports – particularly if labour costs in British industry rose during this period.

None of these arguments destroys the case for import controls, nor is it intended to do so. What I am suggesting is that the alternative strategy will not give rise to rapid growth or stability in the economy, and that it will not be welcomed by British capital. Indeed, I would go so far as to say that British capital will oppose the strategy, and any other socialist measures that Labour might adopt, with all its powers. The only way in which the strategy would have any chance of being implemented at all would be through a programme of public ownership and central planning of production far more comprehensive than Tony Benn has advanced.

Furthermore, the rest of the strategy gives no clear account of how employment might be increased even if growth were achieved. If the only chance of success for the strategy lies in ruthless modernization and improved productivity, then increased employment in manufacturing could not be a high-priority aim. The most successful economies among the advanced industrialized nations have had no such increase in the 1970s, and France in particular has had a 10 per cent decline in manufacturing employment since 1975 despite an 18 per cent increase in industrial production. [15]

But once the notion of rapid growth under the alternative strategy is abandoned, even the vaguest hopes of substantial reductions in unemployment by its measures also disappear. Only the TUC's calculations on public investment give evidence of attempts to quantify the employment effects of Labour's plans. These show an increase of half a million jobs for £24 billion investment over five years. This is both necessary and constructive, even if the calculations (for railway modernization in particular) are a bit optimistic in their hopes of long-term growth of employment.

By the next election, however, unemployment is likely to be nearer 4 than 3 million (not including those in temporary artificial employment). The highest priority for the new government, if it is to represent any credible alternative to monetarism, will be to do something about the inequalities and injustices created by such a rate of unemployment. The alternative strategy offers only a long-term prospect, and a very dubious one, of tackling these. Only measures directly concerned with the redistribution of income, work and leisure will satisfy the demands of the working class. This leads to an examination of Labour's social policies, and particularly of recent developments in Labour's plans for the welfare state.

LABOUR'S SOCIAL POLICIES

Labour's victorious election campaign in February 1974 was focused primarily on social policy issues. Just how important these issues were in its campaign can be gauged from the resounding conclusion to its election manifesto. Summarizing its 'socialist aims, and we are proud of the word', the manifesto announced:

It is indeed our intention to
(a) bring about a fundamental and irreversible shift in the balance of power and wealth in favour of working people and their families;
(b) eliminate poverty wherever it exists in Britain, and commit ourselves to a substantial increase in our contribution to fight poverty abroad;
(c) make power in industry genuinely accountable to workers and the community at large;
(d) achieve far greater economic equality – in income, wealth and living standards;
(e) increase social equality by giving far greater importance to full employment, housing, education and social benefits;
(f) improve the environment in which our people live and work and spend their leisure.[16]

In government, Labour introduced a new and improved pension scheme and rationalized the child benefit and child tax allowance systems. But once these two measures were achieved, the government set about cutting the social services. Capital expenditure on all the social services was reduced between 1975 and 1978. Spending on housing was halved, as was the school-building programme, and spending on capital projects in the National Health Service was lower in real terms in 1978 than it had been in 1971.[17] Of all the social services, only spending on social security was significantly increased, with most of the extra money going to the unemployed, whose numbers doubled under Labour.

The Labour government reduced the proportion of national income spent on the social services. Between 1975 and 1979, in its efforts to boost the profits of private industry by transferring resources from the public sector, the Labour government cut total expenditure on social services (including housing) as a percentage of GDP (at market prices) from 25.6

per cent to 23.6 per cent. As the social security bill rose substantially because of unemployment, this represented a far larger percentage cut, in education and housing particularly.[18] During the first year of the Conservative government, the percentage of GDP spent on social services rose again to 24.5 per cent, mainly because of the further large rise in unemployment.

The Labour government's determination to raise profits also explains its failure to use the taxation system to promote equality. Between 1974 and 1979 the total volume of corporation tax was reduced by 28 per cent. But the total volume of taxes on income and National Insurance contributions increased by 7.6 per cent in the same period, and had at one stage (1976) stood at 15.2 per cent above its 1974 level.[19] Lower-paid individuals and families were more heavily taxed under Labour than they had been under the Conservatives.

Ever since the early 1960s, the most coherent voice of criticism and positive planning for the social services within the Labour Party has been a group of social policy experts who could perhaps best be described as Fabians (Townsend, Abel-Smith, Atkinson, Donnison, Frank Field, and so on). The repeated failures by governments to implement their proposals have brought a gradual shift of emphasis in their argument but not, as far as can be judged from their writings, a willingness to get to grips with the root of the problem.

The Fabians originally presented issues of income redistribution largely in technical terms. It was they who 'rediscovered poverty' in the mid-1960s, showing that the welfare state had neither much altered long-standing inequalities of income nor abolished the hard core of families (mostly with breadwinners at work) living below the officially defined poverty line. Their proposed solutions, then focused mainly on family allowances (later to be called child benefits), were argued in a manner which assumed that the abolition of poverty was an aim of both political parties, and was largely shared by an enlightened electorate, united in its acceptance of the social democratic compromise.

In the early 1970s the Conservative government brought in several measures aimed specifically at family poverty. However, all of these were income-tested selective schemes, which left the National Insurance system unmodified and its inadequacies untouched. In particular, neither the Conservatives nor the subsequent Labour governments did anything to improve the benefits for the long-term unemployed or for single-parent families.

Fabian criticisms of social policy shifted towards pressure for better benefits for these growing groups. They continued to draw attention to the low rates of child benefits, to falling tax thresholds, to persistent inequalities of income and wealth and to the effects of low pay. In addition, they campaigned for a more progressive system of income tax and for taxes on company fringe benefits.

More recently, the Fabians have aimed their pressure directly at the Labour Party, recognizing that the Conservatives are not concerned with social justice. They have analysed Labour governments' records and concluded that many of their failures have stemmed from a basic lack of commitment to income redistribution.

In his book *Inequality in Britain*, Frank Field (now a Labour MP) shows that Labour's parliamentary leadership took little trouble to understand the proposals of the Beveridge Report, and have shown scant interest in the subject since. He quotes a remark made by Arthur Greenwood in the debate on the Report in 1943: 'The abolition of mass unemployment . . . implies a developing prosperity out of which the funds necessary for the services vital to national well-being can be provided.' As Field comments, this attitude 'laid the basis for a post-war consensus about welfare being paid for out of growth rather than through redistribution'.[20]

Peter Townsend was one of the authors of the recent book *Manifesto: a Radical Strategy for Britain's Future*. The book pays a good deal of attention to the notion of a national minimum wage, arguing that it is a necessary precondition for social justice:

The ethic which inspires our view of income distribution must be contrasted with that implicit in present society. It is normal today to think of income as belonging in the first instance to the individual who earns or receives it. The payment of tax to redistribute income to others is seen as an act of collective charity, designed to mitigate poverty and help out the 'less fortunate'. . . . We see income and wealth as being generated collectively. . . . All incomes are part of a social product which passes through the hands of individuals. Redistribution of income to provide opportunities for all is a natural and proper counterpart of the state of mutual inter-dependence in which we live. Postwar social democrats have wrongly assumed that redistribution could be brought about without major changes in the basic structure of pre-tax earnings and wealth. An argument is that it is not good enough simply to seek to modify distribution through taxation and state benefits; wealth and pre-tax earnings must be more equitably distributed in the first place.[21]

The authors argue for a minimum wage of two thirds of the average earnings and an income ceiling of four times the average (at present the top 10 per cent of income receivers in Britain get over 10 times the share of the bottom 10 per cent). They also demand a complete reform of the taxation system, phasing out all tax allowances and reliefs, and taxing all earnings, from whatever source. They conclude: 'in the long run, taxes could be paid entirely by firms (and the self-employed) and pay could be conceived of and bargained for in net-of-tax terms.'[22]

However, two basic weaknesses of the social democratic approach are perpetuated in the new and more radical Fabian programme. The Fabians make no attempt to analyse the problem of declining employment and the consequent loss of earnings by workers. In the entire discussion in Field's work and *Manifesto* there is no mention of possibilities like the shorter working week, overtime bans or the principle of work-sharing. Consequently the problems of falling incomes and employment under automation are never discussed.

This is linked with the basic Keynesianism of *Manifesto's* whole argument. The edifice of its social policy reforms is built on a very shaky foundation of economic expansion. As in every previous Labour programme, social policy aims are ultimately made dependent on growth, and social planning on the success of economic expansion. For instance, *Manifesto* declares, in a section on 'Employment for All':

> Finally, the economic and social objectives must be fully integrated. The recovery of the economy, along the lines we have indicated, will lead to a large reduction in unemployment, greater job security and higher wages. But a positive economic policy will have to be developed in other respects to create a more open access to employment. We should advance from a concept of 'full employment' to one which might more appropriately be described as 'employment for all'. People who want work, including women, older people and disabled people, should be guaranteed rights to employment.[23]

In the absence of any serious analysis of the origins of structural unemployment, this is a dangerously naïve statement. A glance at the facts and figures about unemployment in the advanced industrialized countries since the mid-1960s should have ensured a more serious discussion of the issues. The problems associated with declining employment and rising unemployment are central to every social policy dilemma. The trade union movement has at least attempted to quantify and discuss the problems that have given rise to reduced employment in Britain. Even its muddled and ambivalent analysis (see chapter 12) is better than no analysis at all.

UNEMPLOYMENT, PARTICIPATION AND THE
WELFARE STATE

Another important aspect of social policy that has been too little discussed in the Labour Party is the relationship between citizenship and the welfare state. The Beveridge Plan attempted to reconcile state assistance with full citizenship, but its thinking was necessarily limited by the presuppositions that informed it. Above all, Beveridge was a Keynesian who took full employment as his starting point, and made no attempt to design income maintenance provision (other than family allowances) for able-bodied people of working age. Unemployment benefit, for instance, was designed to be a short-term scheme, to help people live during the period while they were finding another job.

But it is impossible to provide adequately for long-term income support without considering issues of citizenship and participation. To be unemployed is not simply to be deprived of a job; if it were, many more people might be glad to be out of work, as most jobs are boring or unpleasant. It is not even simply to be deprived of the company of workmates, which most people value. The experience of unemployment is to a great extent defined by the identity and status given to the unemployed in that society. In Britain, to be unemployed is to occupy a particular kind of disadvantaged social status, which carries stigma. Added to this, many unemployed people are excluded from active participation in trade union affairs by the rules of their unions. Finally, the conditions attached to the receipt of a minimum income from the state largely reinforce this exclusion from full citizenship.

To qualify for unemployment benefit (or supplementary benefit, when the former runs out after a year) the claimant must make himself available for full-time work, and refrain (within very narrow earning limits) from doing anything that could be classified, under any circumstances, as paid employment, even if he receives no remuneration for doing it. He must follow certain complex claiming procedures, designed to ration benefits to those who fulfil the precise conditions. Under recently introduced measures, if he is in one of several job categories, he may automatically be subjected to surveillance by the authorities in an attempt to detect fraud.

The requirements of the benefits system prescribe a state of orderly passivity. Nothing in the official or unofficial stereotype of the unemployed claimant encourages him or her to active participation in anything except the search for a job.

In the late 1960s (under Labour) and the early 1970s (under the Conservatives) a number of new official systems were created to deal with poverty and other forms of social deprivation – rebates, supplements, special priority areas, and so on. What all these selective systems had in common was the creation of new disadvantaged statuses, characterized by passivity and reduced citizenship. No one tried seriously to measure the cost of these systems in terms of stigma and loss of autonomy by the people who were supposed to benefit from them. Nor did anyone attempt to calculate where this process, once started, might end. For instance, the supplementary benefits scheme (created by a Labour government in 1966) originally supported about 3.5 million claimants and their dependants, and probably now supports twice as many.

The spirit that informed the original development of these selective systems was paternalistic, but their apparent benevolence was basically a poorly disguised form of social control. They distributed strictly limited benefits and services to people who were excluded not only from any share in prosperity but also from any real participation in the mainstream of society. They did this largely out of a mixture of fear and resentment – fear of the potential threat to law and order posed by marginal members of society, and resentment of the burden they imposed by their dependence on the state. Finding no useful role in society for such people, they created new disadvantaged roles as non-participatory claimants, patients or clients.

The difference between that era and the present day is that the process of exclusion and marginalization is no longer disguised as benevolence under the Conservatives. Social policy is aimed at far more explicit rationing, blaming and controlling. But there was no sudden break or discontinuity between the old paternalism and the new, more frosty, climate of restriction. Rather the one merged into the other, as the Labour government between 1975 and 1979 gradually introduced spending cuts and a new approach to the social services, which emphasized that they were draining resources from the potentially productive sectors of the economy.

It is wrong to suggest, as *Manifesto* does in one passage, that this mean spirit in social policy stems mainly from Treasury control over public spending.[24] It reflects a fundamental attitude towards the role of the state in social policy, and the status of those who receive state support or attention. Unemployment has been the major focus of a backlash of public opinion against welfare beneficiaries of all kinds, whipped up by the popular press. But a far more basic reassessment of our approach to the redistribution of income and work is needed if these ancient prejudices are to be overcome.

In a recent research project in several deprived inner-city areas of London, Barry Knight and Ruth Hayes found that only 20 per cent of their sample were involved in neighbourhood affairs or interested in their neighbours, and only 10 per cent were participants in community groups. The more isolated people were, the more they disliked their area, suspected their fellow-residents, were ignorant or critical of the social services. But all their interviewees shared, to a worrying extent, in the current disillusionment with state services, and many favoured authoritarian, right wing 'solutions'.

This is partly because the problems are vast, and are being aggravated by the economic recession, but is partly because – as the present study shows – many social programmes fail to reach the area. People display little knowledge of services, or hold them in low esteem, or resent being branded as a client. Almost every service fares badly in the minds of local people. It is therefore not just a question of more government money for more services or more partnerships. A different approach is also needed. . . . There is a gap between how social agencies see problems and their solutions and how residents of run down inner cities areas see them. Social agencies call for more jobs, more social workers, more community involvement. Locals on the other hand suggest getting rid of the blacks, having more police, or else simply blowing the place up. There is some overlap. Both groups say the areas need better housing and more facilities. However, in the delivery of services the gaps are more important than the overlaps, particularly when initiative for services tend to come from social agencies rather than the local people.[25]

There is some evidence of a new approach to this problem from a number of Labour-controlled local authorities. In Sheffield, for instance, the Council has made strenuous efforts to democratize the services, encouraging participation from clients, voters and trade unionists in debates about social policy issues and how services can best be provided. But the scope of local authorities in issues concerning social deprivation is constantly narrowing, through the impact of national economic factors and of central government controls. Any basic reassessment of social policy and the provision of services must include national economic management and the relationship between central and local government. Some of the issues relevant to this reassessment will be discussed in the last two chapters.

REFERENCES

1 F. Cripps, J. Griffith, F. Morrell, J. Reid, P. Townsend and S. Weir, *Manifesto: A Radical Strategy for Britain's Future*, Pan, 1981, p. 108.
2 C. A. R. Crosland, *The Future of Socialism*, Cape, 1956, pp. 27, 70.
3 Central Statistical Office, *National Income and Expenditure, 1981*, HMSO, 1981, table 4.1, using implied deflator for consumers' expenditure, table 2.6.
4 Ibid., tables 3.1 and 2.6.
5 Ibid., tables 3.3 and 2.6.
6 Ibid., tables 7.1 and 2.6.
7 *Labour Party Manifesto, 1979*, Keesing's Contemporary Archives, Longman, 1979, p. 29636.
8 Labour Party, *Report of the Annual Conference and Special Conference of the Labour Party, 1980*, p. 11.
9 Ibid., p. 14.
10 Ibid., p. 16.
11 Ibid., p. 15.
12 Ibid., p. 30.
13 *National Income and Expenditure, 1981*, table 1.6.
14 *Guardian*, 15 October 1981.
15 OECD *Main Economic Indicators* and *Labour Force Statistics*.
16 F. W. S. Craig (ed.), *British Election Manifestos, 1900–1974*, Macmillan, 1975, pp. 405–6.
17 *National Income and Expenditure, 1979*, table 9.4.
18 *National Income and Expenditure, 1981*, tables 1.1 and 9.4.
19 Ibid., table 7.2.
20 F. Field, *Inequality in Britain: Freedom, Welfare and the State*, Fontana, 1981, pp. 218–19.

21 Cripps *et al.*, *Manifesto*, p. 183.
22 Ibid., p. 193.
23 Ibid., p. 181.
24 Ibid., p. 150.
25 Barry Knight and Ruth Hayes, *Self-Help in the Inner City*, London Voluntary Service Council, 1981, pp. 93–4.

12
The Trade Union Movement

During the 1970s the changing pattern of employment in Britain threatened the living standards of the working class. As industrial employment declined, the only compensatory increase in jobs was in services. Many of the latter were poorly paid, and a large proportion were part-time. Thus as better-paid industrial jobs were lost, the fall in working-class earnings was not made up from new employment. Table 12.1 indicates the fall in total wages and salaries that resulted from the shrinking workforce in manufacturing industry. It shows the indices of the employed labour force and incomes in the 1970s.[1]

It was manual jobs that declined most in industry; the proportion of technical and administrative staff in industrial firms increased in the 1970s. But outside industry this development was much more marked. The kinds of employment that increased most were services, and especially technical and professional services, as table 12.2 shows.[2] By 1980, there were very nearly as many people employed in professional, scientific and miscellaneous services as in the whole of manufacturing industry, and as many employed in insurance, banking, finance and business services as in the construction industry.

The other major change in employment patterns in the 1970s was that employment for women increased as employment for men declined. Between 1972 and 1979 the number of women in work increased from 8,331,000 to 9,492,000. This rise was mainly in the number of badly paid unskilled or semi-skilled jobs in both the private and the public sectors. The majority of these new jobs for women were part-time.

Table 12.1 Indices of employment and incomes by industry (1975 = 100)

	1970	1975	1980
All manufacturing industries			
Employed labour force	111.1	100	93.4
Total wages and salaries (at 1975 prices)	92.3	100	95.0
Food, drink and tobacco			
Employed labour force	94.3	100	105.6
Total wages and salaries	87.5	100	100.8
Chemical, coal and petroleum products			
Employed labour force	90.3	100	105.0
Total wages and salaries	88.9	100	107.0
Metal manufacture			
Employed labour force	127.2	100	84.0
Total wages and salaries	97.8	100	76.8
Engineering and allied industries			
Employed labour force	96.7	100	93.0
Total wages and salaries	97.1	100	101.4
Textiles, leather and clothing			
Employed labour force	101.5	100	82.4
Total wages and salaries	100.0	100	83.7
Other manufacturing			
Employed labour force	97.0	100	94.0
Total wages and salaries	91.0	100	98.7

Table 12.2   *Numbers in employment by industry (thousands)*

	1970	1975	1980
Insurance, banking, finance and business services	956	1,103	1,255
Professional, scientific and miscellaneous services	4,845	5,759	6,226

But as workers have been shed in both public and private sectors since 1979, many women workers have been the first to be made redundant. By March 1981 the total number of women in employment had fallen to 8,722,000, a drop of 8 per cent in less than two years. Of the jobs for women remaining, 41 per cent were part-time.[3] Female unemployment doubled between December 1979 and July 1981.

Employment in national and local government services grew slowly up to 1975, but has declined since. In March 1981 local government employment was 0.3 per cent above its 1972 level, and national government 1.2 per cent higher.[4]

These changes had direct effects on the membership of trade unions. During the 1970s the numbers belonging to many unions declined. Thus the trade union movement faced a very adverse situation for the working class, with falling incomes and employment in its traditional sectors, offset only by an increase in the number of low-paid and white-collar jobs. In all the advanced industrialized world, the British working class was in a uniquely beleaguered situation.

Yet throughout the decade the trade union movement addressed itself predominantly to only one aspect of this problem. Its opposition to any form of incomes policy, and its insistence on free collective bargaining, were the perennial themes of its political message. The paradox of the 1970s was that towards the end of the decade the Conservatives were loud in their support for 'free collective bargaining', while it was the Labour government's attempts to limit pay settlements in the public sector that brought it down in 1979. The decade ended with total working-class incomes declining rapidly under a Conservative government which had taken the trade union movement at its word.

For the origins of this paradox, it is necessary to look back to the mid-1960s. The very first attempt at an incomes policy was made under the Labour government in 1966. It was no coincidence that this was precisely the year in which employment in British industry started to decline. From 1966 onwards the major aim of capital investment in British industry was the saving of labour costs. The Wilson government had abandoned its attempt at a planned expansion, and had reacted with a pay freeze to stave off a balance of payments crisis. For the government as well as for British capital the threat of rising manufactured imports called forth an attempt to hold down industrial wage bills in order to make British products more competitive.

In the ensuing phases of Labour's incomes policy, much emphasis was placed on productivity deals as a basis for pay rises. The trade unions co-operated with this - complaining about slow growth and rising unemployment, but not challenging the basis of the policy. Wilson's economic strategy had been cast in terms of improved productivity through the introduction of new industrial technology. What the trade union movement failed to point out was that unless output grew at the same pace, increases in productivity necessarily caused redundancy and a fall in total working-class incomes.

In the 1970s there were two periods of statutory or semi-statutory wage restraint. Under the Conservatives, the pay freeze was associated with an attempt at rapid expansion which produced even more rapid inflation. Under Labour it was associated with stagnation. In both periods the working class could be seen as having lost ground. However, the trade union movement's analysis of the origins of these setbacks was shallow. It concentrated its resistance to both governments' policies on the loss of the right to negotiate over wage levels, rather than on what was happening to labour as a factor in industrial production as a whole. In fact, workers' share of output of industry declined throughout the period from 1965 onwards, and not only when wages were restrained through incomes policies. Bacon and Eltis calculated that between 1962 and 1973 the proportion of industrial production consumed by industrial workers declined from 17.3 to 16.2 per cent.[5]

By contrast, the trade union movement was remarkably docile in its acceptance of mounting unemployment through the 1970s. Not until the end of the decade was a serious attempt made to analyse the roots of the problem, and even then the trade union leadership remained remarkably ambivalent, as we shall see in this chapter. Unemployment as a structural feature of British industrial development since the mid-1960s seemed almost to escape trade unionists' notice.

This was because the trade union leadership chose to analyse all the developments of this period from the point of view of a Keynesian notion of economic growth, and a classical nineteenth-century liberal view of wage determination. From its Keynesian standpoint the trade union leadership insisted that successive governments could achieve faster growth, and that unemployment was merely one indication of underused productive resources. Time and again, the TUC advocated more rapid expansion than governments of either party were willing to undertake, and used unemployment as evidence for the potential for such expansion.

On the other hand when it came to wage settlements the trade union leadership objected strongly, and often very effectively, to statutory or voluntary limits. Yet incomes policies were part of the stock-in-trade of Keynesian economists and their political followers, particularly among social democractic governments in the 1960s and 1970s. The trade union movement saw unemployment as largely irrelevant to the question of pay settlements, and much of its dealing over wage levels actually increased the unemployment rate. Throughout the 1970s wage bargains based on productivity deals with a large element of redundancy resulted in lost industrial jobs. The trade union leadership took no apparent responsibility for this reinforcement of a trend that was adverse to working-class interests and caused a decline in living standards.

Even the most rudimentary review of economic trends would have revealed the weaknesses of this strategy far earlier. Rising unemployment constantly weakened the bargaining position of those workers still in employment. It is not necessary to be a Marxist to appreciate that the existence of an enormous 'industrial reserve army' is a powerful weapon in the hands of employers who want to limit their workers' pay. On the other hand, even the most doctrinaire and short-sighted Keynesian could hardly have failed to notice that the stagnation of industrial production has become a long-term feature of the British economy, and was a trend that had largely resisted orthodox attempts at expansion. Above all, the significant improvements in productivity achieved in British industry – 31 per cent between 1966 and 1973, faster than required by Labour's Economic Plan of the mid-1960s – had done little to increase industrial output, but much to accelerate redundancy. The failure of the trade union movement to defend working-class interests more effectively in the 1970s can only be ascribed to an overwhelming tendency for leaders raised in the post-war era to rely on modes of thinking adapted to that period of historically rapid economic expansion and social democratic politics.

In this chapter I shall consider the gradual shift in trade union thinking from 1979 onwards, and look at indications for the future of trade union economic policy.

THE TRADE UNIONS AND UNEMPLOYMENT

The TUC *Economic Review* for 1979 was in many ways a remarkable document. Written before the general election of that year, it represented a belated attempt by the trade union movement to trace the origins and consequences of rising unemployment in the British economy. But because the framework to this review continued to be the strange mixture of Keynesian macro-economic thinking and free market micro-economics that had characterized trade union thinking in the previous era, the document reflected the intense ambivalence of the trade union leadership in facing up to the facts it uncovered.

The review started with an account of the fall in employment in British industry since 1966, and particularly in manual employment in manufacturing industry. It noted in passing that the steep rise in the entry into the labour market of married women had contributed to unemployment – failing to recognize that these women had by and large filled posts in the only expanding sectors of the manual employment market, clerical and public services jobs. It went on to present an entirely traditional analysis of the 'causes of unemployment', in terms of 'lack of demand in the economy, causing cyclical unemployment' and a 'world recession' since the oil price crisis of 1973.[6] This passage could have been written by Harold Wilson, such is its banality. However, the review continued:

> . . . it has become increasingly clear that reflation of the economy is not enough to restore full employment. A further factor that has to be considered is what is sometimes called structural unemployment. . . . It is sometimes suggested that there is such a thing as 'technological unemployment', viz. unemployment brought about by technological change and the consequent decrease in demand for labour. While technological change clearly has employment implications . . . it is difficult to isolate the effects of technology on employment levels overall. One measure of technological improvement is the rate of productivity. However . . . high rates of productivity growth are associated with high economic growth and high employment. . . . it is a historical fact that technology and investment have, through the creation of wealth and income, created rather than destroyed employment though not necessarily in the same industries or locations. There is clearly no guarantee, however, that such a relationship will prevail in future. . . . The relationship of productivity with employment and unemployment is difficult to gauge. High rates of productivity growth tend to have beneficial effects on employment in general. . . . there is no clear correlation between high rates of productivity and high levels of unemployment. . . . This, however, by no means proves the case that high productivity growth automatically leads to high employment or low unemployment. All it does prove is

that high rates of productivity growth need not lead to high unemployment.[7]

This comical ambivalence did at least betoken an increasingly vigorous debate within the trade union movement in which established attitudes towards productivity dealing and redundancy were being challenged. Indeed the document *took note* of all the relevant factors that weakened the working class's economic position in the 1970s. It noted the fall in industrial employment, the dangers of new technology (including microtechnology) being used to displace labour, the decline in the British share of world manufactured imports. It noted the rise of the 'super-competitors', recording that 'a number of countries classified as developing countries are now reaching a stage of growth where they are more appropriately described as newly industrializing countries'.[8] It noted the increasing role of transnational corporations in world decisions about locations of production. It noted the importance of social policy as a means of offsetting the decline in working-class incomes from employment. What it resolutely refused to do was to adopt any new analysis of the TUC's overall economic strategy, or adapt its own framework for perceiving these facts.

By the following year the TUC had had time to take stock of the new Conservative government's measures, and particularly of their consequences on unemployment figures. In its *Economic Review* for 1980, the TUC returned to the same theme as the previous year, but with a different emphasis:

> The Government's policies deliberately aim to increase unemployment. The Government callously and foolishly believes that higher unemployment is a cost which the nation must bear if British industry is to become more efficient. There can be no sharper differences of view between the TUC and the Government than on this point.[9]

The framework of the 1980 *Review* was a defence of the record of Keynesian methods of economic management since the war, and a claim that 'we need to add to the Keynesian policy of demand management, not reject it'.[10] The *Review* argued strongly for selective import controls, blaming import penetration for many of Britain's economic problems. It almost outbid the Conservatives in its enthusiasm for higher investment, profitability and productivity in the private sector, but argued that high interest rates and restrictive monetary policies would have the opposite effects.

However, the *Review* also contained certain important new indications of a changing attitude towards unemployment. Alongside the conventional pleas for reflation and higher investment there were strong arguments for a shorter working week. The *Review* announced that since the previous year 'over 3 million work people have negotiated a shorter working week and many others have benefited from earlier retirement or longer holidays'.[11] This statement was linked to a recommendation that new technology should always be assessed for its effects on the size of the workforce – an implicit repudiation of productivity deals leading to redundancy.

A later section returned to the theme of technological innovation under the heading 'Structural Change and Adjustment':

> The effects of new technology combined with the need to tackle the cyclical and structural problems facing the economy require that we use the 1980s to prepare the working population for the employment changes that will be encountered. . . . In many cases, hours reductions can be introduced in ways – restructuring patterns of work and pay to reduce overtime and absenteeism and employ extra shift crews – which, without adding significantly to costs can have immediate beneficial effects on employment and on the provision of services.[12]

The *Review* announced the launching of a TUC campaign for a 35-hour working week.

THE TRADE UNIONS AND THE CONSERVATIVE GOVERNMENT

In many ways it has been the Conservative government that has forced the trade union movement to reconsider its economic strategy and its political alignment. This process has been a slow and painful one. As unemployment clearly emerged as the biggest factor in declining working-class living standards, the trade unions had to take more direct account of it in their policies and actions.

Since the beginning of 1980 two themes have dominated the TUC's pronouncements on economic issues. In the first place, its emphasis has shifted from investment in private industry to investment in the public sector. In the early months of 1980 the TUC was still castigating the government for failing to live up to its promises about revitalizing the private sector, and pointing to the need to 'rebuild our manufacturing base'. In its 1981 *Economic Review,* the TUC's reflationary programme concentrated on public services and on the creation of new jobs, with only £250 million of its £6,000 million package going in aid to private industry. When this was decisively rejected by the government, the TUC moved even further and faster in the same direction. In August 1981 a document called *The Reconstruction of Britain* demanded a £24 billion programme of public investment over five years to rebuild the economy. It pointed out the fall in public investment from £16 billion in 1975–76 to £10 billion in 1980–81, and concentrated as much on house-building, inner-city regeneration and capital expenditure in the social services as it did on industrial reconstruction.

That this new emphasis on the public sector was concerned primarily with employment prospects was clear throughout the document. It claimed that the programme would create 500,000 new jobs, half of them in the construction industry. Indeed, this was rather a modest gain, with unemployment approaching 3 million. As the Keynesian side of their policies was producing this limited return, the TUC was forced to look elsewhere for measures to combat unemployment.

The second theme was shorter working hours. A report in the *Guardian,* published in the same week as the 1981 *Economic Review,* suggested that the TUC had received a confidential survey which revealed that 700,000 jobs could be saved – more than the number that would be created through the proposed public investment programme – if overtime working could be converted into full-time jobs. The survey was said to reveal that the majority of the major unions were in favour of banning overtime (if necessary through legislation) in order to combat unemployment.[13]

That there was considerable conflict about this aim among the trade union leadership was revealed in other press reports in 1981. In April, Len Murray spoke in favour of reductions in the working week, and said that high levels of overtime being worked in sectors where there was unemployment '. . . is not only an affront to unemployed people, but it also undermines the union arguments for significant improvements in basic working time'.[14] However, he did not declare himself unequivocally in favour of overtime bans, and other speakers, including Sir John Boyd of the AUEW, came out strongly against legislation. In August 1981 a TUC report claimed that more than half Britain's manual workers had a standard working week of under 40 hours, which it suggested represented significant progress in the campaign for a shorter working week. However, the same press briefing denied an earlier report that the TUC and Labour leadership had agreed to legislate against overtime. A TUC statement said that progress was being made towards voluntary reductions in overtime, and official policy was still against a statutory ban.

The importance of this issue for the future of the trade union economic strategy was indicated in a number of comments during this period. The whole notion of a ban on overtime ran counter to the spirit of trade union wage bargaining in the 1960s and 1970s, when efforts to raise the total earnings of those still in work – through productivity deals, piecework or any other method, including high overtime working – outweighed any consideration of job-sharing or job-preservation. Once overall employment levels were to be considered, the prospect of falling earnings, especially for those with low basic rates of pay, loomed much larger. Trade unionists were therefore forced to consider other means, including changes in the systems of taxation and benefits, which could guarantee a decent weekly income, yet share work more fully.

SHARING WORK

The present situation in the trade union movement seems to indicate a division between an increasingly aware and radical rank-and-file and the conservative and traditional elements in their leadership. The latter have an even larger stake in the outmoded formulae of the social democratic compromise than the Labour Party leadership, and are even harder to displace.

This traditional leadership will continue to encourage its membership to negotiate over pay and conditions in ways calculated to maximize the earnings of the employed work-force, however small it may become, and however long the dole queue. It will emphasize the need to concentrate on what individual workers can gain from the industrial system, and try to make it work better for them.

But rank-and-file workers will increasingly reject this style of leadership, and focus on issues of class solidarity and struggle. For instance, on 19 September 1981 steel-workers at Ebbw Vale refused overtime work to complete a large contract on the grounds that this would mean increased pay packets for themselves at a time of high unemployment. They urged the employers to take on some unemployed school-leavers to do the extra work.

Seen from the perspective of the 1960s, or from that of workers in a moderately successful capitalist economy, such behaviour by British workers in our present economic situation is absurdly quixotic. But British workers' attitudes are beginning to change. They are beginning to identify with class interests, and put these above higher personal incomes. British capital and a succession of social democratic governments succeeded in persuading them to behave in ways that were against their class interests for 15 years. Rising productivity combined with stagnant output have meant falling employment and rising unemployment, and the level of the latter now begins to threaten every worker's security.

Since the mid-1960s, when the new methods of pay negotiation were introduced, those industries with the best records of improved productivity have often been the ones in which there have been the largest reductions in the workforce. This has not been paralleled in other countries, where productivity growth has led to greater prosperity and employment. Whatever their leadership may tell them about the experiences of workers in other countries, British workers are now concerned to halt the process that they have witnessed over the past 15 years. The pressure towards a more equitable distribution of available work within the trade union movement is therefore a new and significant development. However, the reaction of capital to this development is also important. Two aspects of this should be mentioned.

In the first place, British industrialists have always strongly rejected attempts at reducing the working week, banning overtime or work-sharing. They have consistently insisted that such schemes would damage their already low profitability.

Secondly, where the working week has been reduced, employers have often managed to do this in a way that actually resulted in *fewer*, rather than more, people having jobs. The length of the average working week declined in all the major industrialized countries between 1961 and 1973, but some of the largest reductions in working hours were in Germany and Austria. In Germany the average weekly hours worked in manufacturing declined by 6.4 per cent between 1960 and 1973, but during that time the number of workers employed in manufacturing industry declined also. In Austria the average weekly hours worked in manufacturing was reduced from 43.4 to 36.0 between 1965 and 1973, a reduction of 17.2 per cent in eight years. But the number of workers in manufacturing was virtually the same at the end of this period as it had been at the beginning.[15] Similarly in Britain the TUC is already claiming success in its campaign for a shorter working week, but at a time of enormous reductions in workforces. In the nine months from December 1980 to September 1981, agreements effecting over half a million manual workers and thousands more clerical workers have been reached, so that over 5.5 million manual workers now do less than a 40-hour week, and some clerical workers as little as 32 hours. But the background to this is one of redundancies not increased employment. Not a single case of such agreements resulting in more jobs was reported.[16]

Thus there seems no likelihood that workers' demands for an end to productivity dealing with redundancy and for the sharing out of available work will be acceptable to employers. Negotiations with firms or industries on these points are likely to founder, and only political action, aimed at changing the whole structure of British industry, could possibly bring about the kind of radical change that is being sought.

THE LABOUR MOVEMENT AND UNEMPLOYMENT

As in the Labour Party, there is evidence of a change in the climate of opinion in the trade union movement over unemployment. Another sign of this change is the urgency with which unions who previously excluded unemployed people from membership or participation are now revising their rules.[17] Many unions are actively recruiting unemployed members, and trades councils have sponsored unemployment advice centres. All this is very different from the early 1970s when claimants' unions were formed mainly because the trade unions had so neglected the interests of the non-employed, and the relationship between employed and unemployed was either distant or hostile.

Indeed, in the 1970s it was outside the mainstream of the labour movement that most of the radical thinking about the future of work, income and leisure was taking place. It was the claimants' unions that first drew attention to the absurdities of the benefits systems and the hyprocrisy of governments. It was they who drew attention to the way in which the work ethic (including the notion of 'the right to work') was being used against the working class, to divide it and exploit it. Capital had no need for a large sector of the population in its workforce, but it could whip up resentment against claimants by describing them as idle and a burden on those in employment. The social security system could be discredited as a means of providing a decent and unstigmatized income, and used as a threat to coerce the unemployed into short-term, low-paid jobs. At a political level, the unemployed could be blamed for national economic problems, and taxpaying, ratepaying workers could, out of resentment and fear, be persuaded to vote for Margaret Thatcher.

The claimants' unions pointed out that this basic division between workers' and claimants' interests could never be properly overcome under the current distribution of work and income. So long as the only source of unstigmatized income was employment, social security – in whatever form – was going to be provided grudgingly and under threat. The only solution was to redistribute work more evenly and pay a guaranteed minimum income to *all* citizens, irrespective of whether they were employed or not. If each individual citizen received this minimum provision – rather as each child is entitled to child benefit – then class solidarity could once more be ensured. The claimants' unions predicted that unemployment would rise to a point where workers would recognize the false consciousness implicit in the capitalist work ethic.[18] But they also predicted that capital would never concede the principle of the guaranteed weekly income, and that only a socialist society could implement it.

At the same time, the feminist movement was attacking the sexist basis of the way in which the worlds of both work and state benefits were organized – and of the labour movement's organizations also. Like the claimants' unions, they argued that a system that gave status, power and income only through work undermined the citizenship of most of the population. Since women were at a gross disadvantage in the labour market, their chances of achieving equality were negligible under the present institutions. However, they were equally scathing in their critique of much socialist thinking, which perpetuated the same prejudices, engendered in the relations of production and reproduction.

The third strand of radical thought came from the movement for communes, communities, co-operatives and alternative work projects. They suggest that the unemployment problem is rather like a lake. The streams feeding the lake have increased their flow, because of redundancy in major industries, but the outlets have remained the same. As a result unskilled people in particular stay unemployed for much longer. It is necessary to open new outlets through finding new and co-operative ways of creating work that provides income. They urge people to break out of the modes of thinking based on large, hierarchical units and the disciplined routine of the factory system. They favour a far more participatory, less alienated style of work in small units, and they point out the advantages of part-time employment, and of people pursuing a number of contrasting projects, trainings and skills simultaneously. They would argue in favour of the legalization of the 'black economy', which represents unemployed people's individualistic attempts to break out of the 'lake' and follow their own initiatives.

All these disparate and fragmented elements of radicalism have a contribution to make to the kind of socialist thought that should be going on in the labour movement in the 1980s. The organizational weakness of these small and scattered groups should not disguise the fact that they have anticipated (and pioneered relevant measures for) most of today's problems. But the failure of these groups to achieve wider acceptance of their ideas indicates that the kinds of changes that they want will not be implemented without political action for a socialist society. Capitalist modes of organization and thought are far too powerful to be overthrown by good ideas alone. It is only by a fusion of all these radical new directions into the labour movement itself that this power can be effectively challenged.

REFERENCES

1　Department of Employment, *Employment Gazette,* August 1981, vol. 89, no. 8, table 1.8, and Central Statistical Office, *National Income and Expenditure, 1981,* HMSO, 1981, tables 3.3 and 2.6 (using deflator for consumers' expenditure).
2　*National Income and Expenditure, 1981*, table 1.12.
3　Central Statistical Office, *Annual Abstract of Statistics, 1980,* HMSO, 1980, table 6.1, and Department of Employment, *Employment Gazette,* July 1981, vol. 89, no. 7, table 1.4.
4　*National Income and Expenditure, 1981*, table 1.12.
5　R. Bacon and W. Eltis, *Britain's Economic Problem*: *Too Few Producers*, 2nd edn, Macmillan, 1978, ch. 1.
6　Trades Unions Congress, *TUC Economic Review, 1979*, TUC, 1979, p. 11.
7　Ibid., pp. 11–14.
8　Ibid., p. 36.

9   Trades Unions Congress, *TUC Economic Review, 1980*, TUC, 1980, p. 7.
10 Ibid., p. 74.
11 Ibid., p. 37.
12 Ibid., pp. 67–8.
13 *Guardian*, 11 February 1981.
14 Ibid., 10 April 1981.
15 H. Shutt, *The Jobs Crisis*: *Increasing Unemployment in the Developed World*, Economist Intelligence Unit, Special Report no. 85, 1980, p. 28, table 14.
16 *Guardian*, 31 August 1981.
17 Ibid., 11 July and 21 October 1981.
18 Bill Jordan, *Paupers*: *The Making of the New Claiming Class*, Routledge and Kegan Paul, 1973, pp. 23, 67–86.

13

Conclusions

Many people in Britain will find this book's argument very gloomy. I have suggested that Britain's chances of economic success, as defined in the advanced industrialized countries, are negligible. I have also suggested that under any version of our present 'mixed economy', unemployment in Britain will go on rising.

But the picture I am painting of the future is not meant to be depressing for Britain. It is meant to be realistic about our chances of achieving what capitalism defines as economic success under capitalism's own modes of production and organization. I have tried to show that the logic of international capitalism will require Britain to go on stagnating, while the logic of the capitalist system will continue to increase unemployment and inequality in British society.

Anyone who doubts that the role of a backward 'internal colony' for the prosperous regions of the capitalist world is a very uncomfortable one should study the history of Ireland in the nineteenth century. Once Ireland had been cast in this role, there was no escape from a downward spiral of impoverishment and structural unemployment. Its economic problems were persistently defined by Britain in terms of overpopulation, and both starvation and mass emigration were condoned. While there may not be direct parallels between the economies of nineteenth-century rural Ireland and twentieth-century de-industrializing Britain, there can be little doubt that the political conflicts and tensions produced would be similar. It is in the role of internal colony for capitalist exploitation that the gloom of Britain's future lies.

If we redefine our aims and consider the possibility of trying to create a more just and equal society in Britain, the prospect becomes much less gloomy. Unlike the other countries that have attempted to turn to socialism, Britain would start from a position of relative prosperity and advanced industrialization. Inequalities of income and wealth in Britain, though considerable and growing, are not nearly as great as they were in any of the other countries which have so far attempted the transition to a socialist society, all of which did so during the early stages of new industrialization. Although the process would be painful in Britain, and would provoke enormous resistance, there are strong reasons for supposing that it could be a good deal less traumatic than in other countries, and involve a good deal less authoritarian and repressive measures.

The alternatives under capitalism are extremely bleak. We have already experienced, in 1981, some of the costs of adopting the 'solutions' to Britain's problems prescribed by monetarism. The riots in our inner cities are just a taste of what is likely to follow, as disaffection and lawlessness spread in the wake of despair. Since the government's policies can offer no hope of increased prosperity or employment for these areas, it will be forced to adopt increasingly repressive and punitive tactics. Violence and conflict will certainly be an unavoidable feature of life in Britain under capitalism, and in the long run severe restrictions on freedom will follow from this. As a long-term prospect, therefore, socialism offers a much greater hope of harmony and security in British society.

Furthermore, I shall argue in this chapter that there is a real risk of the rise of a powerful fascist party in Britain in the 1980s, simply because of the social conditions that capitalism will create. Unlike the National Front, such a party would recruit increasingly from disaffected middle-class people. It would argue that its methods alone could solve Britain's economic problems, by cutting wages, coercing the unemployed, repatriating immigrants and dismantling the welfare state. Such a programme will gain increasing credibility with the failure of conventional economic policies.

History has shown that in conditions such as those that prevail in Britain now, socialism is the only effective challenge to fascism. For this reason, more than any other, I am arguing strongly for a socialist future for Britain.

THE BRITISH POLITICAL SYSTEM

In 1981 we are witnessing the apparent fragmentation of the two-party system in British politics, which has existed since the eighteenth century. Roy Jenkins' claim that his group has 'broken the mould' of British politics seems to be justified. Yet I shall argue that appearances are very deceptive. The mould of British politics was broken by recession and unemployment, not by the Gang of Four. Jenkins and his group are engaged in a backward-looking attempt to repair the mould of the post-war social democratic compromise.

The main feature of British politics since 1974 has been a tendency towards polarization along class lines. In the 1950s and 1960s both major parties tried to make appeals to the national interest, and both succeeded at times in attracting voters from all classes. In 1975 the Conservatives under Margaret Thatcher declared themselves for policies which, while superficially similar in their national appeal, were in fact aimed at the defence of capital and the interests of its middle-class adherents.

The Conservatives' 1979 campaign was conducted in a populist style by Thatcher, and won her support from sections of the working class. She took advantage of disillusionment with the Labour government, with a skilful blend of vague right-wing themes and specific economic theories, made to sound remarkably coherent. Large sections of the electorate seemed willing to invest their hopes in her confident abrasive approach, without paying much attention to the specifics of her economic plans. However, within two years of the new government taking office, two things have become clear. Firstly, Thatcher's policies represent a radical break with the 'One Nation' tradition of Toryism, deriving from Disraeli. As more moderate Conservative leaders are constantly reminding her, her recent policies do not advance the interests of the working class, or disadvantaged people, and are increasingly directed at their oppression. Secondly, the working class and large sections of the lower middle class who supported her are rapidly becoming disaffected with the government, and their votes are available for any other political party to capture.

Unlike the Conservatives, the Labour Party did not move towards the representation of class interests in 1975; in fact, it moved exactly in the opposite direction. Having been given a mandate to shift power and wealth towards the working class, its leaders chose instead in government to adopt policies aimed at bolstering private industry and profits. Its policies were so unsuccessful and unpopular that there has been a rapid move to the left among the party membership, which has been resisted by most of the parliamentary leaders. As a result, Labour is in disarray and in a poor position to take advantage of the Conservatives' unpopularity.

The clearest evidence that the mould of post-war British politics had already been broken is Jenkins himself. Since 1979 Labour's leadership has been forced by constituency members and trade unionists to leave the middle ground and move towards more socialist policies. The tide of economic change, and especially the rise in unemployment, have forced the Labour leadership to give some recognition to the real polarization of class interests that is occurring in Britain. But Jenkins and his group have refused to quit the middle ground. It is they who have insisted on standing still, in continuing to adopt policies that were utterly discredited under Wilson and Callaghan. The more the Labour Party has changed, the more they have stayed the same. The Social Democratic Party is the one party in Britain that proclaims, with wide-eyed amazement, that surely nothing need alter, nothing has happened, and that we can return to the certainties of the 1960s without actually doing anything.

THE FAILURE OF ECONOMIC POLICY

The main feature of British politics in the 1980s is that every party is trapped by the expectations they have raised of economic growth. They have all defined political success in terms of the rise of national income, yet no economic strategy can achieve significant expansion for Britain. Each period in office serves only to discredit the theories with which they are associated.

In the first part of this book I have presented detailed

arguments about why major economic systems of thought are inadequate to explain high unemployment and low growth in Britain. Yet both academic economists and politicians are constantly reworking and reformulating these same theories and claiming to have overcome their technical faults, rather than admitting that they cannot achieve growth and higher rates of employment.

Keynesian theory seemed to have been discredited in 1974, after it had contributed to a policy that produced high rates of inflation and only modest growth of income and employment. Some economists have argued that it was abandoned at this point because up to then a measure of inflation was seen as boosting the declining rate of profit, whereas under Heath rapid inflation was associated with a considerable fall in the rate of profit.[1] Keynesian theory had therefore ceased to be useful to capital. But the Labour Party has revived it, in a modified form, and claimed it could produce rapid growth. Throughout this book I have challenged that thesis, and suggested that the alternative economic strategy would fail in this aim, if given a chance to be implemented.

Under Thatcher, monetarism has disastrously failed to produce the revitalization of the economy that was promised to the electorate in 1979. The Conservative government is now hopelessly bogged down in a morass of deflation, trapped by its own high rates of interest and of unemployment. It has neither achieved expansion nor restored profits, and over the final two years of its term of office it must steer a difficult course between the dangers of a violent revolt by the deprived sectors of the population, and the collapse of British industry. If it sticks too rigidly to its monetarist line, there may be a breakdown of law and order; if it relaxes too much, there may be a breakdown in the industrial system.

In order to stay in any kind of control over the whole situation, the Conservative government is having to resort to desperate measures. In chapter 9 (pp. 152–70) I discussed the reasons behind the massive centralization of power, and the reduction in the local authorities' autonomy. In order to protect industry's profits from high rates of local taxation in deprived areas, the government has virtually abolished local decision-making. Similarly, the sacking of James Prior from the Department of Employment, and his replacement by Norman Tebbit, who threatens measures to curb the power of the trade unions, suggests that the Conservatives are determined to try to force down the value of real wages still further in an effort to protect industrial profits.

With its emphasis on law and order, on central control, and its measures on race and nationality, many will see the Conservatives as drifting towards a policy akin to fascism. Some of the scenes at the 1981 Conservative conference, particularly in the debate on police powers, reinforced this impression. Yet I have argued in this book that the danger of fascism in Britain does not lie within the Conservative Party. Even if Margaret Thatcher and her hardline cabinet retain control over the party, the Disraeli tradition of One Nation, reaching back into the eighteenth century and beyond, is too strongly part of the ethos of the Conservative leadership to allow it to reach this degree of authoritarian and anti-democratic oppression.

Thatcher's populism was an ephemeral feature of Conservatism. Her appeal to lower middle-class individualism was far more than an echo of nineteenth-century Liberalism than of the Tory tradition. Rather than moving much further in that direction, the Conservative leadership are likely to exert a moderating and compromising influence.

The danger of a rise in fascism lies rather in the failure of all conventional economic policies, and in progressive disillusionment rather than sudden collapse and despair. It lies in the fact that none of the major political parties have policies that can deal with the consequences of Britain's economic decline, yet all have claimed that they could do so. I believe that the aftermath of the next general election is likely to be the moment at which parts of the volatile lower-middle-class and upper-working class vote finally turn away from the conventional solutions.

It is certainly true that up to now, although a large proportion of this sector of the electorate has changed its vote on as many occasions as there have been elections since 1970, it has always hitherto shifted to other parties which insisted both on operating within the system, and that they could make the system work. The SDP is both the prime example of this and the one that leads me to believe that the next election will be a watershed. Middle-class voters have flocked to the support of the SDP precisely because it seems to represent the pre-1970 world, when Britain's economic problems were susceptible to social democratic solutions, and where social problems such as unemployment were manageable within the welfare consensus. As the repository of these unrealistic fantasies, the SDP–Liberal alliance will be particularly susceptible to a backlash, but this time the volatile section of the electorate will have nowhere else to go. At this point a new party which seems to offer Thatcherism with teeth will have an excellent chance of attracting its support.

While the SDP's fortunes are still waxing, there seems no danger of a fascist party arising. Once it starts to wane, the risk at once occurs. If the Conservatives win the next election, as still seems to me quite possible, they will probably receive little more than a third of the total vote. But this victory would represent a setback for the SDP–Liberal alliance, such has been the expectation that has been generated by the events of 1981. The Conservatives will have no new ideas on policy, and unemployment will soon start to increase again. Such a government might fall fairly quickly and be replaced by the alliance, or even a coalition; in that case, the test of the alliance would simply have been postponed. But if the disillusionment with the setback of having another, similar and unsuccessful Conservative government turned voters against the SDP–Liberal alliance, then a fascist party could gain support at this point.

Alternatively, in the unlikely event of the Labour Party winning a narrow victory under its present leadership, it would have to implement some version of the alternative economic strategy, and would probably be forced by its parliamentary situation to opt for the most Keynesian and least socialist version. Having raised hopes of a quick economic recovery, the new government would soon be faced with impatience and disaffection. If it had support from the SDP and Liberals, this could be a factor in causing people to turn against them and towards a new fascist group.

The third possibility is of an SDP–Liberal government, either following the election, or following a brief and unsuccessful period of Conservative or Labour government. This could take the form of either a government drawn entirely from the two parties of the alliance, or some form of coalition with centrist elements in either or both of the other major parties. As I argued in chapter 10, I consider that this would be the outcome most likely to lead to the emergence of a new and powerful fascist party. Because such a government would be in no better position to handle Britain's long-term economic problems than any other, and because it would raise far more unrealistic expectations than either of the other alternatives, it would be much more vulnerable to an extreme backlash stemming from disillusionment and despair.

This is because the SDP–Liberal alliance has (half unwittingly) become the vehicle for the expression of a set of attitudes, beliefs and hopes which emerged in British political consciousness in the 1970s and which are likely to be crucial to the development of the political crisis which I foresee as occurring in the mid-1980s. Writers such as Tom Nairn and Stuart Hall have identified a social anxiety that developed in the lower middle classes in the 1960s, and which arose from their socio-economic position between big business and organized labour. This social anxiety made them susceptible to 'moral panics' about other social groups and about certain key issues (the 'permissive society', mugging, child abuse). In the 1970s this anxiety expressed itself increasingly in the form of moral fundamentalism, focused on the defence of 'the English way of life', as represented by a commitment to the values of hard work, individual initiative, respectability, responsibility, delayed gratification and social discipline.[2]

Whether or not the SDP–Liberal alliance have sought to arouse a 'moral panic' among the lower middle classes about the 'extremism' of both their major political rivals, they seem in fact to have done so. With the aid of the press, they have particularly been able to portray the Labour Party as in the grip of a stranglehold by the 'irresponsible' left. But this moral panic, when expressed in political terms, is two-edged. The alliance now has to live up to expectations that it will restore Britain to some previous golden age, when English values and the English way of life prevailed.

One of the major preoccupations of lower-middle-class

social anxiety is 'law and order'. The SDP–Liberal alliance (particularly if supported by other groups in Parliament) conjures up visions of social harmony and respect for the law. If in fact unemployment and attendant social unrest continue to increase, as I suggest they must, then this vision could quickly evaporate, and a party that takes a much more radical stand on order, discipline, punishment, control and the suppression of minorities would be in a position to capitalize on the disillusionment.

It could be argued that British people are far too stolid and long-suffering to embrace any such solutions, or to support a party with this political flavour. It is certainly true that the British electorate is far more committed to democratic institutions than the Germans were in the inter-war years. A large proportion of Germans never accepted the Weimar constitution, and it was therefore relatively easy for the Nazis to portray it as an alien imposition, outside the German tradition, and therefore to rally people who wanted total institutional change. According to this argument, Britain would be a far less likely constituency for an anti-democratic right-wing movement.

However, there would be no real need for the new fascist party to emphasize this aspect of its programme in the first instance. For the Nazis it was actually in their interests to attack democratic institutions, which were already unpopular and blamed for Germany's plight. In Britain a neo-fascist party would only have to return to the themes of Thatcherism in a more firm and authoritarian way. Conservative populism has legitimated the politics of racism, of 'law and order' themes such as punishment and hanging, of attacks on the welfare state, the unemployed and the disadvantaged. Only perhaps in the theme of trade union control would the fascists need to hint at radical constitutional innovations, or the loss of traditional British liberties. Even in this respect they would merely be returning to a Thatcherite theme.

The recipe for a successful appeal to the insecurities of the lower-middle class in Britain seems to be a judicious blend of novelty and nostalgia. Thatcherism was novel, in its abrasive style, but nostalgic in many of its moral and political themes. The SDP is a novelty as a new party, but nostalgic in its desire for consensus. It is difficult to see what other novelties the major parties could produce after the next election.

All a more successful neo-fascist party would have to do would be to avoid the more crass crudities of the National Front, to cultivate a more suave and sophisticated image, and to emphasize continuity with a line of neglected prophets, including Enoch Powell. It would need to attract only a proportion of the lower-middle-class vote to become politically significant. It might then hope to attract, as in Germany, certain of the outcasts (mainly from the indigenous inner-city poor) who do not normally participate in the political process, or even cast their votes.

THE ORIGINS OF FASCISM

From where will the leadership of a new fascist party come? My own view is that it would not come from any major figure in any of the present political parties, but would stem from individuals or groups at present outside mainstream politics. This is consistent with my general contention that the Conservative Party, and particularly the Conservative leadership, are not potentially fascist. However, there is a view that has been canvassed that the Labour Party contains within it the seeds of a fascist leadership – indeed another potential Oswald Mosley. In particular, some people have suggested that Tony Benn could play this role.

Benn certainly has the charisma to do so. Furthermore, there are aspects of his political philosophy – his brand of protectionism, nationalism and central planning – that are strongly reminiscent of the Joseph Chamberlain tradition of social imperialism, with Mosley forming the link in that chain. It is a connection that has been made specifically by Andrew Gamble in his book *Britain in Decline*;[3] and others have pointed out that it would scarcely be inappropriate to give Benn's approach the title 'National Socialism'. He is widely accused of manipulating his supporters, of disguising his true motives and intentions, and of deserting democratic traditions.

However, it seems clear to me that Benn could not conceivably take on the mantle of Margaret Thatcher's populist appeal of 1979. Whatever else he might try to do, he is hardly likely to pick up the themes of law and order, remoralization, trade union control and repatriation of immigrants – themes that would probably be important in any brand of fascism that might appeal to the moral fundamentalism of the lower middle classes. In my view the success of a fascist movement would depend on this kind of support. It is, of course, possible that Benn or someone like him might lead a Labour Party that had been deserted by its right-wing 'moderates' in the direction of some version of nationalistic and authoritarian socialism that had echoes of the Chamberlain and Mosley past. My own view is that if he attempted to do so he would quickly be deserted by his rank-and-file. Whatever the shortcomings of Benn's personal philosophy and style, his supporters – or rather those who now prefer him to most of the other alternative leaders in the present Labour Party – would be very unlikely to be duped into following him along a road that led away from democratic socialism.

Why would new fascist leaders arise outside the major parties, and why might people who previously supported the mainstream parties switch their support to them? Since there is no strong fascist tradition in Britain (compared for instance with Spain) why would previously democratic, even moderate, people turn to such a party? The answer seems to me to lie in the fact that fascism would not be wholly irrational in the circumstances that would be likely to prevail in the mid-1980s. Although fascism necessarily contains certain irrational features – such as the belief in mystical or magical powers of great leaders – its economic precepts and social strategies might well fit the kind of crisis that Britain would face in about 1985. *Fascist policies would by then be the only ones that could make British capitalism reasonably successful.*

There is ample evidence from Germany in the Nazi years that Hitler's regime brought about an extraordinary revitalization of German capitalism in the late 1930s by similar policies. Between 1929, when the slump hit Germany, and 1933, when Hitler seized power, unemployment in Germany rose from under 2 million to over 6 million. Real wages fell, probably by about 15 per cent. But profits collapsed catastrophically, and German industry was in ruins. Between 1932 and 1938 total profits increased from 8 billion to 20 billion marks, so that within five years of Hitler's coup they stood considerably above their 1929 level. The share of profits in national income rose from 21 per cent in 1929 to 26.6 per cent in 1938, while the share of wages and salaries fell from 68.8 per cent to 63.1 per cent in the same period.[4]

By banning trade unions and strikes, Hitler enabled capital to increase the working day by 40 per cent without significant increases in real wages from their 1933 level. The total volume of wages and salaries was still lower in 1938 than it had been in 1929, in spite of an increase of nearly 3 million in the number of wage earners, and a much larger increase in the number of man-hours worked. Through extermination and forced labour, as well as through an increase in state employment and in industrial activity, the Nazis achieved full employment in five years, starting from a figure of 6 million unemployed. They also achieved a rate of growth of national income of some 2.5 per cent a year.[5]

A similar pattern emerges from an analysis of fascist rule in Italy, Spain and Japan. In Italy real wages fell by 18 per cent between 1922 and 1938; in Spain they fell by over 40 per cent between 1935 and 1945. In both these cases this fall occurred while output was growing and unemployment falling. For Japan there are no reliable figures, but increases in proportionate spending on food and clothes between 1935 and 1940 give strong evidence of falling real wages.[6]

By the mid-1980s in Britain, capitalism may well be in as bad a condition as it was in Germany in the early 1930s. The only way to revive it would be by means of an authoritarian, centralized regime that would deny workers the right of association, enforce wage cuts and allow an increase in surplus-value through longer working hours at reduced rates of pay. At the same time, the problem of mass unemployment could be tackled by the expulsion of immigrants and by various kinds of forced labour. Rearmament and compulsory military service could also provide increased employment, financed out of reduced spending on social services, housing and health care.

While it is unlikely that the Conservative leadership will

adopt such policies, much of their rhetoric legitimates them. Thatcher and Tebbit will not ban trade unions, but their comments on abuses of union power give credibility to those who would. Whitelaw will not repatriate immigrants, but the Conservatives' policies on race offer encouragement to others who would not hesitate to do so, The Conservatives will not become fascists, but many of their 1979 supporters are likely to turn to a fascist party when they become disillusioned with the failure of Conservative or SDP policies. If the aim of economic management is to restore profits and growth, and fascism is the only way of doing this, then a proportion of voters will come to support a fascist party.

Perhaps the most dangerous suggestion of all made by a Conservative leader was Sir Keith Joseph's in 1974, when he said that Britain's problems were caused by the excessive birthrate in class 5 of the population. The statement cost him dearly, in that it ruined his chances of the leadership, but he was only carrying the logic of monetarism to its conclusion. In the last resort the Conservative analysis of Britain's economic failure leads directly to the conclusion that we have a surplus population, which is of no economic use and which we cannot afford to feed. The unskilled are disproportionately unemployed, and consume a large ratio of our national welfare budget. It would take no great deductive leap from Conservative statements on social policy to conclude that this sector of the population should be reduced, by compulsory sterilization, or more drastic means. A Conservative government would never do this, but a fascist party would.

THE SOCIALIST ALTERNATIVE

If it would take a fascist police state to rescue British capitalism, the Britain's political agenda for the next decade should not be economic growth, but alternatives to fascism. I shall argue that the only effective alternative is socialism.

I have suggested that every other political alternative requires British capitalism to be successful, at least in keeping down unemployment, but cannot make it work. But true socialism, by redefining our political aims, and concentrating on social justice rather than on economic growth, could challenge the whole basis of capitalism, and in so doing defeat the fascist threat.

Many people fear socialism for the reasons that I fear fascism. They think it necessarily entails an authoritarian, centrally controlled state, loss of liberty, the persecution of minorities, police oppression. They look at Russia and the East European countries, and see drab and paranoid regimes, bureaucratic, corrupt, coercive, joyless, philistine and militaristic.

Yet such countries are the products of the circumstances in which they turned to socialism. They were all relatively backward and impoverished, none extensively industrialized, and all at a stage of development where inequalities of income and wealth were extreme. This was particularly so of contrasts between urban and rural standards of living – all had huge peasant farming sectors of their economies. In each case, therefore, the attempt to introduce socialism involved the revolutionary or military seizure of power by a small minority, claiming to represent the interests of industrial workers, which ruthlessly used the institutions of the state to impose its will. Marx's phrase 'the dictatorship of the proletariat' was self-consciously applied, the power elite justifying its measures as a necessary transitional phase in the development of these underdeveloped countries, and doing so in the name of a minority social class – urban workers. All these factors, in combination with the Cold War, help to explain the evolution of the particular style of regime associated with Eastern Europe.

The taunt that is constantly flung at the Labour left (increasingly by the SDP) is that it would reduce Britain to the condition of Poland. It certainly seems paradoxical to be advocating a shift towards a centrally planned regime when those of Eastern Europe, and particularly Poland, are in considerably difficulties. To answer this, we need to consider the nature of the crisis in Poland.

Poland is clearly not only an example of a planned regime that was installed and maintained as described above, but also one in which the Russians presided over its imposition in a highly repressive way. It is also the Eastern European regime which has most conspicuously failed at the task of (literally) delivering the goods to its workers. Although I mistrust political analyses that depend on alleged cultural characteristics, there can be little doubt that the Poles as a nation have many characteristics that have made them very resistant to their regime. Not only is Catholicism exceptionally strong; there is also an important intelligentsia which is both nationalistic and libertarian, and a cultural tradition which reflects these values.

But above all, Polish workers are very independent, and value their autonomy highly. In this respect the Poles closely resemble their British counterparts. In Britain as in Poland there is a streak of anarchism among the rank-and-file of workers, who set no store by grandiose social strategies, and insist on control over their own work and their own lives. For this reason Poland should certainly serve as an example and a warning to any future left-wing regime in Britain. British socialism would have to be both democratic and participatory, and allow far more scope for individual freedom than is permitted in Eastern Europe. But above all, workers would resist a regime which simply transferred power from capital to the state, and did nothing to strengthen workers' control over industrial decision-making and over their own working lives.

The other major accusation against the centrally planned countries is of economic inefficiency. This is far harder to justify than the former charges. If we compare annual growth rates of GNP *per capita* of all the Eastern European countries (including Russia) from 1960 to 1974 with the same rates for all the Western European countries (including Finland, Cyprus, Turkey and Greece) the Eastern European countries show an annual average growth rate of 4.26 per cent and the Western European of 4.34 per cent.[7] Table 13.1 compares rates of growth of various economic indicators between the USSR and the USA, in the period 1950–75.[8]

Nor is it true to suggest that Russia's achievement was at the expense of the satellite countries. All the other Eastern European countries had higher growth rates in GNP *per capita* from 1960 onwards, and East Germany, Poland and Czechoslovakia all have higher average standards of living than the USSR.[9] A more remote comparison of efficiency is

Table 13.1   *Comparative annual average growth rates,*
1950–75 (per cent)

	USSR	USA
Real GNP	5.2	3.3
Industrial production	7.6	3.9
Agricultural production	2.5	1.9
Population	1.4	1.4
Real consumption	4.9–5.4	3.3
Real fixed investment	8.1	2.4
Real *per capita* disposable income	5.3–6.8	2.5

provided by India and China. Between 1960 and 1974, India's rate of growth of GNP *per capita* was 1.1 per cent; China's was 5.2 per cent.[10]

I would not accord any very great significance to these statistics, because I do not think that fair comparisons can be made between rates of growth of countries like the East European ones, which were predominantly rural before their change of regime, and the advanced industrialized countries. A fairer comparison would be with countries like Spain, Portugal and Ireland, which were in the process of industrialization. In such comparisons the Eastern European countries come out as less efficient, having lower rates of growth on average. However, it must be remarked that the Western industrializing countries were developed with the assistance of considerable amounts of capital from the advanced nations.

But above all, none of these countries is remotely comparable with Britain, which is a country in the process of de-industrialization. If Britain adopted the socialist alternative, the aim would not primarily be to rival the rates of growth of Eastern or Western countries, but to achieve greater social justice and national solidarity, and to avoid the threat of fascism.

Another very important consideration in thinking about a socialist future for Britain is the very considerable evidence of continuities between pre-revolutionary and post-revolutionary regimes in the Marxian socialist countries. All the countries that have turned to this form of socialism have done so by displacing regimes that were authoritarian and repressive, and which used violent means to suppress opposition. In every case the succeeding socialist regime has adopted similar tactics after seizing power. But even so, there are great differences between the various socialist regimes, in ideology and in practice, and continuities with the previous era in each country. This leads me to suggest that a British socialist state would in many respects resemble pre-socialist Britain more than it would resemble any other socialist country.

The only comprehensible model of what Britain under socialism might be like seems to me to be offered by conditions during the last war. Having rejected socialist centralization and planning as inefficient and undesirable during the Depression, Britain at once adopted them in wartime. Economic life was controlled and directed by government to a very great extent, and there was also central direction over patterns of deployment of labour. Control over distribution and consumption was designed to ensure fair shares between citizens. The whole system was by and large experienced as efficient and as compatible with liberty as was reasonable to expect in the circumstances of a threat from an alien and repulsive regime – German fascism.

If Britain turned to socialism in the 1980s, it would do so under conditions that were in some ways more auspicious than wartime. Trade with the rest of the world, though problematic, would not be quite as difficult as when U-boats patrolled our coasts. Instead of spending a huge proportion of national income or armaments, a neutral and non-aligned Britain, which had left NATO and got rid of its nuclear weapons, could devote a large proportion of its public spending to the social services. Here the relevant comparison is with Canada, which spends the same proportion of its GNP on state consumption as the USA, but only half as much of this proportion in military expenditure, and consequently enjoys much better social services.

The important similarity between the two situations lies in the necessity of government controlling production, investment and – to a great extent – trade. I have argued throughout this book that there is no way in which British capital can be harnessed to socialist purposes under a 'mixed economy'. Because of historical and structural factors affecting the rate of profit in Britain, it would not be in capital's interests to co-operate with a plan such as Labour's alternative economic strategy. Therefore, the only way in which socialism could succeed in Britain would be by means of a massive programme of public ownership, enabling the central planning of output and investment levels, which otherwise would fall far short of the targets required for a decent standard of living for all.

Furthermore, such a measure would be a necessary condition for all the other aims of socialist policy. Talk of industrial democracy, of work-sharing and the shorter working week is so much moonshine so long as the capitalist system persists. So are notions of a national minimum wage or guaranteed income. British capital would implacably oppose any such measures – indeed it would necessarily do so in its own interests. All these desirable socialist objectives are non-starters without common ownership of the means of production.

Throughout this book I have argued that there can be no social justice without a fundamental redistribution of work, income and leisure; yet capitalism cannot reconcile itself with such a redistribution, let alone bring it about. Only a socialist economic system could achieve socialist policies for social justice. It is as necessary for a socialist government to control decisions in the productive system as it has become for a right-wing government to control the whole of the state system for public expenditure. Socialist control of the means of production to achieve social policy aims is the counterpart of the attempt of the Conservative government to control all the local authority services through massive centralization of budget decision-making.

Would a socialist government be concerned with redistribution? Some people might argue that the evidence from Eastern European countries is of great inequalities and social injustices, and of a power elite that is greedy and selfish as well as brutal and corrupt. All this was certainly true of Russia under Stalin, but it is increasingly less true now. In 1946 the ratio of the share of the top 10 per cent of income receivers to the share of the bottom 10 per cent was 14 : 1. By 1966 it was only 4.5 : 1.[11] The measures adopted in Russia included raising the wages of the lowest income groups, raising the minimum wages of urban workers by more than a third, of rural workers by about a half, of minimum pensions for the disabled by a third, establishing social insurance for the peasants, lowering taxes for low-income families, and narrowing the gap between rural and urban living standards. Official American observers have commented that 'the narrowing of wage differentials in the USSR over the past two decades has been enormous'.[12] One American writer has stated: 'since Stalin's death, I doubt that any country can show a more rapid and sweeping progress towards equality [than the Soviet Union]'.[13] Even if we do not agree with the means by which the Soviet bloc countries have achieved this level of equality (and full employment), we have at least to recognize it.

It should also be emphasized that Britain starts from a situation of moderate advantage in the attempt at social justice, compared with some other advanced countries. In the early 1970s the share of the top 10 per cent of income receivers was 10 times as great as that of the bottom 10 per cent, whereas it was over 20 times as great in France, 15.8 times as great in Australia, and 15.4 times as great in the United States.

Fabian social policy commentators often emphasize inequalities of wealth and income in Britain. While I do not dispute their findings, the relevant point is really that under capitalism these inequalities are certain to grow wider, as economic stagnation is combined with high rates of unemployment. British society is not particularly unequal by capitalist standards, but it is rapidly becoming more so, and the only way to halt this dangerous development, which threatens violence, lawlessness and ultimately fascism, is by a socialist system.

In order to deal specifically with the problem of unemployment a socialist government would have to make structural changes in the economy which took account of all the factors analysed in this book. Higher public investment, though important and constructive, would not on its own provide extra employment for more than a small fraction of the unemployed workforce. In addition, there would be much greater opportunities for employment in the social services (though not in bureaucracies like our present services) for local working people, who could contribute to democratizing them and improving the quality of service to recipients. But the majority of the redistribution of available work would be achieved through reductions in working hours, compensated for by increases in the social wage provided by the state.

Import controls and tariffs need not be an important feature of a socialist economic strategy, even though the government would need to have this weapon in reserve. Ideally, a socialist government could identify the commodities which are more efficiently and cheaply produced in the advanced capitalist world, and those more efficiently and cheaply produced in the industrializing countries, and allow imports of these commodities to continue to increase, while home production declines. But it could also identify and develop growth areas in the British economy. and pursue an investment strategy to make these more competitive, both in the home market and abroad. The socialist strategy would not involve the creation of industrial employment for its own sake, still less the protection of inefficient and outmoded industries. Rather, it would allow the decline of certain sectors of British industrial production, without a parallel decline in the living standards of working people.

The leadership for the socialist alternative is very unlikely to be found among the present Labour Party leadership. The present leadership shares in the moral and intellectual bankruptcy of the whole British establishment. The future leadership of British socialism will probably come from people who are not yet known outside their local labour movements. The first socialist leader of Britain may well at present be an unemployed worker in Liverpool, or a single parent in Leeds. There are clear and recent precedents, from a very different source, for moral and intellectual leadership arising suddenly from complete obscurity. Lech Walesa was an unemployed electrician at the time when the strike of workers in the Gdansk shipyards began.

Above all, a socialist government would seek in the long term to rebuild the social solidarity which is the best bulwark against injustice and class conflict. In this respect, it would seek to rediscover the spirit of national unity which was characteristic of wartime Britain. This notion has become a hypocritical cliché in the mouths of post-war politicians, but it did undoubtedly contribute to the remarkable achievements of the post-war welfare state, many of which have been lost in subsequent years through the divisive effects of capitalist development.

Social solidarity is a relevant factor in low rates of unemployment, even in capitalist countries. This can be seen in the comparatively low rates of unemployment in Sweden, for instance, or New Zealand, neither of them particularly successful economies, yet countries with sufficient social cohesion to enable economic difficulties to be more equitably shared among the population than they have been in Britain, the United States or Australia.

Ultimately, the choice for this country will lie between a society which somewhat resembles Britain during the Second World War, and a society which very much resembles Germany before that war. Britain rejected fascism in the 1930s, and it will eventually do so again. Instead, it will adopt the pattern of government which stood us in good stead during our wartime crisis, and by means of which we defeated the original Nazi threat.

How is a socialist Britain to come about? In 1981 it is still difficult to guess at this. The Labour Party is still a long way short of representing a true socialist alternative, and many of the trade unions are led by people who have an even larger stake in capitalism than the Labour leadership.

I have suggested that whichever party wins the next election, unemployment will continue to rise and the British economy will continue to stagnate or decline. Under these circumstances the middle classes are likely to turn in increasing numbers to a fascist party, which promises what the Conservatives hint at – the coercion of the working class and the revitalization of capitalism.

Whichever party wins the next election, therefore, the British working class is likely to move quickly and decisively towards the socialist alternative. In many ways the election result that would make this most difficult would be the victory of a compromising, 'moderate' Labour Party, under leadership in the Healey mould. However, it seems quite unlikely that the Labour Party will still be under such leadership in 1984, or that it will win the election if it adopts a programme which reflects such a compromise.

I am suggesting that the decisive move towards socialism in Britain could arise in response to the threat of a new and powerful fascist party. While the major new political force in Britain is still the SDP–Liberal alliance, the Labour leadership can continue to argue that its only hope of gaining power lies in moderation and compromise, in fighting the alliance on its own ground. This policy is extremely shortsighted. As soon as the alliance wanes, and a powerful force springs up on the extreme right, a Labour Party that does not clearly represent working-class interests will be in a weak position to challenge it. If indeed the present leadership survives until this time, the Labour Party will require a very sudden change in policy and leadership to face the fascist threat.

It might be argued that fascism always stems from a threat on the left, rather than *vice versa*. In Italy and Germany between the wars, fascism and Nazism won their spurs, and gained support, by attacking the activities of the left which were seen as threatening and disruptive. Whether the left needs actually to be strong or active to provoke fascism is far more debatable. In a situation of economic deterioration and declining standards of living, the left will always tend to advocate, and will often carry out, extra-parliamentary protests which make it highly visible, and which can evoke a moral panic in the middle class. Under these circumstances, even when the left is weak (as it would be after an SDP–Liberal victory, for instance) it could be perceived as threatening, and this could contribute to the emergence of fascism. Whether or not the SDP-Liberal alliance wins the next election, and whether or not the present Labour leadership survives until then, I foresee the emergence of strong forces on the left and right, which will demand direct action, and which will confront each other on the streets in Britain.

My prediction is therefore that some time in the mid-1980s, and probably during the year after the next election (assuming the present government completes its term in office) the country will become increasingly ungovernable. Political and economic disruption will be associated with the activities of fascist groups on the right, and with the organized and angry demands of workers on the left. Under such circumstances there would be an agonizing and anxious moment in which Britain's political future would be determined. I am confident that Britain will ultimately reject fascism and embrace the socialist alternative.

The form of socialism adopted by Britain will necessarily be one that suits our free and democratic political traditions – if it is not, it will fail. It will necessarily involve a more cohesive and participatory society, and will allow people to build their own future rather than have it determined by powerful elites. It will give more power to the people, rather than simply to the state. While the analogy with wartime is relevant, it is not sufficient; lessons must also be drawn from the fate of Poland and the other Eastern European countries. Unlike a declining capitalist Britain, torn by class conflict, a socialist Britain could be a good country in which to live.

REFERENCES

1   See for instance, Bob Rowthorn, *Capitalism, Conflict and In-flation*, Lawrence and Wishart, 1980.
2   T. Nairn, 'Portrait of Enoch Powell', *New Left Review*, no. 61, May–June 1978, pp. 2–7, and S. Hall, C. Critcher, T. Jefferson, J. Clark and B. Roberts, *Policing the Crisis: Mugging, the State, and Law and Order*, Macmillan, 1978.
3   Andrew Gamble, *Britain in Decline*, Macmillan, 1981, pp. 172–84.
4   E. Mandel, *Late Capitalism* (1972), New Left Books, 1976, pp. 159–60.
5   Ibid., pp. 160–1.
6   Ibid., pp. 162–3.
7   John G. Gurley, 'Economic development: a Marxist view', in K. P. Jameson and C. K. Wilber (eds), *Direction in Economic Development*, Notre Dame Press, 1979, p. 218, table 13.
8   Ibid., p. 221, table 15.
9   Ibid., pp. 216–7, table 11.
10   Ibid., p. 218, table 12.

11   Ibid., p. 224, table 18.
12   D. W. Bronson and B. S. Severin, 'Soviet consumer welfare: the Brezhnev era', in Joint Economic Committee of the US Congress, *Soviet Economic Prospects for the Seventies*, GPO Washington, 27 June 1973, p. 379.
13   P. Wiles, *Distribution of Income: East and West*, North-Holland, 1974, p. 25.

Index